Economics

Statistics (data)

World

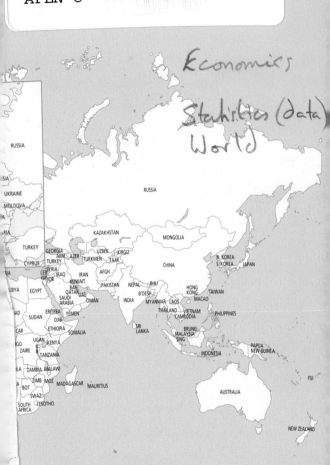

POCKET WORLD IN FIGURES

The Economist

=== POCKET ===

WORLD IN FIGURES

THE ECONOMIST IN ASSOCIATION WITH
HAMISH HAMILTON LTD

Published by the Penguin Group
Penguin Books Ltd, 27 Wrights Lane, London W8 5TZ, England
Penguin Books USA Inc., 375 Hudson Street, New York,
New York 10014, USA
Penguin Books Australia Ltd, Ringwood, Victoria, Australia
Penguin Books Canada Ltd, 10 Alcorn Avenue, Toronto,
Ontario, Canada M4V 3B2
Penguin Books (NZ) Ltd, 182–190 Wairau Road, Auckland 10,
New Zealand

Penguin Books Ltd, Registered Offices: Harmondsworth,
Middlesex, England

First published by The Economist Books Ltd 1991
Second edition published by The Economist Books Ltd 1992
Third edition published by Hamish Hamilton Ltd in association
with The Economist Newspaper Ltd 1993
Fourth edition published by Hamish Hamilton Ltd in association
with The Economist Newspaper Ltd 1994
This edition published by Hamish Hamilton Ltd in association
with The Economist Newspaper Ltd 1995

10 9 8 7 6 5 4 3 2 1

Material researched and compiled by Andrew Bevan, Chris
Coulman, Robert Eves, Carol Howard, Stella Jones,
Jo Malvisi, Liz Mann, David McKelvey, Justene McNeice,
Sara Pritchard, Nick Wiseman

Design and makeup Jonathan Harley, Liz Conway

The greatest care has been taken in compiling this book. However,
no responsibility can be accepted by the publishers or compilers
for the accuracy of the information presented.

Printed in Great Britain by William Clowes Limited,
Beccles and London

A CIP catalogue record for this book is available
from the British Library

ISBN 0-241-13602-4

Notes

This edition of the annual *Economist Pocket World in Figures* has been expanded to include a larger number of country profiles and more rankings. The country profiles cover some 63 major countries, including Russia and Ukraine, and a selection of statistics for the other ex-Soviet republics. The world rankings consider 166: all those with a population of at least 1m or a GDP of at least $1bn. The extent and quality of the statistics available varies from country to country. Every care has been taken to specify the broad definitions on which the data are based and to indicate cases where data quality or technical difficulties are such that interpretation of the figures is likely to be seriously affected. Nevertheless, figures from individual countries will often differ from standard international statistical definitions.

Statistics do not yet fully reflect the changes that have taken place in Germany, Yemen, the Czech Republic and Slovakia, ex-Yugoslavia and the former Soviet Union. Where possible, 1992 or later data have been combined to show Eastern and Western Germany as one and North and South Yemen as one. Data for Cyprus normally refer to Greek Cyprus only. For other countries such as Morocco they exclude disputed areas. Data for the EU refers to its 12 members prior to the recent enlargement of the Union.

Statistical basis

The all-important factor in a book of this kind is to be able to make reliable comparisons between countries. Although this is never quite possible for the reasons stated above, the best route, which this book takes, is to compare data for the same year or period and to use actual, not estimated, figures wherever possible. The research for this edition of *The Economist Pocket World in Figures* was carried out in 1995 using the latest available sources that present data on an internationally comparable basis. Data, therefore, unless otherwise indicated, refers to the year ending December 31 1993.

In the country profiles, population density, population under 15 and over 65, and number of men per 100 women refer to forecasts for 1995; life expectancy, crude birth, death and fertility rates are based on 1995–2000 averages; human development indices are for 1992 and GDP per head in purchasing power parity to 1991; energy data refer to 1991;

structure of manufacturing data to 1991; household data and marriage and divorce data refer to the latest year with available figures, 1985–92. In a number of cases, data are shown for the latest year within a range.

Other definitions
Data shown on country profiles may not always be consistent with those shown on the world rankings because the definitions or years covered can differ. Data may also differ between two different rankings.

Most countries' national accounts are now compiled on a GDP basis so, for simplicity, the term GDP has been used interchangeably with GNP. GDP figures in this book come from the World Bank. It bases its rouble conversions on purchasing power parities.

Statistics for principal exports and principal imports are normally based on customs statistics. These are generally compiled on different definitions to the visible exports and imports figures shown in the balance of payments section.

Definitions of the statistics shown are given on the relevant page or in the glossary at the end of the book. Figures may not add exactly to totals, or percentages to 100, because of rounding or, in the case of GDP, statistical adjustment. Sums of money have generally been converted to US dollars at the official exchange rate ruling at the time to which the figures refer.

Energy consumption data are not always reliable, particularly for the major oil producing countries. Consumption per head data may therefore be higher than in reality. Energy exports can exceed production and imports can exceed consumption if transit operations distort trade data or oil is imported for refining and re-exported.

Abbreviations

bn	billion (one thousand million)	GNP	Gross national product
CAR	Central African Republic	GRT	Gross tonnage
CIS	Commonwealth of Independent	m	million
	States	NDP	Net domestic product
EU	European Union	NMP	Net material product
kg	kilogram	PPP	Purchasing power parity
km	kilometre	UAE	United Arab Emirates
GDP	Gross domestic product	…	not available

Part I
WORLD RANKINGS

Countries: *natural facts*

Countries: *the largest[a]*
'000 sq km

1	Russia	17,078		31	Nigeria	924
2	Canada	9,922		32	Venezuela	912
3	China	9,597		33	Namibia	824
4	United States	9,363		34	Pakistan	804
5	Brazil	8,512		35	Mozambique	785
6	Australia	7,682		36	Turkey	779
7	India	3,169		37	Zambia	753
8	Kazakhstan	2,717		38	Chile	752
9	Sudan	2,506		39	Myanmar	678
10	Saudi Arabia	2,401		40	Afghanistan	652
11	Algeria	2,382		41	Somalia	630
12	Zaire	2,345		42	CAR	625
13	Argentina	2,278		43	Ukraine	604
14	Mexico	1,973		44	Madagascar	594
15	Indonesia	1,919		45	Kenya	583
16	Libya	1,760		46	Botswana	575
17	Iran	1,648		47	France	544
18	Mongolia	1,565		48	Thailand	514
19	Peru	1,285		49	Spain	505
20	Chad	1,284		50	Turkmenistan	488
21	Angola	1,247		51	Yemen	477
22	Mali	1,240		52	Cameroon	476
23	Niger	1,186		53	Papua New Guinea	463
24	South Africa	1,185		54	Morocco	458
25	Colombia	1,139		55	Sweden	450
26	Bolivia	1,099		56	Uzbekistan	447
27	Mauritania	1,031		57	Iraq	438
28	Ethiopia	1,023		58	Paraguay	407
29	Egypt	1,023		59	Zimbabwe	390
30	Tanzania	940		60	Japan	370

Mountains: *the highest[b]*

	Name	Location	Height (m)
1	Everest	Nepal-China	8,848
2	K2 (Godwin Austen)	Pakistan	8,611
3	Kangchenjunga	Nepal-Sikkim	8,586
4	Lhotse	Nepal-China	8,516
5	Makalu	Nepal-China	8,463
6	Cho Oyu	Nepal-China	8,201
7	Dhaulagiri	Nepal	8,167
8	Manaslu	Nepal	8,163
9	Nanga Parbat	Pakistan	8,125
10	Annapurna I	Nepal	8,091
11	Gasherbrum I	Pakistan-China	8,068
12	Broad Peak	Pakistan-China	8,047
13	Xixabangma (Gosainthan)	China	8,046
14	Gasherbrum II	Pakistan-China	8,035

a Includes freshwater.
b Includes separate peaks which are part of the same massif.

Rivers: *the longest*

	Name	Location	Length (km)
1	Nile	Africa	6,695
2	Amazon	South America	6,516
3	Yangtze	Asia	6,380
4	Mississippi-Missouri	North America	6,019
5	Ob'-Irtysh	Asia	5,570
6	Yenisey-Angara	Asia	5,550
7	Hwang He (Yellow)	Asia	5,464
8	Congo	Africa	4,667
9	Parana	South America	4,500
10	Mekong	Asia	4,425
11	Amur	Asia	4,416
12	Lena	Asia	4,400
13	Mackenzie	North America	4,250
14	Niger	Africa	4,030
15	Missouri	North America	3,969
16	Mississippi	North America	3,779
17	Murray-Darling	Australia	3,750
18	Volga	Europe	3,688
19	Kolyma	Asia	3,513
20	Madeira	South America	3,200
21	Yukon	North America	3,185
22	Indus	Asia	3,180
23	Syrdar'ya	Asia	3,078
24	Salween	Asia	3,060
25	Sao Francisco	South America	2,900
26	Rio Grande	North America	2,870
27	Danube	Europe	2,850
28	Brahmaputra	Asia	2,840
29	Euphrates	Asia	2,815
30	Para-Tocantis	South America	2,750

Waterfalls: *the highest*

	Name	Location	Height (m)
1	Angel	Venezuela	979
2	Tugela	South Africa	948
3	Utigard	Norway	800
4	Mongefossen	Norway	774
5	Yosemite	California, USA	739
6	Mardalsfossen	Norway	656
7	Tyssestrengane	Norway	646
8	Cuquenan	Venezuela	609
9	Ribbon	California, USA	491
10	Della	Canada	440

Notes: Estimates of the lengths of different rivers vary widely according to the rules adopted concerning the selection of tributaries to be followed, the path to take through a delta, where different hydrological systems begin and end etc. The Nile is normally taken as the world's longest river but some estimates put the Amazon as longer if a southerly path through its delta leading to the River Para is followed. Likewise, difficulties in waterfall measurements exist depending on which breaks in the fall are counted. The more famous waterfalls, Niagara and Victoria, are surprisingly small, 50m and 108m respectively; their notoriety evolving from their width and accessibility.

Population: *explosions revealed*

Largest populations, 1993
Millions

1	China	1,175.36	31	Argentina	33.48
2	India	900.54	32	Canada	27.82
3	United States	258.06	33	Sudan	27.26
4	Indonesia	187.15	34	Algeria	26.88
5	Brazil	156.41	35	Tanzania	26.74
6	Russia	148.54	36	Morocco	26.72
7	Japan	124.85	37	Kenya	25.38
8	Pakistan	122.83	38	North Korea	23.05
9	Bangladesh	116.70	39	Peru	22.80
10	Nigeria	104.89	40	Romania	22.76
11	Mexico	86.71	41	Afghanistan	22.14
12	Germany	80.77	42	Uzbekistan	21.97
13	Vietnam	70.88	43	Taiwan	20.80
14	Philippines	65.78	44	Venezuela	20.78
15	Iran	61.42	45	Nepal	20.39
16	Turkey	59.46	46	Iraq	19.76
17	Thailand	58.82	47	Malaysia	19.03
18	United Kingdom	58.04	48	Uganda	18.03
19	Italy	57.84	49	Australia	17.71
20	France	57.65	50	Sri Lanka	17.62
21	Egypt	55.75	51	Saudi Arabia	17.39
22	Ethiopia	53.30	52	Kazakhstan	17.17
23	Ukraine	52.14	53	Mozambique	16.92
24	Myanmar	44.70	54	Ghana	16.26
25	South Korea	44.06	55	Netherlands	15.28
26	Zaire	41.00	56	Chile	13.81
27	South Africa	40.68	57	Yemen	13.44
28	Spain	39.13	58	Syria	13.39
29	Poland	38.45	59	Côte d'Ivoire	13.36
30	Colombia	35.68	60	Madagascar	12.73

Largest populations, 2010
Millions

1	China	1,388.47	14	Philippines	88.16
2	India	1,189.08	15	Ethiopia	85.08
3	United States	297.49	16	Egypt	81.49
4	Indonesia	239.60	17	Germany	80.47
5	Pakistan	210.10	18	Turkey	77.88
6	Brazil	199.33	19	Zaire	68.88
7	Nigeria	168.37	20	Thailand	67.13
8	Bangladesh	162.50	21	Myanmar	61.60
9	Russia	143.13	22	France	60.13
10	Japan	127.15	23	United Kingdom	59.92
11	Mexico	117.65	24	South Africa	56.40
12	Vietnam	98.45	25	Italy	55.99
13	Iran	95.22	26	South Korea	50.76

Fastest growing populations, 1985-93
Average annual growth, %

1	Jordan	5.9		Malawi	3.3
2	Qatar	5.3		Syria	3.3
3	Saudi Arabia	4.4		Zaire	3.3
	Yemen	4.4	16	Benin	3.2
5	Oman	3.9		Brunei	3.2
6	Côte d'Ivoire	3.8		Cambodia	3.2
7	Gambia, The	3.7		Ghana	3.2
8	Iran	3.6		Iraq	3.2
	Libya	3.6		Macao	3.2
	Togo	3.6		Niger	3.2
11	Botswana	3.4		UAE	3.2
12	Congo	3.3		Uganda	3.2

Slowest growing populations, 1985-93
Average annual growth, %

1	Kuwait	-2.9		Spain	0.2
2	Bulgaria	-0.8	15	Barbados	0.3
3	Portugal	-0.6		Belarus	0.3
4	Hungary	-0.5		Ukraine	0.3
5	Latvia	-0.1		United Kingdom	0.3
6	Czech Republic	0.0	19	Belgium	0.4
	Ireland	0.0		Croatia	0.4
	Romania	0.0		Finland	0.4
	Suriname	0.0		Georgia	0.4
10	Bosnia & Hercegovina	0.1		Japan	0.4
	Estonia	0.1		Poland	0.4
12	Denmark	0.2		Russia	0.4
	Italy	0.2		Slovakia	0.4

Fastest growing populations, 1995-2010
Average annual growth, %

1	Oman	3.8		Niger	3.2
2	Afghanistan	3.6		Saudi Arabia	3.2
3	Côte d'Ivoire	3.3		Syria	3.2
4	Angola	3.2	9	Jordan	3.1
	Libya	3.2		Liberia	3.1

Slowest growing populations, 1995-2010
Average annual growth, %

1	Bulgaria	-0.4		Russia	-0.2
	Latvia	-0.4		Ukraine	-0.2
3	Estonia	-0.3	9	Belarus	-0.1
	Hungary	-0.3		Germany	-0.1
5	Croatia	-0.2		Italy	-0.1
	Romania	-0.2		Serbia	-0.1

Population density

Highest population density
Population per sq km, 1995

1	Macao	31,063		21	Haiti	259
2	Hong Kong	5,677		22	Israel	255
3	Singapore	4,617		23	Trinidad & Tobago	254
4	Bermuda	1,155		24	United Kingdom	238
5	Malta	1,139		25	Netherlands Antilles	236
6	Bahrain	852		26	Jamaica	232
7	Bangladesh	810		27	Burundi	228
8	Barbados	608		28	Germany	226
9	Taiwan[a]	578		29	Vietnam	223
10	Mauritius	554		30	Philippines	219
11	South Korea	448		31	North Korea	198
12	Puerto Rico	415		32	Italy	192
13	Netherlands	403		33	Switzerland	170
14	Japan	331		34	Dominican Republic	162
15	Belgium	328		35	Nepal	157
16	Rwanda	316		36	Pakistan	154
17	Lebanon	291		37	Luxembourg	149
18	Sri Lanka	280		38	Czech Republic	131
19	El Salvador	274		39	Moldova	129
	India	274		40	Armenia	125

Lowest population density
Population per sq km, 1995

1	Australia	2			Oman	9
	Botswana	2			Papua New Guinea	9
	Mauritania	2			Russia	9
	Mongolia	2		24	Algeria	11
	Namibia	2		25	Argentina	12
6	Canada	3			Paraguay	12
	Iceland	3			Sudan	12
	Libya	3			Zambia	12
	Suriname	3		29	New Zealand	13
10	Chad	5			Norway	13
	Gabon	5		31	Finland	15
12	CAR	6		32	Somalia	16
	Kazakhstan	6		33	Zaire	17
14	Bolivia	7		34	Brazil	18
	Niger	7			Chile	18
16	Congo	8			Peru	18
	Saudi Arabia	8			Uruguay	18
	Turkmenistan	8		38	Sweden	19
19	Angola	9		39	Bahamas	20
	Mali	9			Mozambique	20

a 1993.

Note: Estimates of population density refer to the total land area of a country. In countries such as Japan and Canada, where much of the land area is virtually uninhabitable, the effective population densities of the habitable areas are much greater than the figures suggest.

y living

ggest cities
Population millions, latest year

1	Seoul	10.63
2	Bombay	9.93
3	Sao Paulo	9.48
4	Mexico City	8.83
5	Moscow	8.75
6	Delhi[a]	8.38
7	Tokyo	8.16
8	Jakarta	7.89
9	New York	7.32
10	Cairo	6.80
	London	6.80
12	Istanbul	6.62
13	Lima[a]	6.41
14	Shanghai	6.29
15	Tehran	6.04
16	Bangkok	5.88
17	Beijing	5.53
18	Madras	5.36
19	Rio de Janeiro	5.34
20	Karachi[a]	5.18
21	Tianjin	5.15
22	Santiago	4.86
23	St. Petersburg	4.44
24	Calcutta	4.40
25	Bogota[a]	4.18
26	Shenyang	3.94
27	Baghdad	3.84
28	Pusan	3.80
29	Sydney	3.66
30	Los Angeles	3.49

Quality of life index[b]
New York=100, November 1994

1	Geneva	106.00
2	Vancouver	105.29
3	Vienna	105.24
4	Toronto	105.20
5	Luxembourg	105.19
6	Zurich	105.09
7	Montreal	104.97
8	Dusseldorf	104.78
9	Singapore	104.76
10	Auckland	104.51
11	Oslo	104.50
12	Calgary	104.48
	Munich	104.48
14	Brussels	104.27
15	Amsterdam	104.01
16	Sydney	103.97
17	Frankfurt	103.84
18	Copenhagen	103.73
19	Melbourne	103.70
20	Wellington	103.67
21	London	103.52
22	Stockholm	103.41
23	Perth	103.34
24	Paris	103.14
25	Brisbane	102.92
26	Helsinki	102.88
27	Hamburg	102.70
28	Tokyo	102.31
29	Berlin	102.18
30	Boston	102.09

Highest urban pop.
% pop. living in urban areas, 1995

1	Bermuda	100
	Singapore	100
3	Macao	99
4	Belgium	97
	Kuwait	97
6	Hong Kong	95
7	Israel	93
	Venezuela	93
9	Iceland	92
10	Qatar	91

Lowest urban pop.
% pop. living in urban areas, 1995

1	Burundi	6
	Rwanda	6
	Bhutan	6
4	Uganda	13
	Cambodia	13
	Oman	13
	Ethiopia	13
8	Malawi	14
	Nepal	14
10	Papua New Guinea	18

a Urban agglomeration.
b Based on 42 factors as diverse as personal security and political stability.
Note: Estimates of cities' populations vary according to where geographical boundaries are defined. As far as possible the data refer to the city proper; urban agglomeration includes adjacent suburbs, eg, the population of the extended agglomeration of Paris (which includes 309 communes) is 9.32m; the population of Paris excluding these communes is 2.15m.

Population: *age and sex*

Youngest populations
% aged under 15, 1995

1	Rwanda	49.9	21	Liberia	46.0
2	Yemen	49.3	22	Iran	45.9
3	Malawi	49.2		Nicaragua	45.9
4	Côte d'Ivoire	49.0	24	Togo	45.8
5	Uganda	48.7	25	Madagascar	45.7
6	Zambia	48.5	26	Congo	45.6
7	Niger	48.1	27	Ghana	45.3
	Zaire	48.1		Libya	45.3
9	Tanzania	47.9	29	CAR	45.1
10	Syria	47.6	30	Mauritania	45.0
11	Somalia	47.5		Namibia	45.0
12	Kenya	47.4		Sierra Leone	45.0
	Mali	47.4	33	Botswana	44.9
14	Benin	47.2		Burkina Faso	44.9
15	Angola	47.1		Mozambique	44.9
	Guinea	47.1	36	Laos	44.8
17	Nigeria	46.9	37	Zimbabwe	44.6
18	Oman	46.6	38	Senegal	44.5
19	Ethiopia	46.5	39	Sudan	44.4
20	Burundi	46.3	40	Guatemala	44.3

Oldest populations
% aged over 65, 1995

1	Sweden	17.4	21	Estonia	12.7
2	Norway	15.9	22	United States	12.6
3	Belgium	15.7	23	Uruguay	12.3
4	Italy	15.6	24	Lithuania	12.2
	United Kingdom	15.6	25	Ex-Czechoslovakia	12.1
6	Austria	15.4	26	Canada	12.0
	Denmark	15.4		Ukraine	12.0
	Greece	15.4	28	Barbados	11.8
9	Switzerland	15.1	29	Australia	11.6
10	France	14.9		Ireland	11.6
11	Germany	14.8	31	Romania	11.3
12	Spain	14.7	32	New Zealand	11.2
13	Bulgaria	14.4	33	Iceland	11.1
14	Portugal	14.2	34	Belarus	11.0
15	Finland	14.1	35	Malta	10.9
16	Luxembourg	14.0		Poland	10.9
17	Hungary	13.9	37	Ex-Yugoslavia	10.6
	Japan	13.9	38	Cyprus	10.2
19	Latvia	13.1	39	Hong Kong	10.1
20	Netherlands	13.0	40	Russia	10.0

Most male populations
Number of men per 100 women[a], 1995

1	UAE	194.0	21	Fiji	103.5
2	Qatar	183.3		Iran	103.5
3	Bahrain	133.8		Kuwait	103.5
4	Saudi Arabia	123.8	24	Dominican Republic	103.4
5	Oman	110.7		Egypt	103.4
6	Libya	108.7	26	Singapore	103.2
7	Pakistan	108.3	27	Côte d'Ivoire	103.1
8	Papua New Guinea	107.2		Panama	103.1
9	Hong Kong	106.7	29	Philippines	102.8
	India	106.7	30	Bhutan	102.6
11	Taiwan[b]	106.4	31	Paraguay	102.5
12	Bangladesh	106.0	32	Costa Rica	102.3
13	China	105.7	33	Tunisia	102.2
	Nepal	105.7	34	Liberia	102.1
15	Albania	105.6	35	Guatemala	102.0
16	Brunei	105.2	36	Malaysia	101.8
17	Jordan	105.0		Mongolia	101.8
18	Afghanistan	104.7		Syria	101.8
19	Turkey	104.1	39	Honduras	101.7
20	Iraq	103.7	40	South Korea	101.6

Most female populations
Number of men per 100 women, 1995

1	Ukraine[c]	86.1		Uruguay	95.0
2	Latvia	88.1	24	Ex-Czechoslovakia	95.1
	Russia[c]	88.1		Lebanon	95.1
4	Belarus[c]	88.2		Poland	95.1
5	Estonia	89.5	27	France	95.2
6	Lithuania	90.5	28	Azerbaijan[c]	95.4
7	Georgia[c]	90.6		United States	95.4
8	Moldova[c]	91.1	30	Netherlands Antilles[e]	95.5
9	Cambodia	92.2		Nicaragua	95.5
10	Botswana	92.4	32	Congo	95.7
11	Hungary	92.5		Kirgizstan[c]	95.7
12	Barbados	92.7	34	El Salvador	95.8
13	Austria	93.1	35	Burundi	95.9
14	Portugal	93.4	36	Belgium	96.1
15	CAR	94.1		United Kingdom	96.1
16	Kazakhstan[c]	94.2	38	Bulgaria	96.3
17	Macao[d]	94.4	39	Haiti	96.4
18	Italy	94.6		Switzerland	96.4
19	Germany	94.7	41	Armenia[c]	96.5
20	Finland	94.8	42	Luxembourg	96.7
21	Puerto Rico	94.9	43	Sierra Leone	96.8
22	Lesotho	95.0			

a Large numbers of immigrant workers, mostly men, result in the high male ratios of several Middle East countries.
b 1993.
c mid 1990.
d 1992.
e 1989.

Population: *matters of breeding*

Highest crude birth rates
No. of live births per 1,000 population, 1995-2000

1	Afghanistan	50.5	26	Chad	41.6
2	Niger	50.2	27	Madagascar	41.2
3	Angola	48.4	28	Senegal	41.1
	Uganda	48.4		Tanzania	41.1
5	Côte d'Ivoire	47.6	30	Gambia, The	40.9
	Guinea	47.6	31	Guinea-Bissau	40.6
7	Malawi	47.4		Laos	40.6
	Mali	47.4	33	Libya	40.0
9	Somalia	47.3	34	Cameroon	39.4
10	Sierra Leone	46.3		Ghana	39.4
11	Yemen	46.0	36	CAR	39.3
12	Benin	45.8	37	Syria	38.9
13	Ethiopia	45.4	38	Gabon	38.5
14	Zaire	44.8	39	Sudan	38.4
15	Liberia	44.5	40	Mauritania	38.3
16	Burkina Faso	44.2	41	Jordan	37.5
17	Kenya	42.8	42	Cambodia	37.3
18	Mozambique	42.6		Pakistan	37.3
19	Congo	42.5	44	Bhutan	37.0
	Rwanda	42.5	45	Nicaragua	36.6
21	Nigeria	42.3	46	Nepal	36.4
22	Burundi	42.1	47	Guatemala	36.3
23	Zambia	41.9	48	Zimbabwe	36.0
24	Oman	41.8	49	Iraq	35.8
	Togo	41.8	50	Namibia	35.1

Highest fertility rates
Average no. of children per woman, 1995-2000

1	Yemen	7.14	21	Rwanda	6.00
2	Niger	7.10	22	Nigeria	5.97
3	Côte d'Ivoire	6.88	23	Saudi Arabia	5.94
4	Uganda	6.72	24	Libya	5.92
5	Angola	6.69	25	Congo	5.87
	Malawi	6.69	26	Kenya	5.76
7	Oman	6.67	27	Gabon	5.70
8	Benin	6.60	28	Madagascar	5.65
	Mali	6.60	29	Senegal	5.62
10	Guinea	6.51	30	Pakistan	5.59
	Somalia	6.51	31	Ghana	5.53
12	Afghanistan	6.37	32	Chad	5.51
13	Liberia	6.33	33	Zambia	5.49
14	Burundi	6.28	34	Tanzania	5.48
15	Zaire	6.24	35	Bhutan	5.44
16	Togo	6.08	36	Guinea-Bissau	5.42
17	Burkina Faso	6.06	37	Sudan	5.37
	Mozambique	6.06	38	Syria	5.36
	Sierra Leone	6.06	39	Ethiopia	5.34
20	Laos	6.03	40	Cameroon	5.30

Lowest crude birth rates
Number of live births per 1,000 population, 1995-2000

1	Germany	9.2		Netherlands	12.3
2	Italy	9.6		Switzerland	12.3
3	Greece	9.8	23	France	12.4
	Hong Kong	9.8		Hungary	12.4
	Spain	9.8	25	Finland	12.5
6	Japan	10.5		Luxembourg	12.5
7	Bulgaria	10.6	27	United Kingdom	12.9
	Slovenia	10.6	28	Lithuania	13.0
9	Russia	10.8	29	Poland	13.5
10	Croatia	11.1	30	Sweden	13.6
	Estonia	11.1	31	Bermuda[a]	13.7
12	Latvia	11.3	32	Czech Republic	13.8
13	Austria	11.4	33	Malta	13.9
14	Ukraine	11.5		Singapore	13.9
15	Romania	11.6	35	Canada	14.1
16	Belarus	11.8	36	Australia	14.2
	Belgium	11.8	37	Norway	14.2
	Portugal	11.8		Serbia	14.2
19	Denmark	12.0	39	United States	14.7
20	Bosnia & Hercegovina	12.3	40	Slovakia	14.8

Lowest fertility rates
Average number of children per woman, 1995-2000

1	Hong Kong	1.21	21	Denmark	1.70
2	Spain	1.23	22	Belgium	1.71
3	Italy	1.27		Hungary	1.71
4	Germany	1.30	24	Luxembourg	1.72
5	Greece	1.40	25	Singapore	1.73
6	Slovenia	1.45	26	France	1.74
7	Bulgaria	1.50	27	South Korea	1.80
	Japan	1.50		Taiwan	1.80
	Romania	1.50	29	United Kingdom	1.81
10	Russia	1.53	30	Cuba	1.82
11	Portugal	1.55	31	Barbados	1.83
12	Austria	1.60		Czech Republic	1.83
	Bosnia & Hercegovina	1.60		Lithuania	1.83
14	Estonia	1.61	34	Australia	1.87
	Netherlands	1.61	35	Poland	1.88
16	Latvia	1.64	36	Finland	1.92
	Ukraine	1.64		Slovakia	1.92
18	Belarus	1.65	38	Canada	1.93
	Croatia	1.65	39	China	1.95
20	Switzerland	1.67	40	Macedonia	1.97

Notes: The crude birth rate is the number of live births in one year per 1,000 population. In addition to the fertility rate (see below) it depends on the population's age structure and will tend to be higher if there is a large proportion of women of childbearing age.

The fertility rate is the average number of children born to a woman who completes her childbearing years.

a 1993.

The world economy

Biggest economies
GDP, $bn

1	United States	6,388		49	UAE	39
2	Japan	3,927		50	Egypt	37
3	Germany	1,903		51	Hungary	34
4	France	1,289			Kuwait	34
5	Italy	1,135			Peru	34
6	United Kingdom	1,043		54	Nigeria	33
7	China	581		55	Belarus	29
8	Canada	575		56	Czech Republic	28
9	Spain	534			Morocco	28
10	Brazil	472		58	Bangladesh	26
11	Russia	348			Kazakhstan	26
12	South Korea	338		60	Puerto Rico	25
13	Mexico	325			Romania	25
14	Netherlands	316		62	Libya[a]	24
15	Australia	310		63	North Korea	21
16	India	263			Uzbekistan	21
17	Switzerland	254		65	Iraq[a]	18
18	Argentina	244		66	Tunisia	15
19	Sweden	216			Zaire[a]	15
	Taiwan	216		68	Luxembourg	14
21	Belgium	213		69	Ecuador	13
22	Austria	184			Slovenia	13
23	Denmark	138		71	Uruguay	12
24	Indonesia	137			Vietnam	12
25	Turkey	126		73	Guatemala	11
26	Saudi Arabia	121			Sri Lanka	11
27	Thailand	120		75	Bulgaria	10
28	South Africa	118			Cameroon	10
29	Norway	114			Cuba	10
30	Hong Kong	105			Oman	10
31	Ukraine	100			Slovakia	10
32	Finland	96		80	Liberia[a]	9
33	Poland	87			Myanmar	9
34	Portugal	78		82	Côte d'Ivoire	8
35	Greece	77			Cyprus	8
36	Israel	73			Dominican Republic	8
37	Malaysia	60			Qatar	8
38	Venezuela	59		86	Costa Rica	7
39	Philippines	55			El Salvador	7
	Singapore	55			Ghana	7
41	Pakistan	53			Kenya	7
42	Colombia	50			Panama	7
43	Iran	47			Paraguay	7
44	Ireland	45		92	Angola[a]	6
	New Zealand	45			Iceland	6
46	Algeria	44			Senegal	6
47	Syria[a]	43			Zimbabwe	6
48	Chile	42				

a Estimate.

Regional GDP

$bn 1993		*growth 1985-93*	
World	24,108	World	2.8
Industrial countries	18,899	Industrial countries	2.5
G7	16,259	G7	2.5
EU12	6,785	EU12	2.3
EU15	7,281	Asia[a]	7.3
Asia[a]	1,722	Latin America	2.4
Latin America	889	Eastern Europe	-3.6
Eastern Europe	752	Middle East and Europe[b]	3.8
Middle East and Europe[b]	608	Africa	2.0
Africa	375		

Regional GDP per person

$, 1993		*growth 1985-93*	
World	4,390	Industrial countries	1.8
Industrial countries	21,653	G7	1.8
G7	24,449	EU12	2.0
EU12	19,488	Asia[a]	5.5
EU15	19,685	Latin America	0.4
Asia[a]	599	Eastern Europe	-4.1
Latin America	2,924	Middle East and Europe[b]	0.4
Eastern Europe	2,012	Africa	-0.8
Middle East and Europe[b]	2,285		
Africa	612		

Regional trade: value

Exports, $bn 1993		*Imports, $bn 1993*	
World	3,751	World	3,701
Industrial countries	2,503	Industrial countries	2,408
G7	1,791	G7	1,909
EU12	1,265	EU12	1,285
EU15	1,368	EU15	1,375
Asia[a]	620	Asia[a]	624
Latin America	138	Latin America	153
Middle East and Europe[b]	157	Middle East and Europe[b]	162
Africa	77	Africa	75

Regional trade: volume growth, %

Exports, 1985-93		*Imports, 1985-93*	
World	5.2	Industrial countries	5.4
Industrial countries	4.6	G7	5.7
G7	4.7	EU12	5.5
EU12	4.1	Asia[a]	11.5
Asia[a]	11.9	Latin America	8.5
Latin America	5.4	Middle East and Europe[b]	0.4
Middle East and Europe[b]	6.3	Africa	0.5
Africa	3.0		

a   Excludes Japan.
b   Includes Turkey.

Living standards

Highest GDP per head
$

1	Switzerland	36,399
2	Luxembourg	35,583
3	Japan	31,451
4	Bermuda	28,293
5	Denmark	26,514
6	Norway	26,340
7	Sweden	24,833
8	United States	24,753
9	Iceland	23,985
10	Germany	23,561
11	Kuwait	23,370
12	Austria	23,115
13	UAE	22,512
14	France	22,363
15	Belgium	21,216
16	Netherlands	20,707
17	Canada	20,664
18	Italy	19,623
19	Singapore	19,293
20	Finland	18,978
21	United Kingdom	17,965
22	Hong Kong	17,842
23	Australia	17,502
24	Qatar	15,137
25	Brunei	14,000
26	Israel	13,762
27	Spain	13,646
28	New Zealand	12,912
29	Ireland	12,579
30	Bahamas	11,330
31	Taiwan	10,404
32	Cyprus	10,327
33	Macao[a]	8,750
34	Bahrain	7,931
35	Portugal	7,893
36	South Korea	7,673
37	Greece	7,389
38	Argentina	7,288
39	Malta[b]	7,186
40	Puerto Rico	7,013
41	Saudi Arabia	6,958
42	Netherlands Antilles[a]	6,912
43	Slovenia	6,315
44	Barbados	6,231
45	Oman	5,599
46	Libya[b]	4,722
47	Gabon	4,035
48	Uruguay	3,909
49	Liberia[b]	3,797
50	Mexico	3,748
51	Trinidad & Tobago	3,731
52	Hungary	3,332
53	Syria[b]	3,234
54	Malaysia	3,156
55	Chile	3,074
56	Estonia	3,034
57	Brazil	3,018
58	Mauritius	2,981
59	South Africa	2,902
60	Belarus	2,838
61	Venezuela	2,835
62	Czech Republic	2,732
63	Botswana	2,593
64	Panama	2,586
65	Russia	2,346
66	Poland	2,271
67	Costa Rica	2,153
68	Fiji	2,139
69	Turkey	2,125
70	Thailand	2,044

Lowest GDP per head
$

1	Sudan[b]	63
2	Somalia[c]	78
3	Mozambique	81
4	Tanzania	94
5	Ethiopia[a]	102
6	Afghanistan[a]	111
7	Sierra Leone	145
8	Nepal	156
9	Bhutan	165
10	Vietnam	169
11	Burundi	185
12	Uganda	193
13	Cambodia	197
14	Myanmar	200
	Rwanda	200
16	Chad[a]	214
17	Malawi	219
18	Bangladesh	222
19	Guinea-Bissau	224
20	Haiti[d]	236

a 1992
b Estimate.
c 1990.
d 1991

CONTENTS

Contents

Highest purchasing power[a]
GDP per head in PPP (USA = 100), 1991

1	United States	100.0	36	South Korea	37.6
2	Switzerland	98.4	37	Venezuela	36.7
3	Luxembourg	94.0	38	Estonia	36.6
4	Germany	89.3	39	Greece	34.7
	Japan	87.6	40	Malta	34.2
6	Canada	87.3	41	Latvia	34.1
7	Hong Kong	83.7	42	Malaysia	33.4
8	France	83.3	43	Mauritius	32.4
9	Denmark	80.8		Mexico	32.4
10	Austria	79.9	45	Chile	31.9
11	Belgium	79.1	46	Libya	31.6
13	Iceland	79.0	47	Russia	31.3
	Sweden	79.0	48	Belarus	31.0
14	Norway	77.6	49	Uruguay	30.1
15	Italy	77.0	50	Ex-Czechoslovakia	29.7
16	UAE[b]	76.8	51	Hungary	27.5
17	Netherlands	76.0	52	Colombia	24.7
18	Australia	75.4	53	Lithuania	24.4
19	United Kingdom	73.8	54	Thailand	23.8
20	Finland	72.9	55	Brazil	23.7
21	Singapore	66.6	56	Syria	23.6
22	Brunei[b]	63.3	57	Ukraine	23.4
	Qatar[b]	63.3	58	Argentina	23.1
24	New Zealand	63.1	59	Costa Rica	23.0
25	Israel	60.8	60	Panama	22.2
26	Kuwait	59.3	61	Fiji[b]	22.0
27	Spain	57.3	62	Turkey	21.9
28	Bahamas[b]	54.2	63	Bulgaria	21.7
29	Bahrain	52.1	64	Botswana	21.2
30	Ireland	51.6		Tunisia	21.2
31	Saudi Arabia	49.0	66	Iran	21.1
32	Cyprus	44.5	67	Armenia	20.8
	Barbados	43.7	68	Kazakhstan	20.3
34	Portugal	42.7		Poland	20.3
35	Trinidad & Tobago	37.9	70	Ecuador	18.7

Lowest purchasing power[a]
GDP per head in PPP (USA=100), 1991

1	Ethiopia	1.7		Myanmar[b]	2.9
2	Chad	2.0	12	Burkina Faso	3.0
3	Zaire	2.1	13	Rwanda	3.1
4	Mali	2.2	14	Afghanistan[b]	3.2
5	Guinea	2.3		Comoros	3.2
6	Niger	2.4		Madagascar	3.2
7	Tanzania	2.6	18	Togo	3.3
8	Bhutan	2.8	19	Gambia, The	3.4
9	Burundi	2.9		Guinea-Bissau	3.4
	CAR	2.9		Somalia	3.4

a See glossary for explanation of purchasing power parity.
b Estimate

The quality of life

Human development index

1	Canada	93.2
2	Switzerland	93.1
3	Japan	92.9
4	Norway	92.8
	Sweden	92.8
6	France	92.7
7	Australia	92.6
8	United States	92.5
9	Netherlands	92.3
10	United Kingdom	91.9
11	Germany	91.8
12	Austria	91.7
13	Belgium	91.6
14	Iceland	91.4
15	Denmark	91.2
16	Finland	91.1
17	Luxembourg	90.8
18	New Zealand	90.7
19	Israel	90.0
20	Barbados	89.4
21	Ireland	89.2
22	Italy	89.1
23	Spain	88.8
24	Hong Kong	87.5
25	Greece	87.4
26	Cyprus	87.3
27	Ex-Czechoslovakia	87.2
28	Lithuania	86.8
29	Estonia	86.7
30	Latvia	86.5
31	Hungary	86.3
32	South Korea	85.9
	Uruguay	85.9
34	Russia	85.8
35	Trinidad & Tobago	85.5
36	Bahamas	85.4
37	Argentina	85.3
38	Chile	84.8
	Costa Rica	84.8
40	Belarus	84.7

41	Malta	84.3
42	Portugal	83.8
43	Singapore	83.6
44	Brunei	82.9
45	Ukraine	82.3
46	Venezuela	82.0
47	Panama	81.6
48	Bulgaria	81.5
	Poland	81.5
50	Colombia	81.3
51	Kuwait	80.9
52	Mexico	80.4
53	Armenia	80.1
54	Thailand	79.8
56	Qatar	79.5
57	Malaysia	79.4
58	Bahrain	79.1
59	Fiji	78.7
60	Mauritius	77.8
61	Kazakhstan	77.4
62	United Arab Emirates	77.1
63	Brazil	75.6
64	Jamaica	74.9
65	Georgia	74.7
66	Saudi Arabia	74.2
67	Turkey	73.9
68	Azerbaijan	73.0
69	Romania	72.9
70	Syria	72.7
71	Ecuador	71.8
72	Albania	71.4
	Moldova	71.4
74	Libya	70.3
75	Turkmeninstan	69.7
76	Tunisia	69.0
77	Kirgizstan	68.9
78	Paraguay	67.9
79	Suriname	67.7
80	Iran	67.2

Notes: GDP or GDP per head is often taken as a measure of how developed a country is but its usefuless is limited as it refers only to economic welfare. In 1990 the UN Development Programme published its first estimate of a Human Development Index, which combined statistics on two other indicators – adult literacy and life expectancy – with income levels to give a better, though still far from perfect, indicator of human development. In 1991 average years of schooling was combined with adult literacy to give a knowledge variable. The index is shown here scaled from 0 to 100; countries scoring over 80 are considered to have high human development, those scoring from 50 to 79 have medium human development and those under 50 have low human development.

Economic freedom index

1	Hong Kong	1.25	**42**	Uganda	2.94
	Singapore	1.25	**43**	South Africa	3.00
3	Bahrain	1.60		Turkey	3.00
4	United States	1.90		Venezuela	3.00
5	Japan	1.95	**46**	Botswana	3.05
	Taiwan	1.95		Gabon	3.05
	United Kingdom	1.95		Guatemala	3.05
8	Canada	2.00		Kenya	3.05
	Germany	2.00		Mexico	3.05
10	Austria	2.05		Zambia	3.05
11	Bahamas	2.10	**52**	Israel	3.10
	Czech Republic	2.10	**53**	Algeria	3.15
13	South Korea	2.15		Honduras	3.15
	Malaysia	2.15		Nigeria	3.15
15	Australia	2.20		Pakistan	3.15
	Ireland	2.20	**57**	Bolivia	3.20
17	Estonia	2.25	**58**	Ecuador	3.25
18	France	2.30		Côte d'Ivoire	3.25
	Thailand	2.30		Malta	3.25
20	Chile	2.50		Poland	3.25
	Italy	2.50	**62**	Brazil	3.30
22	Spain	2.60		Fiji	3.30
23	El Salvador	2.65		Ghana	3.30
	Oman	2.65		Philippines	3.30
	Sweden	2.65	**66**	Mongolia	3.33
26	Belize	2.70	**67**	Guinea	3.35
	Panama	2.70		Indonesia	3.35
28	Paraguay	2.75	**69**	Dominican Republic	3.40
	Slovakia	2.75		Malawi	3.40
30	Greece	2.80		Peru	3.40
	Hungary	2.80		Russia	3.40
	Jamaica	2.80	**73**	Bulgaria	3.50
	Portugal	2.80		Cameroon	3.50
	Sri Lanka	2.80		Egypt	3.50
35	Argentina	2.85		Madagascar	3.50
	Tunisia	2.85		Mali	3.50
37	Colombia	2.90		Tanzania	3.50
	Costa Rica	2.90		Zimbabwe	3.50
	Jordan	2.90	**80**	Albania	3.55
	Morocco	2.90		Romania	3.55
	Uruguay	2.90			

Notes: The index of economic freedom, published by the Heritage Foundation, ranks countries on the basis of ten indicators of how government intervention can restrict the economic relations between individuals. The economic indicators are trade policy, taxation, monetary policy, the banking system, foreign-investment rules, property rights, the amount of economic output consumed by the government, regulation policy, the size of the black market and the extent of wage and price controls. A country can score between 1 and 5 in each category, 1 being the most free and 5 being the least free.

Economic growth

Fastest economic growth, 1985-93
Average annual % increase in real GDP

1	China	9.2	21	Papua New Guinea	5.0
2	Thailand	9.1	22	Laos	4.9
3	South Korea	8.9		Uganda	4.9
4	Botswana	8.0	23	Costa Rica	4.8
5	Singapore	7.8		Ghana	4.8
6	Macao[a]	7.4		India	4.8
	Malaysia	7.4		Nepal	4.8
8	Mauritius	7.0		Oman	4.8
9	Chile	6.9	29	Nigeria	4.7
10	Hong Kong	6.8	30	Ireland	4.5
11	Taiwan	6.7		Israel	4.5
12	Bhutan	6.5	32	Colombia	4.2
13	Indonesia	6.4		Tanzania	4.2
14	Lesotho	6.0	34	Bangladesh	4.1
15	Cyprus	5.9		Saudi Arabia	4.1
16	Cambodia[b]	5.8		Sri Lanka	4.1
17	Malta	5.7	37	Syria	4.0
18	Pakistan	5.5	38	Guinea	3.9
19	Turkey	5.1		Kenya	3.9
	Vietnam	5.1		Tunisia	3.9

Slowest economic growth, 1985-93
Average annual % increase in real GDP

1	Georgia[c]	-24.0		Cameroon	-3.8
2	Armenia[c]	-18.5	22	Albania	-3.7
3	Lithuania[c]	-15.7	23	Libya[d]	-3.3
4	Tajikistan[c]	-15.1	24	Haiti	-3.0
5	Azerbaijan[c]	-14.5	25	Ex-Czechoslovakia[d]	-2.5
6	Cuba[c]	-12.4	26	Afghanistan	-2.4
7	Latvia[c]	-11.4		Bulgaria	-2.4
8	Kazakhstan[a]	-10.1	28	Nicaragua	-2.1
9	Moldova[c]	-9.9	29	Togo	-1.7
10	Ex-Yugoslavia[d]	-9.1	30	Hungary	-1.5
11	Ukraine[c]	-8.8	31	Trinidad & Tobago	-1.2
12	Iraq	-8.0	32	Somalia	-1.1
13	Estonia[c]	-7.3	33	North Korea[d]	-0.9
14	Kirgizstan[c]	-7.1	34	Angola[f]	-0.8
15	Russia[e]	-6.7	35	Côte d'Ivoire	-0.7
16	Romania	-4.8	36	Poland	-0.5
17	Turkmenistan[c]	-4.6	37	Bermuda[g]	-0.3
18	Slovenia[e]	-4.1	38	Peru	-0.2
	Zaire	-4.1		Rwanda	-0.2
20	Belarus[c]	-3.8	40	Liberia	-0.1

a	1990-93.	e	1988-93.
b	1988-93.	f	1987-93.
c	1989-93.	g	1987-92.
d	1986-92.		

Fastest economic growth, 1975-84
Average annual % increase in real GDP

1	Botswana	12.4	Malta	7.2
2	Oman	10.3	12 Egypt	7.1
3	Jordan	9.0	13 Malaysia	7.0
4	Hong Kong	8.9	Thailand	7.0
5	Taiwan	8.6	15 Cameroon	6.8
6	Singapore	8.0	16 Paraguay	6.6
	South Korea	8.0	17 Mongolia	6.5
8	Congo	7.6	18 Bahrain	6.2
9	Niger	7.4	19 Vietnam	6.1
10	China	7.2	20 Bhutan	6.0

Slowest economic growth, 1975-84
Average annual % increase in real GDP

1	Kuwait	-1.7	11 Madagascar	-0.2
2	Ghana	-1.5	12 El Salvador	-0.1
3	Nicaragua	-1.4	Zambia	-0.1
	Nigeria	-1.4	14 Switzerland	0.0
5	Chad	-1.3	15 Argentina	0.1
6	Gabon	-0.9	Mozambique	0.1
7	Zaire	-0.8	17 Uganda	0.2
8	Afghanistan	-0.6	18 Papua New Guinea	0.6
9	Lesotho	-0.5	19 Jamaica	0.7
10	Liberia	-0.4	20 Sierra Leone	0.8

Highest industrial growth, 1980-92
Average annual % increase in real terms

1	Bhutan	11.8	6 Oman	9.6
2	South Korea	11.6	7 Mauritius	9.2
3	China	11.1	8 Lesotho	8.5
4	Botswana	10.1	9 Malaysia	8.0
	Thailand	10.1	10 Syria	7.6

Highest services growth, 1980-92
Average annual % increase in real terms

1	Botswana	11.7	6 Bhutan	7.7
2	China	11.0	7 Singapore	7.3
3	South Korea	9.3	8 Indonesia	6.8
4	Taiwan	9.1	9 Chad	6.7
5	Thailand	8.1	10 India	6.3

Highest agricultural growth, 1980-92
Average annual % increase in real terms

1	Saudi Arabia	14.0	6 Algeria	5.3
2	Jordan[a]	8.1	Lesotho	5.3
3	Oman	7.1	Morocco	5.3
4	Chile	5.6	9 Benin	5.2
5	China	5.4	10 Togo	4.9

a 1980-91.

Trading places

Biggest traders
% of total world exports (visible & invisible)

1	United States	13.89	26	Thailand	0.78
2	Japan	10.20	27	Indonesia	0.76
3	Germany	9.47	28	Russia[a]	0.66
4	France	7.03	29	Ireland	0.64
5	United Kingdom	6.35	30	Finland	0.54
6	Italy	4.71	31	South Africa	0.52
7	Belgium/Luxembourg	4.12	32	Turkey	0.50
8	Netherlands	3.41	33	Portugal	0.45
9	Canada	3.10	34	India[b]	0.43
10	Switzerland	2.20	35	Israel	0.41
11	Taiwan	1.91	36	Iran[a]	0.38
12	South Korea	1.82	37	Philippines	0.35
13	Spain	1.80	38	Poland	0.34
14	China[a]	1.55	39	Venezuela	0.32
15	Austria	1.43		Argentina	0.32
16	Denmark	1.34	41	Ex-Yugoslavia[c]	0.31
17	Sweden	1.29		Kuwait	0.31
18	Singapore[a]	1.20	43	Czech Republic[a]	0.30
19	Australia	1.05	44	Greece	0.26
20	Saudi Arabia	1.00	45	New Zealand	0.25
21	Malaysia	0.98	46	Nigeria[a]	0.24
22	Mexico	0.87		Algeria[c]	0.24
	Norway	0.87	48	Egypt	0.23
24	Hong Kong[a]	0.85		Chile	0.23
25	Brazil	0.81	50	Libya[b]	0.22

Most trade dependent
Trade as % of GDP[d]

1	Singapore[a]	101.9
2	Bahrain[a]	96.8
3	Panama	86.5
4	Malaysia	73.6
5	Malta[a]	69.9
6	Botswana[b]	65.6
7	Ireland	54.9
8	UAE[a]	51.5
9	Netherlands Antilles	50.6
10	Namibia[a]	49.3
11	Slovenia	49.0
12	Czech Republic[a]	48.9
13	Oman	48.8
14	Belgium/Luxembourg	47.7
15	Angola[a]	46.9

Least trade dependent
Trade as % of GDP[d]

1	Myanmar[a]	3.3
2	Argentina	5.9
3	Brazil	6.8
4	India[b]	7.1
	Japan	7.1
6	Syria	7.7
7	United States	8.2
8	Russia[a]	8.5
	Rwanda[a]	8.5
10	Uganda	9.6
11	Niger	10.4
12	Cameroon	10.7
	Ethiopia[a]	10.7
14	Peru	11.0
15	CAR	11.1

Notes: The figures are drawn from balance of payment statistics and, therefore, have differing technical definitions from trade statistics taken from customs or similar sources. The invisible trade figures do not show some countries, notably Eastern European, due to unavailable data. For Hong Kong and Singapore, only domestic exports and retained imports have been taken into account.

Biggest visible traders
% of world visible exports

1	United States	12.84	21	Brazil	1.09
2	Germany	10.21	22	Denmark	1.05
3	Japan	9.87	23	Indonesia	1.03
4	France	5.48	24	Russia[a]	1.01
5	United Kingdom	5.09	25	Thailand[a]	0.90
6	Italy	4.73		Norway	0.90
7	Canada	4.05	27	Mexico	0.84
8	Netherlands	3.39	28	Hong Kong[a]	0.82
9	Belgium/Luxembourg	2.92	29	Ireland	0.81
10	Taiwan	2.37	30	South Africa	0.67
11	South Korea	2.27	31	Finland	0.65
12	Switzerland	2.11	32	UAE[a]	0.59
13	China[a]	1.96	33	Iran[a]	0.56
14	Spain	1.65	34	India[b]	0.51
15	Sweden	1.39	35	Turkey	0.44
16	Malaysia	1.29		Portugal	0.43
17	Saudi Arabia	1.26	37	Israel	0.42
18	Australia	1.19	38	Venezuela	0.39
19	Singapore[a]	1.11		Ex-Yugoslavia[c]	0.39
20	Austria	1.10	40	Poland	0.38

Biggest invisible traders
% of world invisible exports

1	United States	15.87	22	Australia	0.78
2	Japan	10.82	23	Turkey	0.63
3	France	9.97	24	Thailand[a]	0.54
4	United Kingdom	8.72	25	Saudi Arabia	0.51
5	Germany	8.07	26	Egypt	0.49
6	Belgium/Luxembourg	6.41		Greece	0.49
7	Italy	4.67		Portugal	0.49
8	Netherlands	3.45	29	Philippines	0.40
9	Switzerland	2.39	30	Israel	0.39
10	Spain	2.07		Malaysia	0.39
11	Austria	2.04	32	Kuwait	0.33
12	Denmark	1.89	33	Finland	0.32
13	Singapore[a]	1.37	34	Ireland	0.31
14	Canada	1.31	35	Brazil	0.27
15	Sweden	1.10		India[b]	0.27
16	Taiwan	1.05	36	Indonesia	0.26
17	South Korea	0.97		Czech Republic[a]	0.26
18	Mexico	0.93	39	Poland	0.25
19	Hong Kong[a]	0.89	40	South Africa	0.23
20	Norway	0.81	41	Argentina	0.22
21	China[a]	0.79	42	Hungary	0.18

a 1992.
b 1990.
c 1991.
d Average of imports and exports of goods as % of GDP.
e 1989.

Current account

Largest surpluses

$bn

1	Japan	131.5		Nigeria[a]	2.3	
2	Switzerland	16.7	17	Libya[c]	2.2	
3	Belgium/Luxembourg	12.6	18	Singapore	2.0	
4	Italy	11.2	19	South Africa	1.8	
5	France	10.2	20	Colombia[a]	0.9	
6	Netherlands	10.0		Portugal	0.9	
7	Hong Kong	9.2	22	South Korea	0.4	
8	Taiwan	6.7	23	Bangladesh	0.2	
9	China[a]	6.4		Kenya	0.2	
10	Kuwait	6.3		Slovenia	0.2	
11	Denmark	5.5	26	Barbados[a]	0.1	
12	Ireland	3.8		Botswana[c]	0.1	
13	Norway	2.5		Malta[a]	0.1	
14	Algeria[b]	2.4		Namibia[a]	0.1	
15	Egypt	2.3		Trinidad & Tobago[a]	0.1	

Largest deficits

$bn

1	United States	-103.9	28	Oman	-1.1
2	Canada	-23.9		Paraguay	-1.1
3	Mexico	-23.4	30	Bahrain[a]	-1.0
4	Germany	-20.0		Finland	-1.0
5	United Kingdom	-16.4		Yemen	-1.0
6	Saudi Arabia	-14.2	33	Austria	-0.9
7	Australia	-10.8		New Zealand	-0.9
8	Argentina	-7.5		Tunisia	-0.9
9	India[c]	-7.0	36	Angola[a]	-0.7
10	Thailand[a]	-6.6		Cameroon	-0.7
11	Iran[a]	-6.5		Greece	-0.7
12	Turkey	-6.4		Guatemala	-0.7
13	Spain	-6.3	40	Brazil	-0.6
14	Poland	-5.8		Mongolia[c]	-0.6
15	Hungary	-4.3		Syria	-0.6
16	Philippines	-3.3		Zaire[c]	-0.6
17	Pakistan	-2.9	44	Bolivia[a]	-0.5
18	Venezuela	-2.2		Bulgaria	-0.5
19	Chile	-2.1		Congo	-0.5
	Malaysia	-2.1		Costa Rica	-0.5
21	Indonesia	-2.0		Jordan	-0.5
22	Peru	-1.8		Morocco	-0.5
	Sweden	-1.8		Nicaragua	-0.5
24	Israel	-1.4		Sudan[a]	-0.5
25	Côte d'Ivoire	-1.2	52	Mozambique[a]	-0.4
	Romania	-1.2		Sri Lanka	-0.4
	Ex-Yugoslavia	-1.2		Tanzania	-0.4

Largest surpluses as % of GDP
%

1	Kuwait	18.6	16	Japan	3.3
2	Gambia, The[a]	10.1	17	Netherlands	3.2
3	Libya[c]	9.2	18	Taiwan	3.1
4	Hong Kong	8.8	19	Trinidad & Tobago[a]	2.4
5	Ireland	8.6	20	Kenya	2.3
6	Barbados[a]	8.1		Malta[a]	2.3
7	Nigeria[a]	6.9	22	Norway	2.2
8	Switzerland	6.6	23	Colombia[a]	2.0
9	Egypt	6.3	24	Lesotho	1.8
10	Belgium	5.9	25	Cambodia[a]	1.7
11	Namibia[a]	5.7	26	Slovenia	1.5
12	Botswana[c]	5.4		South Africa	1.5
13	Algeria[b]	4.5	28	China[a]	1.4
14	Denmark	4.0	29	Portugal	1.2
15	Singapore	3.7		Sierra Leone[b]	1.2

Largest deficits as % of GDP
%

1	Mozambique[a]	-36.8	31	Guatemala	-6.2
2	Mongolia[c]	-36.1		Thailand[a]	-6.2
3	Nicaragua	-32.2	33	Philippines	-6.0
4	Sudan[a]	-30.5	34	Tunisia	-5.9
5	Bahrain[a]	-26.9	35	Afghanistan[d]	-5.8
6	Congo	-21.9	36	Pakistan	-5.5
7	Yemen	-18.9	37	Bulgaria	-5.4
8	Tanzania	-16.2		Gabon	-5.4
9	Paraguay	-15.9		Jamaica	-5.4
10	Somalia[d]	-15.7	40	Ghana	-5.3
11	Côte d'Ivoire	-14.6		Peru	-5.3
12	Guinea-Bissau	-12.4	42	Senegal	-5.2
	Hungary	-12.4	43	Turkey	-5.1
14	Saudi Arabia	-11.8	44	Iran[a]	-5.0
15	Oman	-11.1	45	Chile	-4.9
16	Bolivia[a]	-10.5	46	Madagascar[a]	-4.8
	Mauritania[a]	-10.5	47	Rwanda[a]	-4.7
18	Papua New Guinea[d]	-10.4	48	Romania	-4.6
19	Jordan	-9.6	49	CAR[a]	-4.4
20	Zambia[b]	-9.0	50	Canada	-4.2
21	Honduras[a]	-8.4	51	Malawi	-4.1
22	Angola[a]	-8.2	52	Burkina Faso	-4.0
23	Zaire[c]	-7.9	53	Mali	-3.8
24	Cameroon	-7.7		Venezuela	-3.8
25	Togo	-7.4	55	Sri Lanka	-3.6
26	Mexico	-7.2	56	Australia	-3.5
27	Nepal	-7.0		Malaysia	-3.5
28	Costa Rica	-6.7	58	Cyprus[a]	-3.4
29	Poland	-6.6	59	Argentina	-3.1
30	Chad	-6.4		Uganda	-3.1

a 1992. c 1990.
b 1991. d 1989.

Inflation

Highest inflation, 1993-94
% consumer price inflation

1	Serbia[a]	>1m	31	Iraq[a]	75.0
2	Ukraine[a]	4,734.9	32	Venezuela	60.8
3	Armenia[a]	3,731.8	33	Uruguay[a]	54.1
4	Georgia[a]	3,125.6	34	Lebanon[a]	50.0
5	Turkmenistan[a]	3,102.4		Yemen[a]	50.0
6	Brazil	2,443.0	36	Guinea-Bissau[a]	48.1
7	Tajikistan[a]	2,194.8	37	Ecuador[a]	45.0
8	Zaire[a]	1,986.9	38	Afghanistan[a]	34.0
9	Kazakhstan[a]	1,571.0	39	Poland	32.0
10	Croatia[a]	1,517.0	40	Myanmar[a]	31.8
11	Kirgizstan[a]	1,208.7	41	Cambodia[a]	31.0
12	Belarus[a]	1,188.0	42	Haiti[a]	30.7
13	Angola[a]	1,044.0	43	Somalia[a]	24.3
14	Uzbekistan[a]	851.1	44	Tanzania[a]	23.5
15	Azerbaijan[a]	833.4	45	Slovakia[a]	23.2
16	Moldova[a]	688.5	46	Zimbabwe	23.0
17	Lithuania[a]	410.4	47	Colombia	22.9
18	Russia	307.0	48	Sierra Leone[a]	22.2
19	Macedonia[a]	247.6	49	Jamaica[a]	22.1
20	Zambia[a]	189.0	50	Kenya	22.0
21	Mongolia[a]	183.1	51	China	21.8
22	Nigeria	150.0	52	Peru	21.0
23	Suriname[a]	143.5	53	Algeria[a]	20.5
24	Romania	137.0	54	Nicaragua[a]	20.4
25	Bulgaria[a]	121.9	55	Iran[a]	20.3
26	Latvia[a]	109.0	56	Slovenia	20.0
27	Turkey	106.3	57	Hungary	18.8
28	Sudan[a]	101.4	58	El Salvador[a]	18.6
29	Estonia[a]	89.0	59	Paraguay[a]	18.3
30	Mozambique[a]	76.2	60	Ghana	18.0

Highest inflation, 1989-94
% average annual consumer price inflation

1	Serbia[b]	>1m	16	Azerbaijan[d]	416.0
2	Brazil	1,460.6	17	Uzbekistan[d]	396.6
3	Nicaragua[c]	987.5	18	Zaire[c]	382.8
4	Ukraine[d]	965.8	19	Angola[d]	317.4
5	Armenia[d]	791.9	20	Estonia[d]	309.4
6	Tajikistan[d]	748.2	21	Argentina	279.9
7	Georgia[d]	735.5	22	Latvia[d]	266.7
8	Kazakhstan[d]	679.0	23	Mongolia[d]	232.6
9	Croatia[c]	660.4	24	Slovenia	213.6
10	Turkmenistan[d]	627.2	25	Russia	177.9
11	Moldova[d]	557.5	26	Poland	117.1
12	Belarus[d]	532.2	27	Romania	112.0
13	Kirgizstan[d]	513.7	28	Lebanon[c]	109.6
14	Peru	490.0	29	Zambia[c]	105.0
15	Lithuania[d]	470.5	30	Cambodia[c]	100.9

Lowest inflation, 1993-94
% consumer price inflation

1	Cameroon[a]	-3.9	26	Albania	2.0
2	CAR[a]	-2.9		Bahrain[a]	2.0
3	Niger[a]	-1.2		Denmark	2.0
4	Togo[a]	-1.0	29	Chad[a]	2.1
5	Kuwait[a]	-0.6		Netherlands Antilles[a]	2.1
	Senegal[a]	-0.6	31	Luxembourg	2.2
7	Mali[a]	-0.3		Sweden	2.2
8	Canada	0.2	33	Ireland	2.3
9	Oman[a]	0.5	34	Belgium	2.4
	Panama[a]	0.5	35	Bermuda[a]	2.5
11	Burkina Faso[a]	0.6		United Kingdom	2.5
12	Congo[a]	0.7	37	United States	2.6
	Japan	0.7	38	Bahamas[a]	2.7
14	Switzerland	0.8	39	Côte d'Ivoire[a]	2.8
15	Benin[a]	1.0		Netherlands	2.8
	Saudi Arabia	1.0		Puerto Rico[a]	2.8
17	Barbados[a]	1.1	42	Austria	3.0
	Finland	1.1		Brunei	3.0
19	Gabon[a]	1.2		Germany	3.0
20	Norway	1.4		UAE[a]	3.0
21	Bangladesh[a]	1.5	46	Qatar[a]	3.1
22	Iceland	1.6	47	Ethiopia[a]	3.5
23	France	1.7	48	Singapore	3.6
24	New Zealand	1.8	49	Malaysia	3.7
25	Australia	1.9	50	Italy	3.9

Lowest inflation, 1989-94
% average annual consumer price inflation

1	Niger[c]	-3.5	16	Malta[c]	2.4
2	Kuwait[c]	-1.8	17	Denmark	2.5
3	CAR[c]	-1.2	18	France	2.7
4	Mali[c]	-0.9		Netherlands	2.7
5	Chad[c]	-0.5	20	Belgium	2.9
6	Burkina Faso[c]	0.0		Ireland	2.9
7	Cameroon[c]	0.1		Singapore	2.9
8	Panama[c]	0.9	23	Netherlands Antilles[c]	3.0
9	Bahrain[c]	1.1		Norway	3.0
10	Benin[c]	1.4	25	Canada	3.1
11	Côte d'Ivoire[c]	1.6		New Zealand	3.1
12	Saudi Arabia	1.7	27	Gabon[c]	3.2
13	Brunei[b]	2.1		Luxembourg	3.2
	Congo[c]	2.1		Oman[c]	3.2
	Japan	2.1	30	Austria	3.3

a 1992-93.
b 1990-94.
c 1989-93.

d 1991-93.
e 1991-94.

Notes: Inflation is measured as the % increase in the consumer price index between two dates. The figures shown are based on the average level of the index during the relevant years.

Debt

Highest foreign debt[a]

$m

1	Brazil	132,749	21	Malaysia	23,335
2	Mexico	118,028	22	Morocco	21,430
3	India	91,781	23	Chile	20,637
4	Indonesia	89,539	24	Iran	20,550
5	China	83,800	25	Peru	20,328
6	Russia	83,089	26	Syria	19,975
7	Argentina	74,473	27	Côte d'Ivoire	19,146
8	Turkey	67,862	28	Colombia	17,173
9	South Korea	47,203	29	Sudan	16,560
10	Thailand	45,819	30	Ecuador	14,110
11	Poland	45,306	31	Bangladesh	13,879
12	Egypt	40,626	32	Bulgaria	12,250
13	Venezuela	37,465	33	Ex-Yugoslavia	11,314
14	Portugal	36,942	34	Zaire	11,280
15	Philippines	35,269	35	Nicaragua	10,445
16	Nigeria	32,531	36	Angola	9,655
17	Pakistan	26,050	37	Tunisia	8,701
18	Algeria	25,757	38	Czech Republic	8,661
19	Hungary	24,771	39	Tanzania	7,522
20	Vietnam	24,224	40	Uruguay	7,259

Highest debt service[b]

$m

1	Mexico	20,900	21	Egypt	2,407
2	Indonesia	13,298	22	Russia	2,293
3	Brazil	10,743	23	Nigeria	1,831
4	China	10,105	24	Poland	1,692
5	South Korea	9,173	25	Tunisia	1,350
6	Algeria	9,146	26	Czech Republic	1,274
7	Thailand	9,112	27	Iran	1,255
8	India	8,942	28	Côte d'Ivoire	964
9	Turkey	8,600	29	Ecuador	921
10	Argentina	7,947	30	Papua New Guinea	862
11	Portugal	5,553	31	Uruguay	803
12	Philippines	4,785	32	Kenya	652
13	Hungary	4,436	33	Zimbabwe	627
14	Malaysia	4,229	34	Trinidad & Tobago	620
15	Venezuela	3,938	35	Oman	607
16	Colombia	3,167	36	Jordan	569
17	Chile	2,883	37	Costa Rica	557
18	Peru	2,774	38	Bangladesh	533
19	Morocco	2,614	39	Vietnam	498
20	Pakistan	2,460	40	Jamaica	494

a   Foreign debt is debt owed to non-residents and repayable in foreign currency; the figures shown include liabilities of government, public and private sectors. Developed countries have been excluded.

b   Debt service is the sum of interest and principal repayments (amortization) due on outstanding foreign debt. The debt service ratio is debt service expressed as a percentage of the country's exports of goods and services.

Highest foreign debt burden
Foreign debt as % of GDP

1	Nicaragua	762.0	21	Ethiopia	116.2
2	Mozambique	419.2	22	Zaire[f]	111.9
3	Guinea-Bissau	292.0	23	Gambia, The	110.2
4	Tanzania[c]	285.2	24	Burundi	109.8
5	Somalia[d]	283.9	25	Panama	105.7
6	Sudan[c]	272.8	26	Egypt	104.8
7	Congo	248.6	27	Togo	104.2
8	Mauritania	245.1	28	Ecuador	101.9
9	Côte d'Ivoire	243.9	29	Nigeria	100.7
10	Zambia	231.9	30	Mali	100.5
11	Sierra Leone	218.8	31	Guinea	94.0
12	Vietnam	188.7	32	Malawi	91.5
13	Laos	149.1	33	Angola[d]	84.1
14	Jordan	142.9	34	Morocco	81.7
15	Madagascar	142.6	35	Gabon	80.3
16	Kenya	135.2	36	Bolivia	79.7
17	Honduras	125.6	37	Niger	78.6
18	Bulgaria	124.9	38	Zimbabwe	78.5
19	Jamaica	121.4	39	Uganda	77.0
20	Syria[e]	116.9	40	Ghana	76.9

Highest debt service ratios[b]
%

1	Uganda	121.3		Colombia	29.2
2	Kirgizstan	92.0	22	India	28.4
3	Algeria	76.9	23	Turkey	28.3
4	Peru	63.7	24	Kenya	28.0
5	Bolivia	59.4	25	Trinidad & Tobago[c]	27.7
6	Uruguay	48.8	26	Mauritania	27.3
7	Argentina	47.6	27	Ecuador	25.9
8	Burundi	41.0	28	Tanzania	25.1
9	Hungary	40.8	29	Philippines	24.9
10	Zambia	32.8	30	Pakistan	24.7
11	Mexico	32.7	31	Brazil	24.4
12	Indonesia	32.6	32	Chile	23.4
13	Zimbabwe	32.3	33	Ghana	22.8
14	Papua New Guinea	31.6		Venezuela	22.8
15	Honduras	31.5	35	Malawi	22.1
16	Niger	31.4	36	Cameroon	21.8
17	Morocco	30.7	37	Mozambique	20.6
18	Côte d'Ivoire	30.0	38	Tunisia	20.2
19	Nigeria[c]	29.4	39	Jamaica	20.1
20	Nicaragua	29.2	40	Thailand	18.6

c 1992.   e 1991.
d 1990.   f 1989.

Aid

Largest bilateral and multilateral donors
$m

1	Japan	11,259	13	Australia	953
2	United States	9,721	14	Belgium	808
3	France[a]	7,915	15	Switzerland	793
4	Germany	6,954	16	Austria	544
5	Italy	3,043	17	Saudi Arabia	539
6	United Kingdom	2,908	18	Kuwait	381
7	Netherlands	2,525	19	Finland	355
8	Canada	2,373	20	Portugal	246
9	Sweden	1,769	21	UAE	236
10	Denmark	1,340	22	Taiwan[b]	121
11	Spain	1,213	23	New Zealand	98
12	Norway	1,014	24	Ireland	81

Largest recipients of bilateral and multilateral aid
$m

1	China	3,280	36	Mali	362
2	Egypt	2,256	37	Nepal	360
3	Ex-Yugoslavia	2,131	38	Papua New Guinea	359
4	Indonesia	2,024	39	Nicaragua	337
5	India	1,533	40	Yemen	336
6	Philippines	1,485	41	Niger	334
7	Bangladesh	1,359	42	Algeria	332
8	Israel	1,272	43	Mauritania	331
9	Ethiopia	1,209	44	Vietnam	322
10	Mozambique	1,155	45	Jordan	317
11	Pakistan	1,067	46	Honduras	314
12	Tanzania	978	47	Cambodia	313
13	Kenya	929	48	Angola	300
14	Somalia	881	49	Argentina	279
15	Côte d'Ivoire	840	50	Burundi	276
16	Zambia	811	51	Albania	275
17	Uganda	707	52	Benin	258
18	Cameroon	643	53	Ecuador	237
19	Ghana	624	54	Tunisia	236
20	Thailand	615	55	Brazil	234
21	Morocco	605	56	Chad	230
22	Bolivia	570	57	Afghanistan	214
23	Peru	560	58	Nigeria	206
24	Sri Lanka	553	59	Guatemala	202
25	Malawi	504	60	Laos	198
26	Senegal	496	61	South Africa	193
27	Sudan	485	62	Sierra Leone	192
28	Turkey	460	63	Zaire	191
29	Zimbabwe	428	64	CAR	180
30	Burkina Faso	426	65	Chile	177
31	Guinea	420	66	Iraq	170
32	Mexico	399	67	Syria	168
33	Rwanda	394	68	Namibia	166
34	El Salvador	382	69	Iran	139
35	Madagascar	369	70	Congo	133

Largest bilateral and multilateral donors
% of GDP

1	Kuwait	1.30	13	Australia	0.35
2	Denmark	1.03		Luxembourg	0.35
3	Norway	1.01	15	Switzerland	0.33
4	Sweden	0.98	16	Italy	0.31
5	Netherlands	0.82		United Kingdom	0.31
6	UAE	0.66	18	Austria	0.30
7	France	0.63	19	Portugal	0.29
8	Canada	0.45	20	Japan	0.26
	Finland	0.45	21	New Zealand	0.25
10	Saudi Arabia	0.43		Spain	0.25
11	Belgium	0.39	23	Ireland	0.20
12	Germany	0.37	24	United States	0.15

Largest recipients of bilateral and multilateral aid
$ per head

1	Netherlands Antilles	410	35	Burundi	46
2	Israel	241		Jamaica	46
3	Suriname	200	37	Oman	45
4	Mauritania	155	38	Laos	44
5	Namibia	106		Bhutan	44
6	Somalia	103	40	Burkina Faso	43
7	Gambia, The	94		Sierra Leone	43
	Guinea-Bissau	94	42	Egypt	40
9	Papua New Guinea	87		Niger	40
10	Nicaragua	85		Zimbabwe	40
11	Malta	83	45	Mali	39
12	Gabon	82		Uganda	39
13	Bolivia	81	47	Chad	38
14	Albania	80		Ghana	38
15	Fiji	78		Uruguay	38
16	Jordan	77	50	Kenya	37
17	Zambia	76		Tanzania	37
18	El Salvador	70	52	Mauritius	35
19	Lesotho	69	53	Lebanon	34
20	Mozambique	68	54	Cambodia	33
21	Guinea	67	55	Panama	31
22	Côte d'Ivoire	63		Sri Lanka	31
23	Senegal	62		Togo	31
24	Honduras	56	58	Angola	30
25	CAR	55		Costa Rica	30
26	Malawi	54	60	Madagascar	29
27	Congo	53		Paraguay	29
	Rwanda	53	62	Tunisia	27
29	Ex-Yugoslavia	52	63	Peru	25
30	Cameroon	51		Yemen	25
	Liberia	51	65	Ethiopia	23
32	Benin	50		Morocco	23
33	Cyprus	48		Philippines	23
34	Mongolia	47	68	Zaire	22

a Including overseas territories.   b 1992.

Industry

Largest industrial output
$bn, 1992

1	Japan	1,542		22	Indonesia	51
2	United States	1,385		23	South Africa	44
3	Germany	698		24	Poland	43
4	Italy	391			Thailand	43
5	France	383		26	Ukraine	41
6	United Kingdom	243		27	Norway	40
7	Russia	190		28	Denmark	33
8	Spain	189		29	Iran	31
9	China	172			Portugal	31
10	Brazil	133		31	Finland	28
	South Korea	133		32	Turkey	27
12	Netherlands	93		33	Venezuela	25
13	Mexico	92		34	Greece	24
14	Australia	88			UAE	24
15	Switzerland	84		36	Israel	21
16	Argentina	71		37	Hong Kong	18
	Sweden	71		38	Algeria	17
18	Austria	67			Colombia	17
19	Belgium	66			Philippines	17
20	India	58			Singapore	17
	Saudi Arabia	58				

Highest growth in industrial output
Average annual real % growth, 1980-92

1	Bhutan	11.8		11	Pakistan	7.3
2	South Korea	11.6		12	India	6.4
3	China	11.1		13	Indonesia	6.1
4	Botswana	10.1		14	Chad	6.0
	Thailand	10.1			Singapore	6.0
6	Oman	9.6		16	Turkey	5.8
7	Mauritius	9.2		17	Norway	5.3
8	Lesotho	8.5		18	Bangladesh	5.1
9	Malaysia	8.0			Japan	5.1
10	Syria	7.6		20	Sri Lanka	4.8

Lowest growth in industrial output
Average annual real % growth, 1980-92

1	Trinidad & Tobago	-6.6		11	Peru	-0.5
2	Nicaragua	-3.0		12	Mozambique	-0.4
3	Saudi Arabia	-2.9		13	Philippines	-0.2
4	Panama	-2.6		14	Argentina	-0.1
	Romania	-2.6			South Africa	-0.1
6	Hungary	-2.5		16	Nigeria	0.2
7	UAE	-1.8			Uruguay	0.2
8	Sierra Leone	-1.3		18	Paraguay	0.4
9	Namibia	-1.1		19	Cameroon	0.5
10	Bolivia	-0.8		20	Guatemala	0.6

Largest chemicals output
$bn, 1991

1	United States	127.17	11	Netherlands	9.79
2	Japan	87.34	12	Mexico	8.93
3	Germany	56.15	13	South Korea	7.00
4	United Kingdom	23.41	14	Belgium	6.06
5	France	22.36	15	India	5.89
6	Italy	19.31	16	Puerto Rico	5.64
7	China	18.20	17	Sweden	5.55
8	Brazil	12.61	18	Australia	3.89
9	Canada	12.34	19	Saudi Arabia	3.52
10	Spain	11.00	20	Austria	3.11

Largest machinery and transport output
$bn, 1991

1	Japan	388.19	11	Brazil	19.81
2	United States	328.51	12	Sweden	13.85
3	Germany	191.84	13	Netherlands	13.05
4	Italy	82.06	14	Austria	11.98
5	France	74.52	15	India	10.60
6	United Kingdom	60.47	16	Mexico	10.21
7	China	35.00	17	Belgium	9.52
8	Canada	32.08	18	Australia	8.36
9	South Korea	25.68	19	Singapore	6.08
10	Spain	25.00	20	Argentina	6.01

Largest textiles and clothing output
$bn, 1991

1	United States	52.99	11	Thailand	6.67
2	Japan	48.52	12	Canada	6.17
3	Italy	31.37	13	Mexico	5.74
4	China	19.60	14	India	4.71
5	Germany	18.72	15	Argentina	4.63
6	France	14.90	16	Hong Kong	4.38
7	Brazil	9.91	17	Indonesia	3.85
8	United Kingdom	9.75	18	Iran	3.51
9	South Korea	8.56	19	Belgium	3.03
10	Spain	8.00	20	Turkey	2.96

Largest processed food output
$bn, 1991

1	United States	137.76	11	Brazil	13.51
2	Japan	87.34	12	Argentina	9.25
3	Germany	46.79	13	Netherlands	8.70
4	France	32.29	14	South Korea	8.56
5	United Kingdom	27.31	15	Australia	8.36
6	China	21.00	16	Belgium	7.79
7	Italy	19.31	17	Thailand	7.78
8	Canada	18.51	18	Austria	6.84
9	Spain	18.00	19	Indonesia	5.78
10	Mexico	15.31	20	India	5.10

Agriculture

Most economically dependent on agriculture
% of GDP from agriculture

1	Georgia	70.0		21	Mali	42.0
2	Myanmar	63.0		22	Bhutan	41.0
3	Somalia	62.0			Rwanda	41.0
4	Uganda	56.0		24	Kazakhstan	39.0
5	Burundi	54.0			Niger	39.0
6	Albania	51.8		26	Bangladesh	38.6
7	Laos	51.0		27	Sierra Leone	38.0
8	CAR	50.0		28	Benin	37.0
9	Côte d'Ivoire	49.3		29	Uzbekistan	36.0
10	Nepal	49.0			Vietnam	36.0
	Togo	49.0		31	Madagascar	34.0
12	Armenia	48.0			Nigeria	34.0
	Ethiopia	48.0		33	Sudan	33.8
14	Cambodia	47.0		34	Moldova	33.0
15	Ghana	45.3			Mozambique	33.0
16	Burkina Faso	44.0			Tajikistan	33.0
	Chad	44.0		37	Turkmenistan	32.0
	Guinea-Bissau	44.0		38	India	30.9
19	Kirgizstan	43.0		39	Papua New Guinea	29.8
	Tanzania	43.0		40	Nicaragua	29.2

Least economically dependent on agriculture
% of GDP from agriculture

1	Hong Kong	0.2		21	Canada	3.1
	Singapore	0.2			Italy	3.1
3	Kuwait	0.7			Switzerland	3.1
4	Netherlands Antilles	0.9		24	Oman	3.2
5	Bahrain	1.0		25	Taiwan	3.5
	Germany	1.0		26	Finland	3.6
	Puerto Rico	1.0		27	Netherlands	4.0
8	Luxembourg	1.3			Trinidad & Tobago	4.0
9	Saudi Arabia	1.4		29	Qatar	4.1
10	United Kingdom	1.8		30	Australia	4.2
11	United States	1.9		31	Israel	4.6
12	Japan	2.2			Libya	4.6
	UAE	2.2			Portugal	4.6
14	Austria	2.3		34	Botswana	5.0
	Belgium	2.3			Slovakia	5.0
16	France	2.5		36	Spain	5.1
17	Iceland	2.8		37	Slovenia	5.2
	Norway	2.8		38	Venezuela	5.3
19	Brunei	3.0		39	South Africa	5.8
	Sweden	3.0		40	Cyprus	6.2

Fastest growth
% average annual growth per head, 1980-93

1	Saudi Arabia	13.9	8	Belgium	2.4
2	Malaysia	4.0	9	Cambodia	2.3
3	Lebanon	3.4		Nigeria	2.3
4	Burkina Faso	3.0	11	Algeria	2.1
5	Indonesia	2.7		Denmark	2.1
6	China	2.5	13	Ireland	2.0
	Portugal	2.5		Morocco	2.0

Slowest growth
% average annual growth per head, 1980-93

1	Netherlands Antilles	-12.4	8	Haiti	-3.2
2	Somalia	-6.2	9	Romania	-3.1
3	Liberia	-6.1	10	Botswana	-2.9
4	Singapore	-5.0		Mongolia	-2.9
5	Nicaragua	-4.6	12	Angola	-2.7
6	Macao	-4.5		Suriname	-2.7
7	Afghanistan	-4.0	14	Iceland	-2.6

Biggest producers
'000 tonnes

Cereals

1	China	412,262	6	Indonesia	54,398
2	United States	260,205	7	Canada	52,241
3	India	201,479	8	Brazil	43,044
4	Russia	94,907	9	Ukraine	42,725
5	France	55,817	10	Germany	36,222

Meat

1	China	38,215	6	Germany	5,947
2	United States	31,187	7	India	3,997
3	Russia	7,732	8	Italy	3,975
4	Brazil	7,651	9	Spain	3,700
5	France	6,300	10	Argentina	3,697

Fruit

1	India	31,850	6	Spain	12,649
2	Brazil	31,210	7	France	9,953
3	United States	28,565	8	Turkey	9,645
4	China	23,093	9	Mexico	9,462
5	Italy	18,630	10	Uganda	9,104

Vegetables

1	China	125,509	6	Italy	13,035
2	India	60,010	7	Russia	10,450
3	United States	32,199	8	South Korea	10,276
4	Turkey	18,468	9	Spain	9,945
5	Japan	14,137	10	Iran	7,820

Commodities

Wheat

Top 10 producers '000 tonnes		Top 10 consumers '000 tonnes	
1 China	106,400	1 China	112,000
2 Ex-Soviet Union	83,600	2 Ex-Soviet Union	92,000
3 EU 12	81,100	3 EU 12	66,100
4 United States	65,400	4 India	56,400
5 India	56,800	5 United States	33,700
6 Canada	27,200	6 Pakistan	18,700
7 Australia	16,900	7 Turkey	15,200
8 Turkey	16,800	8 Iran	13,500
9 Pakistan	16,200	9 Egypt	10,000
10 Argentina	9,200	10 Canada	9,100

Rice

Top 10 producers[a] '000 tonnes		Top 10 consumers[b] '000 tonnes	
1 China	177,700	1 China	128,000
2 India	117,012	2 India	75,975
3 Indonesia	48,185	3 Indonesia	30,936
4 Bangladesh	26,800	4 Bangladesh	18,178
5 Vietnam	22,197	5 Vietnam	12,650
6 Thailand	19,200	6 Japan	9,400
7 Myanmar	15,086	7 Thailand	8,500
8 Brazil	10,515	8 Myanmar	8,060
9 Philippines	9,923	9 Brazil	8,000
10 Japan	9,793	10 Philippines	6,725

Sugar[c]

Top 10 producers '000 tonnes		Top 10 consumers '000 tonnes	
1 EU 12	17,384	1 EU 12	13,116
2 India	11,750	2 India	12,989
3 Brazil	10,097	3 Ex-Soviet Union	11,177
4 China	8,093	4 United States	8,192
5 Ex-Soviet Union	7,456	5 China	7,720
6 United States	7,045	6 Brazil	7,575
7 Australia	4,488	7 Mexico	4,500
8 Mexico	4,360	8 Indonesia	2,850
9 Cuba	4,246	9 Pakistan	2,775
10 Thailand	3,825	10 Japan	2,678

Coarse grains[d]

Top 5 producers '000 tonnes		Top 5 consumers '000 tonnes	
1 United States	187,500	1 United States	185,000
2 China	117,000	2 China	108,000
3 Ex-Soviet Union	99,400	3 Ex-Soviet Union	105,000
4 EU 12	84,800	4 EU 12	73,000
5 India	33,700	5 India	34,000

Tea

Top 10 producers '000 tonnes		Top 10 consumers '000 tonnes	
1 India	758	1 India	560
2 China	600	2 China	402
3 Sri Lanka	233	3 Ex-Soviet Union	268
4 Kenya	211	4 United Kingdom	160
5 Indonesia	135	5 Japan	129
6 Turkey	128	6 Pakistan	125
7 Japan	92	7 Turkey	88
8 Ex-Soviet Union	70	8 United States	85
9 Bangladesh	51	9 Iran	83
10 Argentina	46	10 Egypt	61

Coffee

Top 10 producers '000 tonnes		Top 10 consumers '000 tonnes	
1 Brazil	1,780	1 United States	1,080
2 Colombia	678	2 Germany	590
3 Indonesia	438	3 Brazil	540
4 Mexico	253	4 Japan	360
5 Guatemala	212	5 France	330
6 Vietnam	179	6 Italy	290
7 India	175	7 Spain	170
8 Ethiopia	172	8 Netherlands	160
9 Kenya	138	United Kingdom	160
10 Côte d'Ivoire	137	10 Indonesia	140

Cocoa

Top 10 producers '000 tonnes		Top 10 consumers '000 tonnes	
1 Côte d'Ivoire	697	1 United States	587
2 Ghana	312	2 Germany	263
3 Brazil	309	3 United Kingdom	189
4 Indonesia	240	4 France	157
5 Malaysia	225	5 Russia	117
6 Nigeria	145	6 Japan	111
7 Cameroon	90	7 Brazil	76
8 Ecuador	67	8 Italy	68
9 Dominican Republic	52	9 Canada	56
10 Colombia	50	10 Spain	53

a Paddy (unmilled rice, in the husk).
b Milled rice.
c Raw value.
d Includes: maize (corn), barley, sorghum, rye, oats and millet.

Commodities

Copper

Top 10 producers[a] '000 tonnes		Top 10 consumers[b] '000 tonnes	
1 Chile	2,055	1 United States	2,364
2 United States	1,801	2 Japan	1,384
3 Ex-Soviet Union	885	3 China	942
4 Canada	733	4 Germany	895
5 Zambia	432	5 Ex-Soviet Union	600
6 Australia	402	6 Italy	490
7 Poland	383	7 Taiwan	477
8 Peru	375	8 France	474
9 China	346	9 South Korea	400
10 Indonesia	310	10 United Kingdom	325

Lead

Top 10 producers[a] '000 tonnes		Top 10 consumers[b] '000 tonnes	
1 Australia	514	1 United States	1,357
2 United States	362	2 Japan	371
3 China	338	3 Germany	352
4 Peru	218	4 China	290
5 Ex-Soviet Union	203	5 United Kingdom	264
6 Canada	182	6 France	226
7 Mexico	181	7 Italy	223
8 Sweden	111	8 Ex-Soviet Union	200
9 South Africa	100	9 South Korea	177
10 Morocco	75	10 Mexico	162

Zinc

Top 10 producers[a] '000 tonnes		Top 10 consumers[c] '000 tonnes	
1 Canada	1,007	1 United States	1,141
2 Australia	990	2 Japan	719
3 China	775	3 China	530
4 Peru	665	4 Germany	515
5 United States	513	5 Ex-Soviet Union	330
6 Ex-Soviet Union	489	6 South Korea	311
7 Mexico	360	7 Italy	295
8 Ireland	194	8 France	226
9 Spain	170	9 Australia	222
10 Sweden	167	10 Belgium	210

Tin

Top 5 producers[a] '000 tonnes		Top 5 consumers[b] '000 tonnes	
1 China	46.0	1 United States	33.9
2 Indonesia	28.5	2 Japan	28.7
3 Brazil	25.9	3 China	21.1
4 Bolivia	18.6	4 Germany	18.4
5 Peru	13.7	5 Ex-Soviet Union	14.5

Nickel

Top 10 producers[a]
'000 tonnes

1	Ex-Soviet Union	190.0
2	Canada	188.4
3	New Caledonia	98.1
4	Indonesia	65.8
5	Australia	64.7
6	China	32.4
7	South Africa	28.9
8	Cuba	28.8
9	Dominican Republic	23.9
10	Colombia	20.2

Top 10 consumers[b]
'000 tonnes

1	Japan	143.5
2	United States	132.2
3	Germany	75.0
4	Ex-Soviet Union	64.0
5	China	45.0
6	Italy	38.5
7	France	36.5
8	United Kingdom	28.8
9	Finland	26.8
10	Belgium	22.8

Aluminium

Top 10 producers[d]
'000 tonnes

1	United States	3,695
2	Ex-Soviet Union	3,065
3	Canada	2,309
4	Australia	1,376
5	China	1,220
6	Brazil	1,172
7	Norway	888
8	Venezuela	568
9	Germany	552
10	India	466

Top 10 consumers[b]
'000 tonnes

1	United States	4,877
2	Japan	2,175
3	China	1,318
4	Ex-Soviet Union	1,185
5	Germany	1,159
6	France	665
7	South Korea	557
8	Italy	554
9	Canada	493
10	United Kingdom	477

Precious metals

Gold[a]
Top 10 producers
tonnes

1	South Africa	619.5
2	United States	336.0
3	Australia	247.2
4	Ex-Soviet Union	244.0
5	Canada	150.9
6	China	127.0
7	Brazil	75.7
8	Papua New Guinea	61.8
9	Indonesia	46.3
10	Ghana	41.4

Silver[a]
Top 10 producers
tonnes

1	Mexico	2,368
2	Peru	1,616
3	United States	1,604
4	Ex-Soviet Union	1,220
5	Australia	1,152
6	Chile	985
7	Canada	888
8	Poland	850
9	Bolivia	333
10	Sweden	277

a   Mine production.
b   Refined consumption.
c   Slab consumption.
d   Primary refined production.

Commodities

Rubber (natural and synthetic)

Top 10 producers '000 tonnes		Top 10 consumers '000 tonnes	
1 United States	2,170	1 United States	2,968
2 Thailand	1,551	2 Japan	1,653
3 Japan	1,310	3 China	1,145
4 Indonesia	1,301	4 Ex-Soviet Union	1,015
5 Malaysia	1,074	5 Germany	665
6 Ex-Soviet Union	1,020	6 South Korea	578
7 China	710	7 India	555
8 Germany	572	8 France	490
9 France	486	9 Brazil	436
10 India	479	10 Italy	388

Raw wool

Top 10 producers [a] '000 tonnes		Top 10 consumers [b] '000 tonnes	
1 Australia	801	1 China	352
2 Ex-Soviet Union	401	2 Ex-Soviet Union	185
3 New Zealand	284	3 Italy	156
4 China	240	4 Japan	85
5 Argentina	102	5 Turkey	79
6 Uruguay	93	6 United Kingdom	77
7 South Africa	71	7 United States	68
8 Turkey	70	8 India	54
9 United Kingdom	68	9 South Korea	53
10 Pakistan	67	10 Germany	51

Cotton

Top 10 producers '000 tonnes		Top 10 consumers '000 tonnes	
1 China	3,739	1 China	4,523
2 United States	3,513	2 United States	2,268
3 India	2,065	3 India	2,169
4 Pakistan	1,368	4 Pakistan	1,536
5 Uzbekistan	1,358	5 Brazil	835
6 Turkey	602	6 Turkey	700
7 Brazil	483	7 Russia	457
8 Turkmenistan	430	8 Indonesia	445
9 Egypt	416	9 Japan	443
10 Australia	329	10 South Korea	376

Major oil seeds [c]

Top 5 producers '000 tonnes		Top 5 consumers '000 tonnes	
1 United States	57,361	1 United States	38,575
2 China	32,926	2 EU 12	22,992
3 Brazil	25,390	3 China	22,570
4 India	20,000	4 Brazil	18,063
5 Argentina	16,321	5 India	16,935

Oil[d]

Top 15 producers '000 barrels per day, 1993		Top 15 consumers '000 barrels per day, 1993	
1 Saudi Arabia[e]	8,695	1 United States	16,410
2 United States	8,565	2 Japan	5,455
3 Russia	6,995	3 Russia	3,585
4 Iran[e]	3,620	4 China	2,965
5 Mexico	3,135	5 Germany	2,920
6 China	2,900	6 France	1,965
7 Venezuela[e]	2,565	7 Italy	1,905
8 UAE[e]	2,435	8 United Kingdom	1,790
9 Norway	2,340	9 Canada	1,675
10 Canada	2,180	10 South Korea	1,635
11 United Kingdom	2,085	11 Mexico	1,560
12 Kuwait[e]	1,950	12 Brazil	1,360
13 Nigeria[e]	1,910	13 India	1,295
14 Indonesia[e]	1,530	14 Spain	1,090
15 Libya[e]	1,420	15 Indonesia	790

Natural gas

Top 10 producers '000 terajoules, 1992		Top 10 consumers '000 terajoules, 1992	
1 Russia	21,761	1 United States	21,654
2 United States	19,379	2 Russia	15,402
3 Canada	4,767	3 Ukraine	3,769
4 Netherlands	2,881	4 Canada	2,702
5 Turkmenistan	2,345	5 Germany	2,627
6 Algeria	2,177	6 United Kingdom	2,336
7 United Kingdom	2,120	7 Japan	2,199
8 Indonesia	2,022	8 Italy	1,913
9 Uzbekistan	1,670	9 Uzbekistan	1,611
10 Saudi Arabia	1,343	10 Netherlands	1,549

Coal

Top 10 producers Million tonnes, 1992		Top 10 consumers Million tonnes, 1992	
1 China	1,116.4	1 China	1,090.8
2 United States	905.0	2 United States	808.3
3 Russia	317.0	3 Germany	327.5
4 Germany	314.0	4 Russia	316.1
5 India	254.6	5 India	256.8
6 Australia	225.8	6 Poland	176.7
7 Poland	198.4	7 Ukraine	138.9
8 South Africa	174.9	8 South Africa	132.3
9 Ukraine	133.6	9 Japan	116.8
10 Kazakhstan	131.0	10 Australia	103.4

a Greasy basis.
b Clean basis.
c Soybeans, sunflower seed, cottonseed, groundnuts and rapeseed.
d Includes crude oil, shale oil, oil sands and natural gas liquids.
e Opec members.

Energy

Largest producers
Million tonnnes coal equivalent, 1992

1	United States	2,291.5	16	Ukraine	169.3
2	Russia	1,603.5	17	Algeria	157.8
3	China	1,036.8	18	Kazakhstan	155.6
4	Saudi Arabia	674.1	19	France	152.2
5	Canada	416.2	20	Nigeria	137.8
6	United Kingdom	307.7	21	South Africa	134.3
7	Iran	285.7	22	Poland	128.8
8	Mexico	271.0	23	Libya	109.8
9	India	270.1	24	Japan	107.1
10	Germany	228.6	25	Netherlands	104.5
11	Australia	228.5	26	Turkmenistan	87.6
12	Venezuela	223.5	27	North Korea	87.3
13	Norway	206.2	28	Brazil	82.7
14	Indonesia	196.8	29	Kuwait	82.0
15	UAE	194.9	30	Egypt	80.9

Largest consumers
Million tonnes coal equivalent, 1992

1	United States	2,739.6	16	Brazil	124.8
2	Russia	1,096.2	17	Spain	121.5
3	China	972.7	18	South Africa	112.7
4	Japan	589.4	19	Kazakhstan	108.3
5	Germany	472.7	20	Netherlands	108.0
6	Ukraine	312.7	21	Iran	102.3
	United Kingdom	312.7	22	Saudi Arabia	97.1
8	France	310.9	23	North Korea	96.3
9	India	307.8	24	Indonesia	73.2
10	Canada	300.1	25	Uzbekistan	69.1
11	Italy	232.3	26	Belgium	68.7
12	Mexico	166.7	27	Argentina	66.0
13	South Korea	140.8	28	Venezuela	64.9
14	Poland	133.8	29	Romania	63.0
15	Australia	129.8	30	Turkey	61.0

Energy efficiency

Most efficient			Least efficient		
GDP per kg of energy, 1992, $			*GDP per kg of energy, 1992, $*		
1	Benin	22.6	1	Kazakhstan	0.4
2	Myanmar	22.2		Mongolia	0.4
3	Burkina Faso	18.7	3	Albania	0.5
4	CAR	14.6		Bulgaria	0.5
5	Mali	13.9		Romania	0.5
6	Chad	13.4		Russia	0.5
7	Macao	11.7		Suriname	0.5
8	Bhutan	11.1	8	Slovakia	0.6
	Cameroon	11.1		Ukraine	0.6
10	Angola	10.4	10	Armenia	0.7
				Belarus	0.7

Note: Consumption data for small countries, especially oil producers, can be unreliable, often leading to unrealistically high consumption per head rates.

Largest exporters
Million tonnes coal equivalent, 1992

1	Saudi Arabia	535.7	14	Mexico	107.8
2	Russia	480.7	15	United Kingdom	107.6
3	Iran	185.3	16	Libya	92.0
4	Canada	184.5	17	Kuwait	71.7
5	Norway	178.9	18	Kazakhstan	67.6
6	Venezuela	151.4	19	Turkmenistan	65.1
7	UAE	148.9	20	China	58.5
8	United States	139.0	21	Malaysia	53.2
9	Indonesia	125.1	22	Oman	50.9
10	Australia	123.6	23	Singapore	47.5
11	Nigeria	114.5	24	South Africa	43.4
12	Netherlands	113.9	25	Egypt	38.0
13	Algeria	112.2			

Largest importers
Million tonnes coal equivalent, 1992

1	United States	631.9	14	India	58.2
2	Japan	529.9		Brazil	58.2
3	Germany	290.4	16	Canada	54.6
4	Italy	224.4	17	Belarus	52.1
5	France	203.3	18	Turkey	42.5
6	Ukraine	165.9	19	Kazakhstan	39.1
7	South Korea	149.5	20	Sweden	38.5
8	Netherlands	130.6	21	Greece	32.4
9	United Kingdom	123.4		China	32.4
10	Spain	106.9	23	Thailand	31.3
11	Singapore	95.2	24	Poland	29.5
12	Belgium	91.4	25	Portugal	27.1
13	Russia	60.6			

Largest consumption per head
Kg coal equivalent, 1992

1	Qatar	39,576	16	Norway	6,713
2	UAE	26,072	17	Finland	6,566
3	Brunei	17,085	18	Kazakhstan	6,353
4	Bahrain	14,780	19	Iceland	6,215
5	Luxembourg	14,003	20	Saudi Arabia	6,097
6	Canada	10,965	21	Ukraine	5,996
7	United States	10,737	22	New Zealand	5,935
8	Singapore	8,503	23	Germany	5,890
9	Trinidad & Tobago	8,422	24	Czech Republic	5,610
10	Netherlands Antilles	7,531	25	France	5,434
11	Australia	7,376	26	United Kingdom	5,400
12	Russia	7,357	27	Estonia	5,358
13	Netherlands	7,122	28	Belarus	5,095
14	Sweden	6,937	29	Switzerland	4,877
15	Belgium	6,872	30	Japan	4,735

Workers of the world

Highest % of population in labour force
1992-93 or latest

1	Singapore	57.0		Suriname	48.2
2	Denmark	56.6	27	Portugal	47.9
3	Thailand	56.3	28	New Zealand	47.8
4	Latvia	55.1	29	Australia	47.7
5	Japan	53.1	30	Burkina Faso	47.6
6	Burundi	52.9	31	Moldova	47.5
7	Czech Rep	52.6		Panama	47.5
	Russia	52.6	33	Slovakia	47.2
9	Belarus	52.5	34	Austria	46.7
10	Switzerland	51.5	35	Bulgaria	46.3
11	Bahamas	51.0		Netherlands Antilles	46.3
12	Lithuania	50.8		Rwanda	46.3
	Ukraine	50.8	38	Romania	45.9
14	Estonia	50.5	39	Macao	45.4
15	Germany	50.2	40	Colombia	45.2
16	Canada	50.1		Poland	45.2
17	Hong Kong	49.9	42	Bangladesh	45.0
	United States	49.9	43	Colombia	45.2
19	Sweden	49.6		Poland	45.2
20	Finland	49.5	45	Uruguay	45.0
21	Norway	49.4	46	France	44.8
	United Kingdom	49.4	47	Bahrain	44.6
23	Hungary	48.6		Paraguay	44.6
24	CAR	48.2	49	Jamaica	44.5
	Cyprus	48.2	50	South Korea	44.4

Most male workforce
% male workers, 1992-93 or latest

1	Iran	90.4	21	Ireland	68.4
2	Pakistan	86.3	22	Honduras	68.3
3	Bahrain	82.0	23	Côte d'Ivoire	67.7
	Syria	82.0	24	Chile	67.5
5	Tunisia	79.1	25	Nigeria	66.7
6	Kuwait	75.7	26	Sri Lanka	66.1
7	Senegal	74.4	27	Mauritius	65.9
8	Guatemala	74.2		Nicaragua	65.9
9	Morocco	73.9	29	Malaysia	64.5
10	Ecuador	73.6	30	Luxembourg	63.5
	Egypt	73.6	31	Spain	63.2
12	Malta	73.2	32	Hong Kong	63.1
13	Argentina	72.1	33	Greece	63.0
14	India	71.4		Trinidad & Tobago	63.0
15	Panama	70.8	35	Italy	62.9
16	Costa Rica	70.1	36	Philippines	62.8
17	Turkey	69.2	37	Netherlands	62.4
18	Mexico	69.1	38	Suriname	62.2
19	Brazil	69.0	39	Cyprus	62.1
20	Venezuela	68.8	40	Indonesia	61.8

Lowest % of population in labour force
1992-93 or latest

1	Iran	26.0			Costa Rica	38.1
2	Syria	27.8		27	Chile	38.6
3	Pakistan	28.0		28	Kuwait	38.9
4	Egypt	29.2			Mexico	38.9
5	Tunisia	29.8		30	Bolivia	39.4
6	Nigeria	31.1			Côte d'Ivoire	39.4
7	Puerto Rico	32.4			Spain	39.4
8	Morocco	32.5		33	Peru	39.9
9	Botswana	33.3		34	Trinidad & Tobago	40.5
10	Guatemala	33.5		35	Barbados	40.6
11	Senegal	34.0			El Salvador	40.6
12	Nicaragua	34.7			Greece	40.6
13	Ecuador	34.8		38	Brazil	40.8
	Honduras	34.8			Philippines	40.8
15	Fiji	35.2		40	Sri Lanka	41.0
16	Turkey	35.3		41	Ethiopia	41.3
17	Malta	36.1		42	Indonesia	41.9
18	Venezuela	36.3			Netherlands	41.9
19	Israel	36.9		44	Belgium	42.1
20	India	37.5		45	Slovenia	42.4
	South Africa	37.5		46	Italy	42.5
22	Malaysia	37.6		47	Taiwan	42.6
23	Zimbabwe	37.7		48	Cambodia	43.1
24	Ireland	37.8		49	Malawi	43.3
25	Argentina	38.1		50	Luxembourg	43.5

Most female workforce
% female workers, 1992-93 or latest

1	Cambodia	55.7		21	Slovenia	46.6
2	Lithuania	53.8		22	Denmark	46.5
3	Rwanda	53.5			Jamaica	46.5
4	Burundi	52.6		24	Poland	46.1
5	Malawi	51.0			Slovakia	46.1
6	Latvia	50.0		26	Norway	45.4
7	Estonia	49.9		27	El Salvador	45.3
8	Ukraine	49.2		28	Canada	45.2
9	Belarus	49.0			United States	45.2
10	Burkina Faso	48.7		30	Netherlands Antilles	45.1
11	Russia	48.5		31	Portugal	44.7
12	Barbados	48.4			Romania	44.7
	Bulgaria	48.4		33	Hungary	44.5
14	Sweden	48.1		34	France	44.1
15	Zimbabwe	47.8		35	United Kingdom	43.8
16	Czech Rep	47.6		36	New Zealand	43.6
17	Bahamas	47.5		37	Colombia	43.4
18	Finland	46.9		38	Paraguay	42.4
	Thailand	46.9			Uruguay	42.4
20	CAR	46.8		40	Belgium	42.3

Banking and business

Largest banks
By capital, $m

1	Sumitomo Bank	Japan	22,120
2	Sanwa Bank	Japan	19,577
3	Fuji Bank	Japan	19,388
4	Dai-Ichi Kangyo	Japan	19,360
5	Sakura Bank	Japan	18,549
6	Mitsubishi Bank	Japan	17,651
7	Industrial & Commercial Bank of China	China	16,782
8	Crédit Agricole	France	14,718
9	HSBC Holdings	United Kingdom	14,611
10	Citicorp	United States	13,625
11	Industrial Bank of Japan	Japan	13,596
12	Union Bank of Switzerland	Switzerland	13,264
13	BankAmerica Corp	United States	12,058
14	Deutsche Bank	Germany	11,723
15	International Nederland Group	Netherlands	11,068
16	Tokai Bank	Japan	10,903
17	Long-Term Credit Bank of Japan	Japan	10,850
18	Bank of Tokyo	Japan	10,570
19	Crédit Lyonnais	France	10,386
20	Asahi Bank	Japan	10,311
21	Bank of China	China	10,273
22	ABN-AMRO Bank	Netherlands	10,194
23	Chemical Banking Group	United States	10,075
24	Banque Nationale de Paris	France	9,739
25	J.P. Morgan & Co	United States	9,611
26	C.S.Holding(Crédit Suisse)	Switzerland	9,337
27	Compagnie Financière de Paribas	France	9,284
28	Swiss Bank Corp	Switzerland	9,139
29	Barclays Bank	United Kingdom	9,055
30	NationsBank	United States	8,809
31	National Westminster Bank	United Kingdom	8,713
32	Mitsubishi Trust & Banking Corporation	Japan	8,511
33	Sumitomo Trust & Banking	Japan	8,395
34	Chase Manhattan Corp	United States	7,981
35	Rabobank Nederland	Netherlands	7,912
36	Société Générale	France	7,857
37	Dresdner Bank	Germany	7,077
38	Banc One Corp	United States	6,736
39	Westdeutsche Landesbank Girozentrale	Germany	6,656
40	Banco do Brasil	Brazil	6,446

Notes: Capital is essentially equity and reserves.
Figures for Japanese banks refer to the year ended March 31, 1994. Figures for all
other countries refer to the year ended December 31, 1993.

Largest businesses
By sales, $bn

1	General Motors	United States	133.6
2	Ford Motor	United States	108.5
3	Exxon	United States	97.8
4	Royal Dutch/Shell Group	United Kingdom/Netherlands	95.1
5	Toyota Motor[a]	Japan	85.3
6	Hitachi[b]	Japan	68.6
7	Intl. Business Machines	United States	62.7
8	Matshushita[b]	Japan	61.4
9	General Electric	United States	60.8
10	Daimler-Benz	Germany	59.1
11	Mobil	United States	56.6
12	Nissan Motor[b]	Japan	53.8
13	British Petroleum	United Kingdom	52.5
14	Samsung	South Korea	51.3
15	Philip Morris	United States	50.6
16	IRI[c]	Italy	50.5
17	Siemens[d]	Germany	50.4
18	Volkswagen	Germany	46.3
19	Chrysler	United States	43.6
20	Toshiba[b]	Japan	42.9
21	Unilever	United Kingdom/Netherlands	41.8
22	Nestlé[e]	Switzerland	38.9
23	Elf Aquitaine	France	37.0
24	Honda Motor	Japan	35.8
25	ENI[c]	Italy	34.8
26	Fiat	Italy	34.7
27	Sony[b]	Japan	34.6
28	Texaco	United States	34.4
29	NEC[b]	Japan	33.2
30	E.I. Du Pont de Nemours	United States	32.6
31	Chevron	United States	32.1
32	Philips Electronics	Netherlands	31.7
33	Daewoo	South Korea	30.9
34	Procter & Gamble[a]	United States	30.4
35	Renault[c,e]	France	30.0
36	Fujitsu[b]	Japan	29.1
37	Mitsubishi Electric[b]	Japan	28.8
38	ABB Asea Brown Boveri	Switzerland	28.3
39	Hoechst	Germany	27.8
40	Alcatel Alsthom	France	27.6

a Year ended June 30, 1993.
b Year ended March 31, 1994.
c Government owned.

d Year ended September 30, 1993.
e Figures in accordance with
  International Accounting

Notes: All companies shown have derived at least half of their sales from
manufacturing and/or mining. Figures refer to the year ended December 31, 1993,
except where specified. They include sales of consolidated subsidiaries but exclude
excise taxes collected by manufacturers, thus differing, in some instances, from
figures published by the companies themselves.

Stockmarkets

Largest market capitalisation
$m, end 1993

1	United States	5,223,768	26	Argentina	43,967
2	Japan	2,999,756	27	Denmark	41,785
3	United Kingdom	1,151,646	28	China	40,567
4	Germany	463,476	29	Philippines	40,327
5	France	456,111	30	Turkey	37,496
6	Hong Kong	385,247	31	Indonesia	32,953
7	Canada	326,524	32	Austria	28,437
8	Switzerland	271,713	33	Norway	27,380
9	Malaysia	220,328	34	New Zealand	25,597
10	South Africa	217,110	35	Finland	23,562
11	Australia	203,964	36	Luxembourg	19,337
12	Mexico	200,671	37	Portugal	12,417
13	Taiwan	195,198	38	Greece	12,319
14	Netherlands	181,876	39	Pakistan	11,602
15	South Korea	139,420	40	Kuwait	10,103
16	Italy	136,153	41	Colombia	9,237
17	Singapore	132,742	42	Venezuela	8,010
18	Thailand	130,510	43	Peru	5,113
19	Spain	119,264	44	Jordan	4,891
20	Sweden	107,376	45	Egypt	3,800
21	Brazil	99,430	46	Morocco	2,662
22	India	97,976	47	Sri Lanka	2,498
23	Belgium	78,067	48	Oman	1,605
24	Israel	50,773	49	Ecuador	1,566
25	Chile	44,622	50	Jamaica	1,469

Highest growth in market capitalisation, $ terms
% increase, 1985-93

1	Indonesia	28,065	21	India	582
2	Thailand	6,932	22	Peru	573
3	Portugal	6,367	23	Israel	566
4	Philippines	5,928	24	Spain	528
5	Mexico	5,160	25	Austria	518
6	Turkey[a]	3,910	26	France	477
7	Colombia	2,120	27	Jamaica	452
8	Chile	2,118	28	Bangladesh	302
9	Argentina	2,058		Finland	302
10	South Korea	1,789	30	Zimbabwe	298
11	Taiwan	1,771	31	South Africa	292
12	Uruguay	1,573	32	Belgium	274
13	Greece	1,510	33	United Kingdom	251
14	Malaysia	1,258	34	Australia	239
15	Singapore	1,099	35	Japan	207
16	Hong Kong	1,016	36	Netherlands	206
17	Morocco	944	37	Switzerland	202
18	Pakistan	747	38	Kenya[b]	200
19	Venezuela	610	39	New Zealand	192
20	Sri Lanka	584	40	Sweden	188

Highest growth in value traded, $ terms
% increase, 1985-93

1	Indonesia	305,167	24	Bangladesh	1,400
2	Turkey[a]	178,685	25	Spain	1,294
3	Portugal	96,600	26	Hong Kong	1,252
4	Greece	15,859	27	France	1,088
5	Thailand	15,205	28	Costa Rica[c]	1,000
6	Sri Lanka	12,733	29	Austria	856
7	Taiwan	6,973	30	Jordan	745
8	Malaysia	6,481	31	Pakistan	681
9	Philippines	6,013	32	New Zealand	626
10	Venezuela	5,945	33	Kuwait	575
11	Singapore	5,802	34	Uruguay[a]	550
12	South Korea	4,987	35	United Kingdom	519
13	Chile	4,807	36	Cote d'Ivoire	500
14	Peru	4,300	37	Belgium	497
15	Israel	3,954	38	Zimbabwe	489
16	Morocco	3,731	39	Italy	377
17	Luxembourg	2,967	40	Norway	366
18	Mexico	2,546	41	South Africa	360
19	Colombia	2,340		Tunisia	360
20	Denmark	1,547	43	Sweden	352
21	Argentina	1,539	44	India	341
22	Finland	1,516	45	Australia	330
23	Jamaica	1,500	46	Germany	323

Highest growth in number of listed companies[d]
% increase, 1985-93

1	Portugal	663	20	Italy	43
2	Indonesia	625	21	South Africa	40
3	Turkey[a]	280	22	Jamaica	32
4	Thailand	247	23	Philippines	30
5	Costa Rica	131	24	Greece	25
6	Taiwan	124	25	Canada	23
7	Bangladesh	122	26	Mexico	21
8	Egypt	113	27	Cote d'Ivoire	20
9	Israel	109	28	Japan	18
10	South Korea	103	29	Sri Lanka	17
11	Malaysia	85	30	Chile	15
12	Nigeria	81	31	Finland	14
13	Pakistan	80	32	Spain	13
14	Austria	73		Zimbabwe	13
	Hong Kong	73	34	Australia	7
16	Switzerland	64	35	Denmark	6
17	India	57		Netherlands	6
18	Peru	47	37	Kenya	4
19	Singapore	46	38	Brazil	2

a 1986-93.
b 1988-93.
c 1987-93.
d Only 38 stockmarkets experienced an increase in number of listed companies.

Transport: *roads and cars*

Longest road networks
Km, 1993 or latest

1	United States	6,277,859	16	Indonesia	244,164
2	India	2,962,470	17	Argentina	215,578
3	Brazil	1,824,364	18	Austria	200,000
4	Japan	1,130,892	19	Pakistan	194,922
5	Canada	849,404	20	South Africa	182,329
6	France	811,600	21	Ukraine	170,518
7	Australia	810,264	22	Kazakhstan	165,002
8	Germany	636,282	23	Philippines	160,709
9	Romania	461,880	24	Hungary	158,711
10	Turkey	388,093	25	Saudi Arabia	151,532
11	Poland	368,364	26	Zaire	145,000
12	United Kingdom	362,328	27	Belgium	137,876
13	Spain	337,139	28	Sweden	135,920
14	Italy	305,388	29	Ex-Yugoslavia	122,571
15	Mexico	245,433	30	Greece	116,150

Densest road networks
Km of road per km^2 land area, 1993 or latest

1	Belgium	4.50	16	France	1.47
2	Singapore	4.42	17	Ireland	1.31
3	Bahrain	4.40	18	Poland	1.18
4	Japan	2.99	19	Cyprus	1.17
5	Netherlands	2.80	20	Italy	1.02
6	Ukraine	2.66	21	Latvia	1.00
7	Luxembourg	1.98	22	Mauritius	0.98
8	Romania	1.94	23	Greece	0.88
9	Germany	1.80	24	Lithuania	0.85
10	Hungary	1.70	25	Portugal	0.79
	Switzerland	1.70	26	Slovenia	0.73
12	Denmark	1.65	27	Spain	0.67
13	United Kingdom	1.57	28	Albania	0.64
14	Hong Kong	1.51		United States	0.64
15	Austria	1.50	30	South Korea	0.62

Highest car ownership
Number of cars per 100 people, 1993 or latest

1	United States	57	11	Sweden	41
2	Luxembourg	54	12	Austria	40
3	Italy	50	13	Belgium	39
4	Canada	49	14	Netherlands	38
5	Germany	47		Norway	38
6	Australia	46	16	Finland	37
7	New Zealand	45	17	United Kingdom	36
	Switzerland	45	18	Spain	34
9	Iceland	44	19	Cyprus	33
10	France	42		Japan	33

Most crowded road networks
Number of vehicles per km of road network, 1993 or latest

1	Hong Kong	284	16	Malaysia	49
2	Taiwan	211	17	Egypt	48
3	Singapore	152		Switzerland	48
4	Kuwait	140	19	Spain	47
5	Brunei	96	20	Mexico	46
6	Italy	91	21	Slovenia	45
7	Israel	87	22	Luxembourg	44
8	Thailand	73	23	Bulgaria	39
	Ukraine	73	24	Jordan	37
10	United Kingdom	67		Mauritius	37
11	Netherlands	66	26	France	36
12	Germany	62		Macedonia	36
13	Japan	56	28	Saudi Arabia	34
14	Czech Republic	52	29	Austria	32
15	Bahrain	51		Belgium	32

Most used road networks
'000 vehicle-km per year per km of road network, 1993 or latest

1	Hong Kong	6,078.8	16	United States	571.6
2	Kuwait	3,474.6	17	France	558.2
3	Madagascar	2,468.4	18	Finland	554.8
4	Israel	1,749.7	19	Denmark	542.9
5	Thailand	1,227.6	20	Lithuania	499.3
6	United Kingdom	1,224.0	21	Slovenia	438.0
7	Bahrain	1,189.7	22	Oman	425.7
8	Italy	1,187.5	23	Portugal	392.2
9	Netherlands	922.5	24	Colombia	383.4
10	South Korea	881.2	25	Bulgaria	356.0
11	Luxembourg	766.2	26	Belgium	353.3
12	Sweden	745.3	27	Poland	301.0
13	Iraq	745.0	28	Spain	298.7
14	Germany	713.5	29	Honduras	289.2
15	Japan	599.7	30	Macedonia	273.0

Most accidents
Number of people injured per 100m vehicle-km, 1993 or latest

1	Malawi	2,730	11	Hong Kong	209
2	Rwanda	1,764	12	Canada	207
3	South Korea	625		Morocco	207
4	Jordan	658	14	Israel	154
5	Costa Rica	406	15	Belgium	143
6	Turkey	336	16	Japan	130
7	Kenya	330	17	South Africa	129
8	Honduras	317	18	Latvia	125
9	Portugal	234	19	Macedonia	114
10	Egypt	217	20	Spain	104

Transport: *planes and trains*

Most air passenger-km
Million passenger-km[a] per year

1	United States	773,311	21	Malaysia	17,445
2	United Kingdom	124,882	22	India	14,420
3	Japan	106,360	23	New Zealand	14,163
4	Russia	76,444	24	Philippines	13,085
5	France	59,201	25	South Africa	10,790
6	Australia	57,525	26	Pakistan	9,898
7	Germany	52,941	27	Argentina	9,221
8	China	45,000	28	Israel	8,747
9	Singapore	41,262	29	Sweden	8,428
10	Canada	40,426	30	Portugal	7,917
11	Netherlands	38,544	31	Greece	7,899
12	South Korea	31,786	32	UAE	7,794
13	Italy	29,759	33	Turkey	7,464
14	Brazil	29,500	34	Norway	7,242
15	Spain	27,105	35	Venezuela	6,708
16	Thailand	22,874	36	Belgium	6,484
17	Indonesia	19,472	37	Kazakhstan	5,731
18	Saudi Arabia	18,572	38	Austria	5,629
19	Mexico	18,216	39	Finland	5,529
20	Switzerland	17,704	40	Colombia	5,296

Busiest airports
Number of passengers '000, 1992

1	Chicago	O'Hare	64,441
2	Dallas	Dallas/Ft. Worth	51,944
3	Los Angeles	Los Angeles Intl.	46,965
4	London	Heathrow	44,968
5	Tokyo[b]	Haneda	41,981
6	Atlanta[b]	Hartsfield	37,915
7	San Francisco	San Francisco Intl.	31,789
8	Frankfurt	Frankfurt/Main	30,085
9	Denver[b]	Stapleton	28,285
10	New York	Kennedy	27,761

Busiest international airports
Number of international passengers '000, 1992

1	London	Heathrow	38,257
2	Frankfurt	Frankfurt/Main	23,271
3	Paris	Charles de Gaulle	22,444
4	Hong Kong	Hong Kong Intl.	22,061
5	Tokyo	New Tokyo Intl. (Narita)	19,022
6	London	Gatwick	18,690
7	Amsterdam	Schipol	18,609
8	Singapore	Changi	16,882
9	New York	Kennedy	15,110
10	Zurich	Zurich	12,007

a Air passenger–km data refer to the distance travelled by each aircraft of national origin.
b 1991.

Longest railway networks
'000 km

1	United States	239.7	21	Sweden		9.7
2	Russia	87.5	22	Czech Republic		9.4
3	India	62.5		Ex-Yugoslavia[e]		9.4
4	China	54.0	24	Pakistan[c]		8.8
5	Germany	40.4	25	Turkey		8.4
6	Australia[a]	35.8	26	Hungary		7.8
7	Argentina[b]	34.2	27	Chile[d]		6.3
8	France	32.6	28	Finland		5.9
9	Mexico[a]	26.5	29	Austria		5.6
10	Poland	24.9	30	Belarus		5.5
11	South Africa	23.6	31	Zaire[a]		5.1
12	Ukraine	22.6	32	Iran		5.0
13	Canada[c]	22.4	33	Philippines[a]		4.9
14	Brazil[d]	22.1	34	Cuba[d]		4.8
15	Japan	20.2		Sudan[a]		4.8
16	United Kingdom	16.5	36	Egypt		4.5
17	Italy	15.9		North Korea[a]		4.5
18	Canada	13.5	38	Bulgaria		4.3
19	Spain	12.6		New Zealand[c]		4.3
20	Romania	11.3	40	Indonesia[e]		4.2

Most rail passengers
Km per year per person

1	Japan	2,017	11	Slovakia	862
2	Belarus	1,880	12	Romania	851
3	Russia	1,826	13	Czech Republic	824
4	Switzerland	1,769	14	Italy	826
5	Ukraine	1,456	15	Egypt	801
6	Austria	1,168	16	Lithuania	722
7	France	1,011	17	Germany	715
8	Netherlands	994	18	South Korea	705
9	Latvia	918	19	Bulgaria	689
10	Denmark	884	20	Sweden	666

Most rail freight
Million tonnes-km per year

1	United States	1,619,560	11	Australia[a]	50,670
2	Russia	1,607,700	12	France	45,033
3	China	1,192,300	13	Belarus	42,919
4	India	252,388	14	Mexico[f]	32,988
5	Ukraine	246,356	15	Japan	25,075
6	Canada[d]	101,806	16	Czech Republic	23,750
7	Brazil[b]	92,838	17	Romania	21,849
8	South Africa	83,478	18	Italy	18,792
9	Germany	64,626	19	Sweden	18,133
10	Poland	63,246	20	Turkmenistan	16,820

a	1989.	d	1988.
b	1987.	e	1990.
c	1992.	f	1991.

Transport: *sail away*

Largest merchant fleets
Number of vessels over 100 GRT [a], mid-1994

1	Japan	9,981	21	Ukraine	1,140
2	Panama	5,680	22	Malta	1,051
3	United States	5,282	23	Netherlands	1,017
4	Russia	5,253	24	Turkey	975
5	China	2,576	25	India	887
6	Norway	2,271	26	Canada	881
7	South Korea	2,083	27	France	847
8	Indonesia	2,044	28	Mexico	635
9	Greece	1,926	29	Peru	632
10	Spain	1,813	30	Australia	627
11	United Kingdom	1,625		Taiwan	627
12	Liberia	1,605	32	Sweden	593
13	Cyprus	1,585	33	Malaysia	592
14	Italy	1,470	34	Poland	576
15	Philippines	1,465	35	Brazil	564
16	Honduras	1,391	36	Morocco	483
17	Germany	1,208	37	Argentina	448
18	Denmark	1,202	38	Chile	436
19	Singapore	1,192		Vietnam	436
20	Bahamas	1,147	40	Romania	435

Largest ports
Total cargo traffic, '000 tonnes [b]

1	Rotterdam	282,207	21	Pusan[e]	66,547
2	Singapore	273,700	22	Hamburg	65,850
3	Kobe	168,694	23	Vancouver	60,762
4	Chiba	159,530	24	Philadelphia[e]	58,831
5	Shanghai[c]	139,590	25	Yokkaichi	55,512
6	Nagoya	134,381	26	Le Havre	54,917
7	Yokohama	123,700	27	Port Hedland	52,970
8	Antwerp	101,855	28	London	50,932
9	Osaka[d]	95,109	29	Newcastle	50,870
10	Kitakyushu	93,097	30	Norfolk	48,083
11	Marseilles	87,317	31	Tees and Hartlepool	42,741
12	Houston[d]	86,747	32	Tampa	42,716
13	Ulsan[d]	84,576	33	Genoa[d]	41,381
14	Kaohsiung[d]	79,497	34	New York	41,352
15	Tokyo[c]	79,335	35	Arzew	41,214
16	Long Beach[e]	72,398	36	Dunkirk	40,827
17	Inchon[e]	70,959	37	Sullom Voe	39,374
18	Los Angeles[e]	70,910	38	Warri	39,284
19	Corpus Christi	69,437	39	Grimsby-Immingham	39,271
20	Hampton Roads[c]	68,530	40	Trieste	36,619

a   Gross Tonnage (GRT) = total volume within the hull and above deck. 1 GRT=100 cu ft.
b   Total cargo loaded and discharged.
c   1990.
d   1992.
e   1991.

Tourism

Most tourist arrivals
Number of arrivals, '000

1	France	60,100	21	Thailand	5,761
2	United States	45,793	22	Netherlands	5,757
3	Spain	40,085	23	Morocco	4,027
4	Italy	26,379	24	Macao	3,850
5	Hungary	22,804	25	Bulgaria	3,827
6	United Kingdom	19,186	26	Ireland	3,814
7	China	18,982	27	Tunisia	3,656
8	Austria	18,257	28	Argentina	3,532
9	Poland	17,000	29	Indonesia	3,403
10	Mexico	16,534	30	South Africa	3,358
11	Canada	15,105	31	South Korea	3,331
12	Germany	14,348	32	Belgium	3,285
13	Switzerland	12,400	33	Australia	2,996
14	Czech Republic	11,500	34	Romania	2,911
15	Greece	9,413	35	Puerto Rico	2,857
16	Hong Kong	8,938	36	Norway	2,556
17	Portugal	8,434	37	Croatia	2,363
18	Malaysia	6,504	38	Egypt	2,112
19	Turkey	5,904	39	Uruguay	2,003
20	Singapore	5,804	40	Japan	1,925

Biggest tourist spending
$m

1	United States	41,260	11	Belgium	6,363
2	Germany	37,514	12	Switzerland	5,803
3	Japan	26,860	13	Mexico	5,562
4	United Kingdom	17,244	14	Spain	4,706
5	Italy	13,053	15	Sweden	4,464
6	France	12,805	16	South Korea	4,105
7	Canada	10,629	17	Australia	4,100
8	Netherlands	8,974	18	Norway	3,565
9	Austria	8,180	19	Denmark	3,214
10	Taiwan	7,585	20	Singapore	3,022

Largest tourist receipts
$m

1	United States	56,501	11	Canada	5,897
2	France	23,410	12	Singapore	5,793
3	Italy	20,521	13	Thailand	5,014
4	Spain	19,425	14	Netherlands	4,690
5	Austria	13,566	15	China	4,683
6	United Kingdom	13,449	16	Australia	4,655
7	Germany	10,509	17	Poland	4,500
8	Hong Kong	7,562	18	Portugal	4,176
9	Switzerland	7,001	19	Belgium	4,071
10	Mexico	6,167	20	Indonesia	3,988

Education

Highest primary enrolment
Number enrolled as % of relevant age group, 1991

1	Gabon[a]	134	17	Philippines	110
2	Peru	126		Turkey	110
3	China	123	19	Paraguay	109
4	Portugal	122		Spain	109
5	Botswana	119		Syria	109
	Namibia	119	22	Hong Kong	108
7	Ecuador[b]	118		Singapore	108
8	Tunisia	117		Sri Lanka	108
	Zimbabwe	117		Uruguay	108
10	Indonesia	116	26	Argentina	107
11	UAE	115		Australia	107
12	Mexico	114		Canada	107
13	Thailand	113		France	107
14	Iran	112		Germany	107
15	Colombia	111		South Korea	107
	Togo	111		Lesotho	107

Lowest primary enrolment
Number enrolled as % of relevant age group, 1991

1	Afghanistan[b]	24	14	Mozambique	63
2	Ethiopia	25	15	Chad	65
	Mali	25	16	Benin	66
4	Bhutan[c]	26		Malawi	66
5	Niger	29		Morocco	66
6	Burkina Faso	30	19	CAR	68
7	Liberia[a]	35	20	Côte d' Ivoire	69
8	Guinea	37		Tanzania	69
9	Pakistan	46	22	Burundi	70
10	Sierra Leone	48	23	Nigeria	71
11	Sudan[c]	49		Papua New Guinea	71
12	Mauritania	55		Rwanda	71
13	Senegal	59		Uganda	71

Highest tertiary enrolment[d]
Number enrolled as % of relevant age group, 1991

1	Canada	99		Netherlands	38
2	United States	76	12	Denmark	36
3	Finland	51		Germany	36
4	New Zealand	45		Peru	36
	Norway	45		Spain	36
6	Argentina	43	16	Austria	35
	France	43	17	Ireland	34
8	South Korea	40		Israel	34
9	Australia	39		Sweden	34
10	Belgium	38	20	Italy	32

Notes: The gross enrolment ratios shown are the actual number enrolled as a percentage of the number of children in the official primary age group. They may exceed 100 when children outside the primary age group are receiving primary education either because they have not moved on to secondary education or because they have started primary education early.

Least literate
% adult literacy rate, 1992

1	Burkina Faso	19.9		Oman	35.0
2	Sierra Leone	23.7	15	Mali	35.9
3	Benin	25.0	16	Pakistan	36.4
4	Guinea	26.9	17	Bangladesh	36.6
5	Nepal	27.0	18	Cambodia	37.8
	Somalia	27.0	19	Guinea-Bissau	39.0
7	Sudan	28.2	20	Namibia	40.0
8	Gambia, The	30.0		Senegal	40.0
9	Niger	31.2	22	CAR	40.2
10	Afghanistan	31.6	23	Bhutan	40.9
11	Chad	32.5	24	Yemen	41.1
12	Mozambique	33.5	25	Angola	42.5
13	Mauritania	35.0		Liberia	42.5

Highest mean years of schooling
1992

1	United States	12.4	15	Japan	10.8
2	Canada	12.2	16	New Zealand	10.7
3	Norway	12.1	17	Luxembourg	10.5
4	Australia	12.0	18	Israel	10.2
	France	12.0	19	Hungary	9.8
6	United Kingdom	11.7	20	Barbados	9.4
7	Germany	11.6	21	South Korea	9.3
	Switzerland	11.6	22	Argentina	9.2
9	Austria	11.4		Ex-Czechoslovakia	9.2
	Sweden	11.4		Iceland	9.2
11	Belgium	11.2	25	Estonia	9.0
12	Netherlands	11.1		Latvia	9.0
13	Denmark	11.0		Lithuania	9.0
14	Finland	10.9		Russia	9.0

Lowest mean years of schooling
1992

1	Burkina Faso	0.2		Guinea	0.9
	Niger	0.2		Oman	0.9
3	Bhutan	0.3		Senegal	0.9
	Chad	0.3		Sierra Leone	0.9
	Somalia	0.3		Yemen	0.9
6	Burundi	0.4	19	Papua New Guinea	1.0
	Guinea-Bissau	0.4	20	CAR	1.1
	Mali	0.4		Ethiopia	1.1
	Mauritania	0.4		Rwanda	1.1
10	Gambia, The	0.6		Uganda	1.1
11	Benin	0.7	24	Nigeria	1.2
12	Sudan	0.8	25	Angola	1.5
13	Afghanistan	0.9			

a 1988. b 1989. c 1990.
d Tertiary education includes all levels of post-secondary education including
courses leading to awards not equivalent to a university degree, courses leading to
a first university degree and postgraduate courses.

Life: *the chances*

Highest life expectancy
Years, 1995-2000

1	Japan	80	34	Brunei	75
2	Hong Kong	79		Chile	75
	Iceland	79		Jamaica	75
	Sweden	79		UAE	75
	Switzerland	79	38	Bahamas	74
6	Australia	78		Georgia	74
	Canada	78		Netherlands Antilles	74
	Cyprus	78		Panama	74
	France	78	42	Albania	73
	Greece	78		Argentina	73
	Italy	78		Armenia	73
	Netherlands	78		Bahrain	73
	Spain	78		Bosnia & Hercegovina	73
14	Austria	77		Fiji	73
	Belgium	77		Macao	73
	Costa Rica	77		Macedonia	73
	Finland	77		Serbia	73
	Germany	77		Slovenia	73
	Israel	77		Sri Lanka	73
	Luxembourg	77		Trinidad & Tobago	73
	Malta	77		Uruguay	73
	Norway	77		Venezuela	73
	United Kingdom	77	56	Azerbaijan	72
	United States	77		Croatia	72
25	Barbados	76		Malaysia	72
	Cuba	76		Mauritius	72
	Denmark	76		Mexico	72
	Ireland	76		North Korea	72
	Kuwait	76		Qatar	72
	New Zealand	76		South Korea	72
	Portugal	76		Suriname	72
	Puerto Rico	76		Tajikistan	72
	Singapore	76			

Highest male life expectancy
Years, 1995-2000

1	Japan	76.8	6	Greece	75.5
2	Iceland	76.3	7	Australia	75.4
3	Hong Kong	76.2		Israel	75.4
4	Sweden	76.1		Switzerland	75.4
5	Cyprus	75.6	10	Spain	75.3

Highest female life expectancy
Years, 1995-2000

1	Japan	82.9	6	France	81.3
2	Hong Kong	82.3		Iceland	81.3
3	Sweden	81.9	8	Australia	81.2
4	Switzerland	81.7		Canada	81.2
5	Italy	81.4	10	Spain	81.0

Lowest life expectancy
Years, 1995-2000

1	Sierra Leone	41		Laos	54
2	Uganda	43		Mauritania	54
3	Malawi	45	34	Sudan	55
4	Afghanistan	46	35	Gabon	56
	Guinea-Bissau	46	36	Nepal	57
	Zambia	46		Togo	57
7	Burkina Faso	47	38	Bangladesh	58
	Gambia, The	47		Ghana	58
	Guinea	47		Haiti	58
	Mozambique	47		Liberia	58
	Rwanda	47		Papua New Guinea	58
12	Mali	48	43	Cameroon	59
13	Angola	49		Madagascar	59
	Benin	49	45	Myanmar	60
	Niger	49	46	Namibia	61
	Somalia	49	47	Bolivia	62
17	CAR	50	48	India	63
	Chad	50		Lesotho	63
	Congo	50	50	Pakistan	64
	Côte d'Ivoire	50	51	Indonesia	65
	Ethiopia	50		South Africa	65
22	Burundi	51	53	Egypt	66
	Senegal	51		Libya	66
	Zimbabwe	51		Mongolia	66
25	Nigeria	52		Morocco	66
	Tanzania	52	57	Botswana	67
	Yemen	52		Guatemala	67
	Zaire	52		Peru	67
29	Bhutan	53		Turkmenistan	67
30	Cambodia	54		Vietnam	67
	Kenya	54			

Lowest male life expectancy
Years, 1995-2000

1	Sierra Leone	39.4	6	Rwanda	45.2
2	Uganda	42.2	7	Burkina Faso	45.3
3	Guinea-Bissau	43.9	8	Gambia, The	45.4
4	Malawi	44.3		Mozambique	45.4
5	Afghanistan	45.0		Zambia	45.4

Lowest female life expectancy
Years, 1995-2000

1	Sierra Leone	42.6	6	Guinea	47.0
2	Uganda	44.3	7	Guinea-Bissau	47.1
3	Malawi	45.4	8	Rwanda	48.0
4	Afghanistan	46.0	9	Burkina Faso	48.1
5	Zambia	46.8	10	Mozambique	48.3

Death: *the chances*

Highest death rates[a]
Number of deaths per 1,000 population

1	Sierra Leone	22.9		Sweden	10.9
2	Afghanistan	20.3		United Kingdom	10.9
3	Malawi	19.6	53	Haiti	10.8
4	Guinea-Bissau	19.5		Moldova	10.8
5	Uganda	19.4		Norway	10.8
6	Guinea	18.3	56	Cameroon	10.7
7	Burkina Faso	18.0		Poland	10.7
8	Mozambique	17.6		Slovenia	10.7
9	Gambia, The	17.3	59	Slovakia	10.6
10	Mali	17.1	60	Belgium	10.5
11	Angola	16.9		Ghana	10.5
12	Rwanda	16.7		Portugal	10.5
13	Somalia	16.6	63	Uruguay	10.4
14	Benin	16.4	64	Bangladesh	10.2
15	Chad	16.3		Finland	10.2
16	Zambia	16.2	66	Austria	10.1
17	Ethiopia	15.9		Greece	10.1
18	CAR	15.7		Madagascar	10.1
19	Côte d'Ivoire	15.3	69	Italy	9.9
20	Congo	15.2		Luxembourg	9.9
21	Hungary	14.5		Papua New Guinea	9.9
	Senegal	14.5	72	Myanmar	9.8
23	Burundi	14.4	73	France	9.6
24	Gabon	14.3		Serbia	9.6
25	Nigeria	13.9	75	Spain	9.3
	Zaire	13.9	76	Namibia	9.2
27	Yemen	13.7	77	Bolivia	9.1
28	Ukraine	13.6	78	Georgia	9.0
29	Bhutan	13.5		Switzerland	9.0
	Tanzania	13.5	80	India	8.9
31	Latvia	13.4	81	Barbados	8.8
32	Bulgaria	13.3		Ireland	8.8
33	Estonia	13.2		Netherlands	8.8
	Laos	13.2	84	United States	8.7
	Zimbabwe	13.2	85	Lesotho	8.6
36	Mauritania	13.1	86	Japan	8.3
37	Russia	13.0	87	New Zealand	8.2
38	Czech Republic	12.9	88	Argentina	8.0
39	Liberia	12.6		Malta	8.0
40	Cambodia	12.1	90	South Africa	7.9
41	Belarus	12.0	91	Pakistan	7.8
42	Sudan	11.9	92	Canada	7.7
43	Denmark	11.8	93	Indonesia	7.6
	Kenya	11.8	94	Puerto Rico	7.5
45	Croatia	11.7	95	Australia	7.4
46	Lithuania	11.6		Macedonia	7.4
47	Romania	11.5	97	Bosnia & Hercegovina	7.3
48	Nepal	11.4	98	Brazil	7.2
	Togo	11.4		Cyprus	7.2
50	Germany	10.9		Kazakhstan	7.2

Highest infant mortality[b]
Number of deaths per 1,000 live births

1	Afghanistan	162		26	CAR	105
	Mozambique	162		27	Nepal	99
3	Sierra Leone	143			Sudan	99
4	Liberia	142		29	Laos	97
5	Guinea-Bissau	140		30	Pakistan	95
6	Malawi	134		31	Gabon	94
7	Guinea	133		32	Haiti	93
8	Burkina Faso	132			Madagascar	93
	Gambia, The	132		34	Tanzania	92
	Somalia	132		35	Bangladesh	91
11	Mali	130			Côte d'Ivoire	91
12	Bhutan	129			Zaire	91
13	Angola	124		38	Togo	85
14	Niger	123		39	Nigeria	84
15	Chad	122		40	Bolivia	82
	Ethiopia	122		41	Ghana	81
	Uganda	122		42	India	79
18	Mauritania	117		43	Myanmar	72
	Rwanda	117		44	Libya	68
20	Cambodia	116			Senegal	68
21	Congo	114		46	Indonesia	66
22	Benin	110		47	Iran	65
23	Zambia	107		48	Guatemala	62
24	Burundi	106		49	Cameroon	61
	Yemen	106			Kenya	61

Lowest death rates[a]
Number of deaths per 1,000 pop.

1	Kuwait	2.2
2	UAE	2.9
3	Brunei	3.5
4	Qatar	3.7
5	Bahrain	3.8
	Costa Rica	3.8
7	Saudi Arabia	4.2
8	Oman	4.3
9	Fiji	4.6
10	Venezuela	4.7

Lowest infant mortality[b]
Number of deaths per 1,000 pop

1	Ireland	5
	Japan	5
	Singapore	5
	Sweden	5
5	Finland	6
	Germany	6
	Hong Kong	6
	Iceland	6
	Netherlands	6
	Norway	6
	Switzerland	6
12	Australia	7
	Austria	7
	Brunei	7
	Canada	7
	Denmark	7
	France	7
	New Zealand	7
	United Kingdom	7

Notes: The data for the number of deaths per 1,000 population are crude rates, i.e. not adjusted for differences in age structure. Thus a country with a high proportion of older people will have a higher rate than one with a younger population. This explains why a number of developed countries have apparently high death rates.

Both death and, in particular, infant mortality rates can be underestimated in certain countries where not all deaths are officially recorded.

a 1995–2000.
b 1992.

Death: *the causes*

Cancer

%

1	Lithuania	26.5
2	Netherlands	26.0
3	Switzerland	25.4
4	France	25.1
5	United Kingdom	25.0
6	Canada	24.9
7	Belgium	24.6
	Denmark	24.6
9	Italy	24.1
10	New Zealand	23.9
11	Luxembourg	23.7
12	Australia	23.1
	Iceland	23.1
14	Austria	22.8
15	Germany	22.7
16	Czech Republic	22.5
	Ireland	22.5
18	Japan	22.3
	United States	22.3
20	Uruguay	21.9

Heart attack

%

1	Lithuania	47.3
2	Armenia	42.3
3	Belarus	36.2
4	Iceland	35.8
5	Latvia	35.5
6	Sweden	35.4
7	Malta	35.0
	United States	35.0
9	Austria	34.9
	Finland	34.9
11	Bahrain	34.6
	Ex-Yugoslavia	34.6
13	Argentina	33.4
14	Australia	33.0
15	Ireland	32.4
	Israel	32.4
17	Germany	32.1
18	New Zealand	32.0
19	Cuba	31.8
20	Kazakhstan	31.7

Infectious disease

%

1	Guatemala	16.5
2	Mexico	5.0
3	Venezuela	4.6
4	Sri Lanka	3.9
5	Suriname	3.8
6	Kuwait	3.4
7	Brazil	3.3
	Chile	3.3
9	Jamaica	3.2
10	Argentina	2.9
11	Bahamas	2.7
12	Barbados	2.4
	Puerto Rico	2.4
	Singapore	2.4
15	Israel	2.2
16	Costa Rica	2.1
17	Mauritius	1.9
18	Trinidad & Tobago	1.8
19	Kazakhstan	1.7
	Kirgizstan	1.7

Motor accident

%

1	Kuwait	2.8
2	Latvia	2.7
3	Suriname	2.4
4	Lithuania	2.3
5	Portugal	2.1
6	Venezuela	2.0
7	Brazil	1.9
	Kirgizstan	1.9
9	Russia	1.8
10	Belarus	1.7
	Greece	1.7
	Mexico	1.7
13	Armenia	1.6
	Kazakhstan	1.6
	Luxembourg	1.6
	Spain	1.6
	Ukraine	1.6
18	Costa Rica	1.5
	Hungary	1.5
20	Poland	1.4

Notes: Data refer to the chances a newborn baby has of eventually dying from one of the causes shown. Statistics are only available for a limited number of countries and many less developed countries are excluded.

Stroke
%

1	Portugal	25.2
2	Russia	21.7
3	Bulgaria	21.5
4	Latvia	21.1
5	Greece	21.0
6	Kirgizstan	20.7
7	Jamaica	19.3
8	Kazakhstan	18.8
9	Ukraine	17.6
10	Czech Republic	17.3
11	Armenia	16.9
12	Romania	16.3
13	Luxembourg	16.1
14	Ex-Yugoslavia	15.5
15	Mauritius	15.3
16	Japan	15.1
17	Italy	14.4
18	Spain	14.3
19	Belarus	14.2
	Hungary	14.2

Injury and poisoning
%

1	Russia	9.9
2	Latvia	9.8
3	Lithuania	9.0
4	Hungary	8.7
	Suriname	8.7
6	Cuba	7.9
	Kazakhstan	7.9
8	France	7.8
	Kirgizstan	7.8
10	Ukraine	7.7
11	Mexico	7.5
12	Belarus	7.4
13	Finland	7.3
14	Chile	7.2
15	Switzerland	7.0
16	Czech Republic	6.7
17	Brazil	6.5
18	Sri Lanka	6.4
19	Bahamas	6.3
20	Poland	6.2

AIDS
Cases per 100,000 inhabitants[a]

1	Bahamas	522.18	21	Ghana	75.66
2	Bermuda	359.68	22	Haiti	72.76
3	Zambia	348.70	23	Honduras	60.33
4	Malawi	342.59	24	Spain	56.94
5	Namibia	325.94	25	Zaire	55.48
6	Zimbabwe	262.31	26	Switzerland	50.85
7	Congo	254.90	27	France	49.39
8	Uganda	243.40	28	Burkina Faso	42.66
9	Barbados	160.77	29	Suriname	41.73
10	United States	150.52	30	Gabon	38.22
11	Tanzania	144.78	31	Guinea-Bissau	36.43
12	Rwanda	142.94	32	Canada	35.64
13	Côte d'Ivoire	139.77	33	Italy	35.15
14	Burundi	126.58	34	Brazil	34.02
15	Trinidad & Tobago	119.58	35	Dominican Republic	31.66
16	Kenya	118.72	36	Jamaica	27.74
17	CAR	114.80	37	Gambia, The	27.18
18	Botswana	100.93	38	Australia	27.02
19	Togo	86.24	39	Denmark	26.10
20	Netherlands Antilles	84.69	40	Chad	26.05

a AIDS data refer to the total number of cases reported to the World Health Organisation up to the end of 1993. The number of cases diagnosed and reported depends on the quality of medical practice and administration and is likely to be under-recorded in a number of countries.

Health

Highest population per doctor
1990

1	Kenya	71,430		Côte d'Ivoire	16,670
2	Nigeria	66,670		Nepal	16,670
3	Zimbabwe	62,500	23	Angola	14,290
4	Guinea	50,000		Benin	14,290
	Malawi	50,000		Sierra Leone	14,290
	Mozambique	50,000		Somalia	14,290
	Rwanda	50,000	27	Bhutan	13,110
8	Burkina Faso	33,330	28	Cameroon	12,500
	Chad	33,330		Myanmar	12,500
	Ethiopia	33,330		Papua New Guinea	12,500
	Niger	33,330		Togo	12,500
	Tanzania	33,330	32	Mauritania	11,900
13	Cambodia	25,000	33	Gambia, The	11,690
	CAR	25,000	34	Sudan	11,110
	Ghana	25,000		Zambia	11,110
	Uganda	25,000	36	Liberia	9,340
17	Mali	20,000	37	Madagascar	8,330
	Senegal	20,000		Philippines	8,330
19	Lesotho	18,610	39	Congo	8,320
20	Burundi	16,670	40	Guinea-Bissau	7,260

Lowest population per doctor
1990

1	Georgia	170	21	Bulgaria	320
2	Latvia	200	22	Argentina	330
3	Estonia	210	23	Hungary	340
	Italy	210	24	France	350
	Russia	210		Israel	350
6	Lithuania	220		Tajikistan	350
7	Austria	230		Uruguay	350
	Ukraine	230	28	Germany	370
9	Armenia	250		North Korea	370
	Azerbaijan	250		Sweden	370
	Belarus	250	31	Denmark	390
	Kazakhstan	250	32	Finland	410
	Moldova	250		Netherlands	410
14	Cuba	270	34	United States	420
15	Kirgizstan	280	35	Australia	440
	Spain	280	36	Canada	450
	Uzbekistan	280	37	Poland	490
18	Turkmenistan	290		Portugal	490
19	Belgium	310	39	Norway	500
	Ex-Czechoslovakia	310	40	Qatar	530

Highest calorie intake

Calories per person, per day, latest available year

1	Greece	4,152	31	Ireland	3,023
2	Denmark	3,675	32	Iran	3,020
3	Germany	3,537	33	Spain	3,014
4	United States	3,495	34	Portugal	3,009
5	France	3,491	35	Algeria	2,940
6	Belgium	3,460	36	Norway	2,938
7	Sweden	3,443	37	Saudi Arabia	2,930
8	Switzerland	3,435	38	Mauritius	2,900
9	Italy	3,323	39	Brunei	2,860
10	Austria	3,320		Hong Kong	2,860
11	Egypt	3,310	41	North Korea	2,840
12	Libya	3,290	42	South Korea	2,830
	UAE	3,290	43	Bahamas	2,780
14	Barbados	3,220	44	Finland	2,775
15	Canada	3,207	45	Fiji	2,770
16	Turkey	3,200		Trinidad & Tobago	2,770
17	Lebanon	3,140	47	Brazil	2,730
18	Cuba	3,130	48	Costa Rica	2,710
	South Africa	3,130		Jordan	2,710
20	Singapore	3,120	50	Uruguay	2,690
	Syria	3,120	51	Paraguay	2,680
	Tunisia	3,120	52	Malaysia	2,670
23	Iraq	3,100	53	Japan	2,647
24	Australia	3,094	54	China	2,640
25	Argentina	3,070	55	Indonesia	2,610
26	United Kingdom	3,062	56	Papua New Guinea	2,590
27	Mexico	3,060	57	Côte d'Ivoire	2,570
28	Netherlands	3,050	58	Jamaica	2,560
29	Kuwait	3,040	59	Chile	2,480
30	Morocco	3,030	60	Laos	2,470

Highest health spending

As % of GDP, 1990

1	United States	13.3
2	Canada	9.9
3	France	9.1
	Germany	9.1
5	Finland	8.9
6	Sweden	8.8
	Switzerland	8.8
8	Netherlands	8.7
9	Australia	8.6
	Nicaragua	8.6

Lowest health spending

As % of GDP, 1990

1	Somalia	1.5
2	Singapore	1.9
3	Indonesia	2.0
	Philippines	2.0
5	Syria	2.1
	Vietnam	2.1
7	Sierra Leone	2.4
	Zaire	2.4
9	Laos	2.5
10	Cameroon	2.6
	Egypt	2.6
	Iran	2.6

Till death us do part

Highest marriage rates[a]
Number of marriages per 1,000 population

1	Cuba	17.7		Mongolia	7.5
2	Bermuda	15.0		Romania	7.5
3	Bangladesh	11.3	33	Hong Kong	7.4
4	Mauritius	10.4	34	Mexico	7.3
5	Azerbaijan	10.1		Portugal	7.3
6	Kazakhstan	10.0	36	Brunei	7.2
	Uzbekistan	10.0		Czech Republic	7.2
8	Turkmenistan	9.8		Latvia	7.2
9	Kirgizstan	9.7	39	Canada	7.1
10	Bahamas	9.6		Malta	7.1
	Belarus	9.6		Thailand	7.1
	Fiji	9.6	42	Georgia	7.0
13	Puerto Rico	9.4		Paraguay	7.0
14	Singapore	9.3	44	Chile	6.9
	United States	9.3		Tunisia	6.9
16	Lithuania	9.2	46	New Zealand	6.8
	Tajikistan	9.2	47	Costa Rica	6.7
18	Moldova	9.0		Netherlands Antilles	6.7
19	Albania	8.9	49	Australia	6.6
	South Korea	8.9		Luxembourg	6.6
	Sri Lanka	8.9		Switzerland	6.6
22	Cyprus	8.7		Ukraine	6.6
	Jordan	8.7	53	Israel	6.5
24	Russia	8.6		United Kingdom	6.5
25	Iraq	8.5		Uruguay	6.5
26	Egypt	8.4	56	Netherlands	6.4
	Turkey	8.4	57	Denmark	6.3
28	Barbados	7.9	58	Armenia	6.1
29	Syria	7.7		Ecuador	6.1
30	Iran	7.5		Greece	6.1

Youngest brides[a]
Average age, years

1	Niger	15.8
2	Guinea	16.0
3	Mali	16.4
4	Chad	16.5
5	Bangladesh	16.7
6	Mozambique	17.6
7	Gabon	17.7
	Uganda	17.7
9	Afghanistan	17.8
	Malawi	17.8
	Yemen	17.8

Oldest brides[a]
Average age, years

1	Barbados	30.4
	Sweden	30.4
3	Jamaica	29.7
4	Denmark	28.6
5	Iceland	28.3
6	Norway	27.5
7	Finland	26.8
8	Netherlands	26.7
	Switzerland	26.7
10	Hong Kong	26.6

a   Latest available year.

Note: Marriage rates refer to registered marriages only and, therefore, reflect the customs surrounding registry and efficiency of administration. The data are based on latest available figures and hence will be affected by the population age structure at the time.

Highest divorce rates[a]
Number of divorces per 1,000 population

1	United States	4.8		31	France	1.9
2	Cuba	4.2			Kirgizstan	1.9
3	Lithuania	4.1		33	Netherlands	1.8
4	Latvia	4.0		34	Germany	1.7
	Russia	4.0		35	Azerbaijan	1.6
6	Ukraine	3.9			Tunisia	1.6
7	Puerto Rico	3.8		37	Kuwait	1.5
8	Estonia	3.7			Tajikistan	1.5
9	Belarus	3.4			Uzbekistan	1.5
	Moldova	3.4		40	Barbados	1.4
11	Bermuda	2.9			Egypt	1.4
	Canada	2.9			Georgia	1.4
	United Kingdom	2.9			Japan	1.4
14	Kazakhstan	2.8			Turkmenistan	1.4
15	New Zealand	2.7		45	Bahamas	1.3
16	Australia	2.6			Bulgaria	1.3
17	Denmark	2.5			Israel	1.3
	Finland	2.5			Jordan	1.3
19	Ex-Czechoslovakia	2.4			Romania	1.3
	Hungary	2.4			Singapore	1.3
	Norway	2.4		51	Bahrain	1.2
	Suriname	2.4		52	Costa Rica	1.1
23	Iceland	2.3			Portugal	1.1
	Sweden	2.3		54	Hong Kong	1.0
25	Netherlands Antilles	2.2			Slovenia	1.0
	Uruguay	2.2			Venezuela	1.0
27	Austria	2.1		57	Armenia	0.9
	Belgium	2.1			South Korea	0.9
	Switzerland	2.1			Trinidad & Tobago	0.9
30	Luxembourg	2.0		60	Albania	0.8

Youngest grooms[a]
Average age, years

1	Nepal	21.5
	Niger	21.5
3	Yemen	22.2
4	Mozambique	22.6
	Rwanda	22.6
6	Malawi	22.9
7	Chad	23.0
8	CAR	23.3
9	India	23.4
10	Cuba	23.5
	Madagascar	23.5

Oldest grooms[a]
Average age, years

1	Jamaica	33.8
2	Barbados	32.7
3	Botswana	30.8
4	Iceland	29.9
5	Japan	29.6
	Macao	29.6
7	Netherlands	29.3
8	Hong Kong	29.2
9	Finland	28.5
10	Denmark	28.4
	Singapore	28.4

Households and prices

Biggest households[a]
Population per dwelling

1	Gabon	8.3		Sudan	5.6
2	Iraq	7.1	25	India	5.5
3	Algeria	7.0		Mauritania	5.5
4	Yemen	6.8		Tunisia	5.5
5	Guinea	6.7	28	Benin	5.4
	Jordan	6.7		Zaire	5.4
	Pakistan	6.7	30	Congo	5.3
8	Bahrain	6.6		Philippines	5.3
9	Kuwait	6.5		Tanzania	5.3
10	Niger	6.4	33	Cameroon	5.2
11	Syria	6.3		Colombia	5.2
12	Burkina Faso	6.2		Guatemala	5.2
	Liberia	6.2		Iran	5.2
14	Côte d'Ivoire	5.8		Malaysia	5.2
15	Afghanistan	5.9		Myanmar	5.2
	Morocco	5.9		Paraguay	5.2
17	Brunei	5.8		Sri Lanka	5.2
	Fiji	5.8		Turkey	5.2
	Nepal	5.8	42	Ecuador	5.1
20	Bangladesh	5.7		Kenya	5.1
	Togo	5.7		Peru	5.1
22	Mali	5.6		Venezuela	5.1
	Qatar	5.6			

Highest cost of living[b]
September 1994 USA=100

1	Japan	221	17	Netherlands	110
2	Libya	181		United Kingdom	110
3	Switzerland	140	19	Finland	108
4	Norway	137	20	Luxembourg	106
5	France	128	21	Congo	105
6	Austria	123	22	Gabon	104
7	Nigeria	119	23	Israel	103
	Taiwan	119	24	Ireland	101
9	Denmark	118	25	Papua New Guinea	100
10	Russia	114		United States	100
11	Hong Kong	113	27	Côte d'Ivoire	97
	Singapore	113		Spain	97
13	Belgium	112	29	Greece	95
	South Korea	112	30	Australia	94
	Sweden	112		China	94
16	Germany	111			

a Latest available year.
b The cost of living index shown is compiled by The Economist Inteligence Unit for use by companies in determining expatriate compensation: it is a comparison of the cost of maintaining a typical international lifestyle in the country rather than a comparison of the purchasing power of a citizen of the country. The index is based on typical urban prices an international executive and family will face abroad. The prices are for products of international comparable quality found in a supermarket

Smallest households[a]
Population per dwelling

1	Denmark	2.2	24	Australia	3.0
	Sweden	2.2		Japan	3.0
3	Western Germany	2.3	26	Greece	3.1
4	Latvia	2.4		Poland	3.1
	Norway	2.4		Romania	3.1
6	Bermuda	2.6	29	Malta	3.2
	Finland	2.6		Ukraine	3.2
	France	2.6	31	Puerto Rico	3.3
	Netherlands	2.6		Uruguay	3.3
	Switzerland	2.6	33	Gambia, The	3.4
	United States	2.6		Hong Kong	3.4
12	Austria	2.7	35	Cyprus	3.5
	Belgium	2.7		Israel	3.5
	Canada	2.7		Spain	3.5
	Hungary	2.7	38	Barbados	3.6
16	Ex-Czechoslovakia	2.8		Ireland	3.6
	Italy	2.8		Macao	3.6
	Luxembourg	2.8		Ex-Yugoslavia	3.6
	New Zealand	2.8	42	Bahamas	3.8
	United Kingdom	2.8		Belarus	3.8
21	Bulgaria	2.9		Bolivia	3.8
	Portugal	2.9		South Korea	3.8
	Russia	2.9			

Lowest cost of living[b]
September 1994 USA=100

1	India	45	16	Sri Lanka	66
2	Iran	47	17	Ecuador	67
	Venezuela	47	18	Chile	68
	Zimbabwe	47		South Africa	68
5	Pakistan	54		Turkey	68
6	Algeria	56	21	Peru	70
	Romania	56	22	Colombia	71
	Vietnam	56		Kuwait	71
9	Czech Republic	57	24	Tunisia	72
10	Hungary	58	25	Guatemala	74
11	Poland	63	26	Morocco	75
12	Kenya	64		Saudi Arabia	75
	Paraguay	64		Uruguay	75
14	Bangladesh	65	29	Panama	76
	Philippines	65	30	UAE	77

or department store. Prices found in local markets and bazaars are not used unless the available merchandise is of the specified quality and the shopping area itself is safe for executive and family members. New York City prices are used as the base, so USA = 100.

Consumer goods: *ownership*

TV

Number of people per receiver, 1991

1	Bermuda	0.9		Switzerland		2.5
2	United States	1.2	27	Latvia		2.6
3	Malta	1.4		Qatar		2.6
	Oman	1.4	29	Lithuania		2.7
5	Canada	1.6		Russia		2.7
	Japan	1.6		Singapore		2.7
7	Germany	1.8	32	Estonia		2.8
8	Denmark	1.9	33	Netherlands Antilles		3.0
9	Finland	2.0		Ukraine		3.0
10	Australia	2.1	35	Iceland		3.2
	Austria	2.1		Trinidad & Tobago		3.2
	Ex-Czechoslovakia	2.1	37	Ireland		3.4
	Netherlands	2.1		Poland		3.4
14	Belgium	2.2	39	Hong Kong		3.6
	Sweden	2.2	40	Belarus		3.7
16	New Zealand	2.3	41	Barbados		3.8
	United Kingdom	2.3		Puerto Rico		3.8
18	Hungary	2.4	43	Israel		3.9
	Italy	2.4		Luxembourg		3.9
	Kuwait	2.4		Saudi Arabia		3.9
	Norway	2.4	46	Bulgaria		4.0
22	Bahrain	2.5	47	Lebanon		4.2
	France	2.5	48	Uruguay		4.3
	South Korea	2.5	49	Brunei		4.4
	Spain	2.5	50	Bahamas		4.5

Telephone[a]

Number of people per telephone

1	Sweden	1.0		Greece	1.9
	United States	1.0		Japan	1.9
3	Switzerland	1.1	25	Australia	2.0
4	Bermuda	1.2		Israel	2.0
	Denmark	1.2		UAE	2.0
6	Canada	1.3	28	Barbados	2.3
	Finland	1.3		Spain	2.3
	Norway	1.3	30	South Korea	2.4
	United Kingdom	1.3	31	Singapore	2.5
10	Luxembourg	1.4	32	Bahrain	2.8
	New Zealand	1.4	33	Ireland	2.9
12	Iceland	1.5		Netherlands Antilles	2.9
	Netherlands	1.5		Qatar	2.9
	Western Germany	1.5		Taiwan	2.9
15	Austria	1.6	37	Bulgaria	3.1
	Hong Kong	1.6	38	Macao	3.3
17	Belgium	1.7	39	Ex Czechoslovakia	3.4
	France	1.7	40	Brunei	4.0
19	Bahamas	1.8	41	Germany	4.1
	Italy	1.8	42	Uruguay	4.7
	Malta	1.8	43	Turkey	5.0
22	Cyprus	1.9	44	Hungary	5.1

Home computer[a]
% of households owning

1	Netherlands	25	**11**	Ireland	12
2	United Kingdom	18		Italy	12
3	Finland	16		Japan	12
	Norway	16		Luxembourg	12
	United States	16		Sweden	12
	Western Germany	16	**16**	Austria	11
7	Belgium	15	**17**	Spain	8
8	Denmark	14	**18**	Portugal	7
	France	14	**19**	Greece	6
	Switzerland	14			

Video cassette recorder
% of households owning

1	Japan	98		Sweden	56
2	United Kingdom	72	**11**	France	54
3	Canada	70	**12**	Belgium	48
	United States	70		Ireland	48
5	Switzerland	68	**14**	South Korea	46
6	Austria	59	**15**	Denmark	45
	Finland	59		Spain	45
8	Netherlands	58	**17**	Norway	43
9	Germany	56	**18**	Italy	38

Dishwasher[a]
% of households owning

1	United States	51	**11**	Belgium	26
2	Luxembourg	50		Denmark	26
3	Iceland	45	**13**	Italy	18
4	Norway	37	**14**	Ireland	15
5	Austria	35	**15**	Portugal	14
6	Western Germany	34	**16**	Greece	11
7	France	33		Netherlands	11
8	Switzerland	32		Spain	11
9	Finland	31		United Kingdom	11
	Sweden	31			

Microwave[a]
% of households owning

1	United States	80	**11**	Belgium	21
2	Japan	79	**12**	Ireland	20
3	Finland	53	**13**	Luxembourg	16
4	United Kingdom	48	**14**	Switzerland	15
5	Sweden	37	**15**	Denmark	14
6	Western Germany	36	**16**	Spain	9
7	Norway	34	**17**	Italy	6
8	Austria	31	**18**	Portugal	4
9	France	25	**19**	Greece	2
10	Netherlands	22			

a Latest available year up to 1992.
Note: A number of difficulties arise when dealing with household penetration data. Definitions of articles may vary.

Culture and crime

Books published[a]
Per year

1	China	90,156
2	United Kingdom	86,573
3	Germany	67,277
4	United States	49,276
5	France	45,379
6	Spain	41,816
7	Italy	29,351
8	Russia	28,716
9	South Korea	27,889
10	Switzerland	14,663
11	India	14,438
12	Belgium	13,913
13	Sweden	12,813
14	Netherlands	11,844
15	Denmark	11,761
16	Finland	11,033
17	Poland	10,727
18	Australia	10,723
19	Ex-Yugoslavia	9,797
20	Ex-Czechoslovakia	9,362

Library book loans[a]
'000 per year

1	United Kingdom	564,525
2	Ukraine	519,600
3	Germany	324,857
4	Japan	203,133
5	China	180,660
6	Canada	176,185
7	Netherlands	174,182
8	Poland	154,891
9	France	120,000
10	Ex-Czechoslovakia	96,074
11	Finland	85,700
12	Denmark	78,280
13	Sweden	73,307
14	Romania	54,025
15	Hungary	47,996
16	Mexico	45,701
17	Bulgaria	24,088
18	Norway	19,130
19	Spain	16,981
20	South Korea	13,911

Cinema attendances[a]
Per head per year

1	China	12.3
2	Ukraine	11.9
3	Hong Kong	10.3
	Ex-Soviet Union[b]	10.3
5	Mongolia	9.4
6	Iceland	5.2
7	India	5.0
8	Latvia	4.3
9	United States	3.9
10	Vietnam	3.8
11	Ex-Czechoslovakia	3.2
12	Canada	3.0
13	Bulgaria	2.9
	Romania	2.9
15	Cuba	2.8
16	Norway	2.5
17	Australia	2.4
18	Switzerland	2.3
19	Albania	2.2
20	France	2.1
	Hungary	2.1

Daily newspapers
Circulation per '000 pop., 1992

1	Hong Kong	819
2	Norway	606
3	Japan	576
4	Iceland	519
5	Finland	515
6	Sweden	511
7	Macao	510
8	South Korea	407
9	Austria	400
10	Switzerland	387
11	Luxembourg	384
12	United Kingdom	383
13	Singapore	336
14	Denmark	332
15	Germany	331
16	Romania	322
17	Belgium	310
18	New Zealand	304
19	Netherlands	303
20	Netherlands Antilles	301

a Data for books, libraries and cinemas are for 1992 or the latest available year.
b Excluding Ukraine.

Biggest wine drinkers
Average annual consumption of litres per head

1 Portugal	77.2
2 Italy	63.4
3 France	62.6
4 Greece	56.8
5 Argentina	55.9
6 Switzerland	43.4
7 Spain	37.7
8 Austria	31.4
9 Belgium	28.1
10 Malta[a]	27.9
11 Ex-Yugoslavia[a]	27.6
12 Luxembourg	27.2
13 Germany	26.8
14 Chile	26.6
15 Hungary	25.8
16 Denmark	24.6
17 Australia	19.3
18 New Zealand	17.0
19 Netherlands	15.2
20 Ex-Czechoslovakia	13.8

Biggest smokers
Average annual consumption of cigarettes per head, per day

1 Malta[a]	8.2
2 Hungary	8.0
3 Greece	7.6
4 Poland	7.5
5 Japan	7.4
6 Ex-Czechoslovakia	6.8
7 Switzerland	6.3
8 South Korea	6.1
9 United States	5.5
10 Australia	5.3
Ex-Yugoslavia[a]	5.3
12 Austria	5.0
13 Ireland	4.7
14 Italy	4.6
Taiwan	4.6
16 Belgium	4.5
France	4.5
18 Germany	4.4
Luxembourg	4.4
United Kingdom	4.4

Murders[b]
Number per 100,000 pop., 1990

1 Bahamas	52.61
2 Philippines	30.12
3 Guatemala	27.40
4 Jamaica	20.85
5 Botswana	19.50
6 Zimbabwe	17.88
7 Peru	12.01
8 Barbados	11.67
9 Sri Lanka	11.60
10 Malta	10.44
11 Paraguay	10.00
12 Thailand	9.50
13 United States	9.40
14 Ex-Soviet Union	8.67
15 Trinidad & Tobago	8.42
16 Papua New Guinea	7.78
17 Sweden	7.02
18 Taiwan	6.40

Drug offences[b]
Number per 100,000 pop., 1990

1 Bahamas	460.2
2 Sweden	326.1
3 Switzerland	279.7
4 Denmark	271.2
5 Canada[c]	258.9
6 Trinidad & Tobago	236.6
7 Barbados	216.0
8 Norway	213.9
9 Jamaica	212.8
10 Luxembourg	201.9
11 Germany	165.3
12 Israel	161.8
13 France	99.9
14 Mauritius	89.5
15 Botswana[c]	85.5
16 Brunei	80.3
17 Sri Lanka	71.2
18 Austria	69.5

a 1992.
b Crime statistics are based on offences recorded by the police. The number will therefore depend partly on the efficiency of police administration systems, the definition of offences, and the proportion of crimes reported, and therefore may not be strictly comparable.
c 1988.

Environment: *trees and disasters*

Top deforesters
Average annual rate, km² 1981-90

1	Brazil	-36,710	21	Ghana	-1,380
2	Indonesia	-12,120	22	Vietnam	-1,370
3	Zaire	-7,320	23	Madagascar	-1,350
4	Mexico	-6,780		Mozambique	-1,350
5	Bolivia	-6,250	25	Cambodia	-1,310
6	Venezuela	-5,990	26	CAR	-1,290
7	Thailand	-5,150		Laos	-1,290
8	Sudan	-4,820	28	Nicaragua	-1,240
9	Tanzania	-4,380	29	Cameroon	-1,220
10	Paraguay	-4,030	30	Côte d'Ivoire	-1,190
11	Myanmar	-4,010		Nigeria	-1,190
12	Malaysia	-3,960	32	Gabon	-1,160
13	Columbia	-3,670	33	Papua New Guinea	-1,130
14	Zambia	-3,630	34	Honduras	-1,120
15	India	-3,390	35	Mali	-1,060
16	United States	-3,170	36	Chad	-890
17	Philippines	-3,160	37	Guinea	-870
18	Peru	-2,710	38	Guatemala	-810
19	Ecuador	-2,380	38	Botswana	-770
20	Angola	-1,740		Pakistan	-770

Top reafforesters
Average annual rate, km² 1980s

1	China	45,520	6	Japan	2,400
2	Ex-Soviet Union	45,400	7	Sweden	2,070
3	United States	17,750	8	North Korea	2,000
4	Canada	7,200	9	Finland	1,580
5	Brazil	4,490	10	India	1,380

Fastest forest depletion
% average annual decrease in forested area, 1981-90

1	Jamaica	5.3		Nicaragua	1.7
2	Haiti	3.9		Panama	1.7
3	Bangladesh	3.3	17	Guatemala	1.6
4	Pakistan	2.9	18	Togo	1.4
	Philippines	2.9		Vietnam	1.4
	Thailand	2.9	20	Ghana	1.3
7	Costa Rica	2.6		Ireland	1.3
8	Dominican Republic	2.5		Malawi	1.3
9	Paraguay	2.4		Sri Lanka	1.3
10	El Salvador	2.1	24	Benin	1.2
11	Honduras	1.9		Mexico	1.2
	Trinidad & Tobago	1.9		Myanmar	1.2
13	Malaysia	1.8		Tanzania	1.2
14	Ecuador	1.7		Venezuela	1.2

Most forested countries

% of total area covered with forest, 1992

1	Suriname	91		Sweden	62
2	Papua New Guinea	83	13	Guinea	59
3	Gabon	74		Malaysia	59
	North Korea	74	15	Brazil	57
	Zaire	74		CAR	57
6	Finland	69		Indonesia	57
7	Japan	67	18	Bhutan	55
8	Fiji	65	19	Laos	53
	South Korea	65		Peru	53
10	Cambodia	64		Senegal	53
11	Congo	62			

Oil tanker spills

	Country affected	Oil spilled ('000 tonnes)	Name	Flag	Year
1	Trinidad & Tobago	276	Atlantic Express	Greece	1979
2	South Africa	256	Castello de Belvar	Spain	1983
3	France	228	Amoco Cadiz	Liberia	1978
4	Canada	140	Odyssey	Liberia	1988
5	United Kingdom	121	Torrey Canyon	Liberia	1967
6	Oman	120	Sea Star	South Korea	1972
7	Greece	102	Irenes Serenade	Greece	1980
8	Spain	101	Urquiola	Spain	1976
9	United States	99	Hawaiian Patriot	Liberia	1977
10	Turkey	95	Independenta	Romania	1979

Industrial disasters, 1984-93[a]

	Location	Origin of accident	Deaths
1984	St J Ixhuatepec	gas explosion	503
	Bhopal, India	chemical leakage	2,800
	Cubatao, Brazil	pipeline explosion	508
1986	Chernobyl, Soviet Union	reactor explosion	31
	Miamisburg, USA	rail accident	...
1987	Shangsi, China	fertiliser misuse	...
1988	Islamabad, Pakistan	explosives	100
	Arzamas, Soviet Union	explosives	73
	Tours, France	chemical leakage	...
	North Sea, UK	oil explosion	167
	Sverdlosk, Soviet Union	explosives	5
1989	Ionava, Soviet Union	chemical explosion	6
	Acha Ufa, Soviet Union	gas explosion	575
1990	Ufa, Soviet Union	chemical explosion	...
	Bangkok, Thailand	explosion (lorry)	54
	Patna, India	explosion (train)	100
1991	Thailand	explosives	171
	Livorno, Italy	oil explosion	140
	Sterlington, USA	gas explosion	8
1992	Kozlu,Turkey	gas explosion	270
1993	Shenzhen,China	chemical leakage	70

a Not ranked due to difficulties in comparing the effects of each.

Environment: *pollution and waste*

Carbon dioxide emissions
Kg per head

1	Qatar	44,700	21	Ireland	9,230
2	UAE	36,490		Netherlands	9,230
3	Iraq[a]	27,860	23	Libya	9,120
4	Luxembourg	27,500	24	Japan	8,790
5	United States	19,530	25	Poland	8,060
6	Bahrain	19,400	26	Austria	7,800
7	Canada	15,210	27	Oman	7,400
8	Australia	15,100	28	Israel	7,290
9	Singapore	15,060		Greece	7,180
10	Trinidad & Tobago	14,730	30	South Africa	7,180
11	Saudi Arabia	13,960	31	Iceland	7,000
12	Norway	13,740		Italy	6,960
13	Ex-Soviet Union	12,310	33	New Zealand	6,960
14	Denmark	12,240	34	France	6,560
15	Ex-Czechoslovakia	12,200		Bulgaria	6,300
16	Germany	12,130	36	Sweden	6,230
17	North Korea	10,960	37	Switzerland	6,160
18	Finland	10,410	38	Venezuela	6,160
19	Belgium	10,220	39	Hungary	6,050
20	United Kingdom	10,000		South Korea	6,050

Nitrogen oxide emissions
Kg per head

1	United States	73.4	11	Ireland	36.2
2	Canada	69.1	12	Italy[a]	34.5
3	Luxembourg	56.6	13	Belgium	29.9
4	Finland	56.5	14	Austria	27.3
5	Denmark	54.8	15	France	26.3
6	Norway	50.9	16	Switzerland	25.5
7	United Kingdom	47.6	17	Spain	23.4
8	Sweden	44.7	18	Portugal	14.4
9	Germany	40.1	19	Japan	10.5
10	Netherlands	36.3			

Sulphur dioxide emissions
Kg per head

1	Canada	118.7	11	Luxembourg	25.7
2	United States	81.2	12	France	22.9
3	Germany	70.7	13	Portugal	21.4
4	United Kingdom	61.8	14	Netherlands	13.5
5	Spain	56.1	15	Sweden	12.2
6	Ireland	52.9	16	Norway	10.7
7	Belgium	41.8	17	Austria	10.6
8	Finland	38.3	18	Switzerland	8.9
9	Denmark	35.0	19	Japan	7.0
10	Italy[a]	34.4			

Solid hazardous waste generated
Kg per head

1	Luxembourg	1,989	11	France	69
2	United States	705		Netherlands	69
3	Ex-Czechoslovakia	701	13	Finland	62
4	Hungary	392	14	Sweden	57
5	Canada	218	15	Italy	56
6	Portugal	106	16	Norway	47
7	Belgium	93	17	United Kingdom	44
8	Austria	78		Spain	44
9	Switzerland	76	19	Greece	43
10	Germany	74	20	New Zealand	32

Solid industrial waste generated
Kg per head

1	Luxembourg	3,485	11	Italy	701
2	United States	3,049	12	Norway[b]	519
3	Belgium	2,712	13	Sweden	474
4	Japan	2,529	14	Denmark	467
5	Canada	2,300	15	Netherlands	447
6	Finland	2,111	16	Greece	428
7	Austria	1,748	17	Ireland	425
8	Western Germany	1,002	18	Ex-Yugoslavia	301
9	France	891	19	Spain	130
10	United Kingdom	874	20	Portugal	64

Solid municipal waste generated
Kg per head

1	United States	721	11	Sweden	374
2	Finland	624	12	Germany	350
3	Canada	601	13	United Kingdom	348
4	Netherlands	497		Italy	348
5	Denmark	475	15	Belgium	343
6	Norway	472	16	Poland	338
7	Hungary	463	17	France	328
8	Luxembourg	445	18	Austria	325
9	Switzerland	441	19	Spain	322
10	Japan	411	20	Iceland	314

a Excluding emissions from industrial processes.
b Wastes from the chemical industry only.

The statistics for all tables (including those on page 82) except carbon dioxide emissions, fresh water resources and water use cover OECD and emerging Eastern European countries only. They normally refer to various years in the mid to late 1980s, though some refer to an earlier period.

Environment: recycling and water

Glass recycling
Recovery rates, %

1	Netherlands	66.7	11	Finland	35.7
2	Switzerland	64.7	12	Portugal	30.0
3	Denmark	60.4	13	France	28.5
4	Austria	60.0	14	Spain	27.0
5	Belgium	55.0	15	Ireland	23.0
6	Japan	54.4	16	United Kingdom	21.0
7	New Zealand[a]	53.0	17	United States	19.9
8	Italy	48.0	18	Greece	15.0
9	Germany	45.0	19	Canada	12.0
10	Sweden	44.0	20	Norway	10.0

Paper recycling
Recovery rates, %

1	Spain	51.0	11	Austria	36.8
2	Netherlands	50.3	12	Denmark	35.4
3	Japan	49.6	13	United Kingdom	31.0
4	Switzerland	49.4	14	Greece	30.0
5	France	45.7	15	United States	28.6
6	Sweden	42.9	16	Norway	26.0
7	Finland	40.8	17	Canada	20.0
8	Germany	39.6	18	New Zealand	19.0
9	Portugal	39.1	19	Belgium	14.7
10	Italy	38.0	20	Ireland	3.0

Freshwater resources
Cubic metres per head, '000

1	Iceland	653.9	11	Bhutan	58.9
2	Suriname	456.6	12	Panama	57.3
3	Papua New Guinea	197.5	13	CAR	44.4
4	Gabon	132.6	14	Nicaragua	44.3
5	New Zealand	114.9	15	Venezuela	42.4
6	Canada	106.0	16	Bolivia	39.9
7	Norway	94.5	17	Fiji	38.6
8	Liberia	84.3	18	Guinea	37.0
9	Congo	76.4	19	Sierra Leone	36.6
10	Laos	64.4	20	Chile	34.4

Water use
Cubic metres per head, latest year

1	Turkmenistan	6,216	11	Afghanistan	1,775
2	Iraq	4,575	12	Canada	1,688
3	Uzbekistan	4,007	13	Madagascar	1,642
4	Kirgizstan	2,663	14	Chile	1,623
5	Tajikistan	2,376	15	Bulgaria	1,545
6	Kazakhstan	2,264	16	Iran	1,362
7	Azerbaijan	2,215	17	Australia	1,306
8	Estonia	2,085	18	Spain	1,188
9	Pakistan	2,053	19	Lithuania	1,179
10	United States	1,868	20	Suriname	1,156

a   Refillable glass bottles only.   See also note on page 85.

=Part II=
COUNTRY PROFILES

ALGERIA

| Area | 2,381,745 sq km | Currency | Algerian dinar (AD) |
| Capital | Algiers | | |

People

Population	26.9m	Life expectancy: men	68 yrs
Pop. per sq km	11	women	70 yrs
Av. ann. growth		Adult literacy	60.6%
in pop. 1985–93	2.6%	Fertility rate (per woman)	3.4
Pop. under 15	41.3%		
Pop. over 65	3.4%		*per 1,000 pop.*
No. of men per 100 women	100	Crude birth rate	27.4
Human Development Index	55	Crude death rate	5.6

The economy

GDP	AD1,027bn	GDP per head	$1,650
GDP	$44bn	GDP per head in purchasing	
Av. ann. growth in real		power parity (USA=100)	13
GDP 1985–93	0.3%		

Origins of GDP[a]		Components of GDP[a]	
	% of total		*% of total*
Agriculture	12.0	Private consumption	48.5
Industry, of which:	49.3	Public consumption	15.9
manufacturing	10.1	Investment	29.8
Services	17.9	Exports	30.7
		Imports	-25.0

Structure of manufacturing

	% of total		*% of total*
Agric. & food processing	22	Other	48
Textiles & clothing	19	Av. ann. increase in industrial	
Metal products & machinery	11	output 1980–92	1.1%

Energy

	'000 TCE		
Total output	157,838	% output exported	71.1
Total consumption	42,000	% consumption imported	4.1
Consumption per head,			
kg coal equivalent	1,594		

Inflation and finance

Consumer price		*av. ann. increase 1989–93*	
inflation 1993	20.5%	Narrow money (M1)	10.5%
Av. ann. inflation 1989–93	20.6%	Broad money	14.2%

Exchange rates

	end 1994		*end June 1994*
AD per $	42.89	Effective rates	*1990 = 100*
AD per SDR	62.62	– nominal	...
AD per Ecu	34.74	– real	...

Principal exports[a]

	$bn fob		$bn fob
Energy & products	10.9	Total including others	**11.1**

Main export destinations

	% of total		% of total
Italy	17.2	France	12.1
United States	15.2	Netherlands	7.3
Germany	12.6	Spain	7.0

Principal imports[a]

	$bn cif		$bn cif
Semi-finished products	3.1	Agric. products & foodstuffs	2.0
Machinery & industrial		Consumer goods	1.1
equipment	2.1	Total incl. others	**8.3**

Main origins of imports

	% of total		% of total
France	29.9	Spain	11.1
United States	12.7	Germany	5.3
Italy	11.9	Japan	3.5

Balance of payments[a], reserves and debt, $m

Visible exports fob	12,330	Overall balance	1,047
Visible imports fob	-6,852	Change in reserves	436
Trade balance	5,478	Level of reserves	
Invisibles inflows	463	end Dec.	1,743
Invisibles outflows	-3,790	No. months import cover	3.1
Net transfers	216	Foreign debt	25,757
Current account balance	2,367	– as % of GDP	57.4
– as % of GDP	4.5	Debt service	9,146
Capital balance	-2,068	Debt service ratio	76.9

Family life

No. of households	3.3m	Divorces per 1,000 pop.	...
Av. no. per household	7.0	Cost of living, Sept. 1994	
Marriages per 1,000 pop.	5.7	New York = 100	56

a 1992.
b 1990.

ARGENTINA

Area	2,777,815 sq km	Currency	Peso (P)
Capital	Buenos Aires		

People

Population	33.5m	Life expectancy: men	70yrs
Pop. per sq km	12	women	77yrs
Av. ann. growth		Adult literacy	95.5%
in pop. 1985–93	1.2%	Fertility rate (per woman)	2.6
Pop. under 15	28.3%		
Pop. over 65	9.6%		*per 1,000 pop.*
No. of men per 100 women	98	Crude birth rate	19.6
Human Development Index	85	Crude death rate	8.0

The economy

GDP	P244bn	GDP per head	$7,288
GDP	$244bn	GDP per head in purchasing	
Av. ann. growth in real		power parity (USA=100)	23
GDP 1985–93	3.1%		

Origins of GDP		**Components of GDP**	
	% of total		*% of total*
Agriculture	7.2	Private consumption[a]	82.9
Industry, of which:	34.7	Public consumption	...
manufacturing	26.6	Investment	21.0
Services	66.2	Exports	9.5
		Imports	-13.4

Structure of manufacturing

	% of total		*% of total*
Food & agric.	20	Other	57
Textiles & clothing	10	Av. ann. increase in industrial	
Machinery & transport	13	output 1980–92	-0.1%

Energy

	'000 TCE		
Total output	78,415	% output exported	13.1
Total consumption	66,005	% consumption imported	7.8
Consumption per head			
kg coal equivalent	1,994		

Inflation and finance

Consumer price		*av. ann. increase 1989–93*	
inflation 1994	4.4%	Narrow money (M1)	431%
Av. ann. inflation 1989–94	279.9%	Broad money	386%

Exchange rates

	end 1994		*end June 1994*
P per $	1.00	Effective rates,	*1990 = 100*
P per SDR	1.46	– nominal	...
P per Ecu	0.81	– real	...

Principal exports

	$bn fob		$bn fob
Agricultural products	2.9	Cattle & meat	1.1
Processed foods	2.4	Minerals	0.9
Oils	1.1	Total incl. others	**12.0**

Main export destinations

	% of total		% of total
Brazil	13.3	Germany	6.0
United States	11.7	Italy	4.3
Netherlands	10.1		

Principal imports

	$bn cif		$bn cif
Machinery & industrial		Metals	1.1
equipment	4.8	Plastics	0.8
Transport equipment	2.3	Total incl. others	**14.8**
Chemicals	1.8		

Main origins of imports

	% of total		% of total
United States	21.6	Italy	5.2
Brazil	18.8	Japan	4.7
Germany	7.3		

Balance of payments, reserves and debt, $bn

Visible exports fob	13.1	Overall balance	2.5
Visible imports fob	15.5	Change in reserves	2.6
Trade balance	-2.4	Level of reserves	
Invisibles inflows	4.1	end Dec.	14.0
Invisibles outflows	-9.6	No. months import cover	10.8
Net transfers	0.4	Foreign debt	74.5
Current account balance	-7.5	– as % of GDP	29.6
– as % of GDP	-3.1	Debt service	7.9
Capital balance	7.4	Debt service ratio	47.6

Family life

No. of households	7.1m	Divorces per 1,000 pop.	...
Av. no. per household	3.9	Cost of living, Sept. 1994	
Marriages per 1,000 pop.	5.8	New York = 100	92

a   Including public consumption.

AUSTRALIA

Area	7,682,300 sq km	Currency	Australian dollar (A$)
Capital	Canberra		

People

Population	17.7m	Life expectancy: men	75 yrs
Pop. per sq km	2	women	81 yrs
Av. ann. growth		Adult literacy	99.0%
in pop. 1985–93	1.5%	Fertility rate (per woman)	1.9
Pop. under 15	21.7%		
Pop. over 65	11.6%		*per 1,000 pop.*
No. of men per 100 women	100	Crude birth rate	14.2
Human Development Index	93	Crude death rate	7.4

The economy

GDP	A$456bn	GDP per head	$17,502
GDP	$310bn	GDP per head in purchasing	
Av. ann. growth in real		power parity (USA=100)	75
GDP 1985–93	2.6%		

Origins of GDP[a]		Components of GDP[a]	
	% of total		*% of total*
Agriculture & mining	8.5	Private consumption	62.1
Industry, of which:	25.5	Public consumption	18.1
manufacturing	18.8	Investment	19.7
Services	66.0	Exports	19.3
		Imports	-19.8

Structure of manufacturing

	% of total		*% of total*
Agric. & food processing	19	Other	56
Textiles & clothing	6	Av. ann. increase in industrial	
Machinery & transport	19	output 1980–92	2.2%

Energy

	'000 TCE		
Total output	228,454	% output exported	54.1
Total consumption	129,791	% consumption imported	16.2
Consumption per head,			
kg coal equivalent	7,376		

Inflation and finance

Consumer price		*av. ann. increase 1989–93*	
inflation 1994	1.9%	Narrow money (M1)	13.4%
Av. ann. inflation 1989–94	3.8%	Broad money	0.2%

Exchange rates

	end 1994		*end June 1994*
A$ per $	1.29	Effective rates	*1990 = 100*
A$ per SDR	1.88	– nominal	112.1
A$ per Ecu	1.59	– real	...

Principal exports[a]

	$bn fob		$bn fob
Ores & minerals	9.0	Wool	3.7
Coal & oil	7.4	Cereals	2.8
Gold	3.8	Total incl. others	**44.2**

Main export destinations

	% of total		% of total
Japan	24.6	United States	7.9
Asean[b]	13.7	Developing countries	42.5
EU	11.3		

Principal imports[a]

	$bn cif		$bn cif
Machinery	13.8	Chemicals	2.4
Motor vehicles & other		Energy & products	2.3
transport equipment	7.1		
Consumer goods	9.3	Total incl. others	**44.6**

Main origins of imports

	% of total		% of total
United States	21.7	Asean[b]	7.8
EU	19.9	Developing countries	32.5
Japan	18.1		

Balance of payments, reserves and aid, $bn

Visible exports fob	42.2	Capital balance	9.5
Visible imports fob	42.4	Overall balance	-0.04
Trade balance	-0.2	Change in reserves	-0.1
Invisibles inflows	14.6	Level of reserves	
Invisibles outflows	-25.6	end Dec.	11.5
Net transfers	0.3	No. months import cover	3.3
Current account balance	-10.8	Aid given	1.0
– as % of GDP	-3.5	– as % of GDP	0.35

Family life

No. of households	5.3m	Divorces per 1,000 pop.	2.6
Av. no. per household	3.0	Cost of living, Sept. 1994	
Marriages per 1,000 pop.	6.6	New York = 100	94

a Year ending June 30, 1994.
b Brunei, Indonesia, Malaysia, Philippines, Singapore, Thailand.

AUSTRIA

Area	83,855 sq km	Currency	Schilling (ASch)
Capital	Vienna		

People

Population	7.9m	Life expectancy: men	74 yrs
Pop. per sq km	94	women	80 yrs
Av. ann. growth		Adult literacy	99.0%
in pop. 1985–93	0.7%	Fertility rate (per woman)	1.6
Pop. under 15	17.6%		
Pop. over 65	15.4%		*per 1,000 pop.*
No. of men per 100 women	93	Crude birth rate	11.4
Human Development Index	92	Crude death rate	10.1

The economy

GDP	ASch2,140bn	GDP per head	$23,115
GDP	$184bn	GDP per head in purchasing	
Av. ann. growth in real		power parity (USA=100)	80
GDP 1985–93	2.4%		

Origins of GDP		**Components of GDP**	
	% of total		*% of total*
Agriculture	2.3	Private consumption	55.7
Industry, of which:	34.1	Public consumption	19.0
manufacturing	26.9	Investment	24.1
Services	63.3	Exports	38.1
		Imports	-36.9

Structure of manufacturing

	% of total		*% of total*
Agric. & food processing	16	Other	50
Textiles & clothing	6	Av. ann. increase in industrial	
Machinery & transport	28	output 1980–92	2.2%

Energy

	'000 TCE		
Total output	8,712	% output exported	18.2
Total consumption	32,432	% consumption imported	83.2
Consumption per head,			
kg coal equivalent	4,171		

Inflation and finance

Consumer price		*av. ann. increase 1989–93*	
inflation 1994	3.0%	Narrow money (M1)	5.5%
Av. ann. inflation 1989–94	3.3%	Broad money	7.4%

Exchange rates

	end 1994		*end June 1994*
ASch per $	11.10	Effective rates	*1990 = 100*
ASch per SDR	16.20	– nominal	104.2
ASch per Ecu	11.02	– real	99.5

Principal exports

	$bn fob		$bn fob
Machinery & transport		Chemicals	3.6
equipment	15.7	Raw materials	1.6
Manufactured goods	11.5	Food, drink & tobacco	1.2
Consumer goods	5.8	Total incl. others	**40.2**

Main export destinations

	% of total		% of total
Germany	38.9	United Kingdom	3.3
Italy	7.8	EU	63.3
Switzerland	6.4	Efta	8.9
France	4.4	Eastern Europe	12.7

Principal imports

	$bn cif		$bn cif
Machinery & transport		Chemicals	5.1
equipment	18.4	Fuel & energy	2.4
Consumer goods	9.2	Food & drink	2.3
Manufactured products	9.0	Total incl. others	**48.6**

Main origins of imports

	% of total		% of total
Germany	41.5	Switzerland	4.1
Italy	9.0	EU	67.1
Japan	4.4	Efta	6.7
France	4.4	Eastern Europe	7.5

Balance of payments, reserves and aid, $bn

Visible exports fob	39.3	Capital balance	1.7
Visible imports fob	47.1	Overall balance	2.2
Trade balance	-7.8	Change in reserves	2.0
Invisibles inflows	38.5	Level of reserves	
Invisibles outflows	-30.6	end Dec.	15.5
Net transfers	-0.9	No. months import cover	3.9
Current account balance	-0.9	Aid given	0.5
– as % of GDP	-0.5	– as % of GDP	0.30

Family life

No. of households	2.8m	Divorces per 1,000 pop.	2.1
Av. no. per household	2.7	Cost of living, Sept. 1994	
Marriages per 1,000 pop.	5.7	New York = 100	123

BANGLADESH

Area	144,000 sq km	Currency	Taka (Tk)
Capital	Dhaka		

People

Population	116.7m	Life expectancy: men	58 yrs
Pop. per sq km	810	women	58 yrs
Av. ann. growth		Adult literacy	36.6%
in pop. 1985–93	2.2%	Fertility rate (per woman)	3.9
Pop. under 15	40.3%		
Pop. over 65	3.0%		*per 1,000 pop.*
No. of men per 100 women	106	Crude birth rate	32.9
Human Development Index	31	Crude death rate	10.2

The economy

GDP	Tk1,029bn	GDP per head	$222
GDP	$26bn	GDP per head in purchasing	
Av. ann. growth in real		power parity (USA=100)	5
GDP 1985–93	4.1%		

Origins of GDP[a]		Components of GDP[a]	
	% of total		*% of total*
Agriculture	30.4	Private consumption	78.9
Industry, of which:	15.7	Public consumption	13.8
manufacturing	9.9	Investment	12.7
Services	53.9	Exports	11.2
		Imports	-16.7

Structure of manufacturing

	% of total		*% of total*
Agric. & food processing	23	Other	34
Textiles & clothing	38	Av. ann. increase in industrial	
Metal products & machinery	5	output 1980–92	5.1%

Energy

	'000 TCE		
Total output	6,943	% output exported	0.0
Total consumption	9,975	% consumption imported	33.6
Consumption per head,			
kg coal equivalent	84		

Inflation and finance

Consumer price		*av. ann. increase 1989–93*	
inflation 1993	1.5%	Narrow money (M1)	11.9%
Av. ann. inflation 1989–93	5.8%	Broad money	13.9%

Exchange rates

	end 1994		*end June 1994*
Tk per $	40.25	Effective rates	*1990 = 100*
Tk per SDR	58.76	– nominal	...
Tk per Ecu	40.25	– real	...

Principal exports

	$m fob		$m fob
Textiles & clothing	1,411.1	Leather	158.0
Fish & fish products	253.2	Raw jute	64.0
Jute goods	238.9	Total incl. others	**2,347**

Main export destinations[a]

	% of total		% of total
United States	33.9	United Kingdom	5.9
Germany	8.2	France	5.6
Italy	6.0	Singapore	4.1

Principal imports

	$m cif		$m cif
Textiles	1,007.7	Chemicals	228.9
Machinery & transport equipment	423.4	Cereal & dairy products	74.0
Energy products	284.2	Total incl. others	**3,374.0**

Main origins of imports[a]

	% of total		% of total
South Korea	8.9	Japan	7.3
Singapore	7.4	India	6.6
China	7.3	United States	6.0

Balance of payments, reserves and debt, $bn

Visible exports fob	2.3	Overall balance	0.7
Visible imports fob	3.6	Change in reserves	0.7
Trade balance	-1.3	Level of reserves	
Invisibles inflows	0.6	end Dec.	2.4
Invisibles outflows	-1.1	No. months import cover	8.0
Net transfers	1.9	Foreign debt	13.9
Current account balance	0.2	– as % of GDP	56.3
– as % of GDP	0.8	Debt service	0.53
Capital balance	-0.2	Debt service ratio	13.5

Family life

No. households	14.8m	Divorces per 1,000 pop.	...
Av. no. per household	5.7	Cost of living, Sept. 1994	
Marriages per 1,000 pop.	11.3	New York = 100	65

a 1992.

BELGIUM

Area	30,520 sq km	Currency	Belgian franc (BFr)
Capital	Brussels		

People

Population	10.0m	Life expectancy: men		74 yrs
Pop. per sq km	328	women		81 yrs
Av. ann. growth		Adult literacy		99.0%
in pop. 1985–93	0.4%	Fertility rate (per woman)		1.7
Pop. under 15	17.9%			
Pop. over 65	15.7%			*per 1,000 pop.*
No. of men per 100 women	96	Crude birth rate		11.8
Human Development Index	92	Crude death rate		10.5

The economy

GDP	BFr7,369bn	GDP per head	$21,216
GDP	$213bn	GDP per head in purchasing	
Av. ann. growth in real		power parity (USA=100)	79
GDP 1985–93	2.2%		

Origins of GDP[b]		Components of GDP[a]	
	% of total		*% of total*
Agriculture	2.3	Private consumption	63.9
Industry, of which:	31.4	Public consumption	15.4
manufacturing	22.0	Investment	18.1
Services	62.3	Exports	66.5
		Imports	-63.0

Structure of manufacturing

	% of total		*% of total*
Agric. & food processing	8	Other	53
Textiles & clothing	7	Av. ann. increase in industrial	
Machinery & transport	22	output 1980–92	2.2%

Energy

	'000 TCE		
Total output	16,859	% output exported[c]	168.6
Total consumption	68,702	% consumption imported[c]	133.1
Consumption per head,			
kg coal equivalent	6,872		

Inflation and finance

		av. ann. increase 1989–93	
Consumer price			
inflation 1994	2.4%	Narrow money (M1)	4.4%
Av. ann. inflation 1989–94	2.9%	Broad money	8.6%

Exchange rates

	end 1994		*end June 1994*
			1990 = 100
BFr per $	31.84	Effective rates	
BFr per SDR	47.34	– nominal	105.8
BFr per Ecu	32.38	– real	103.6

Principal exports[a][b]

	$bn fob		$bn fob
Machinery & transport		Textiles & clothing	8.8
equipment	33.4	Precious stones & jewellery	7.7
Chemicals	18.1	Petroleum & products	4.0
Metals & products	13.8		
Agric. products &			
foodstuffs	10.7	Total incl. others	**123.4**

Main export destinations

	% of total		% of total
Germany	22.8	Italy	5.9
France	19.3	United States	3.9
Netherlands	13.7	Japan	1.0
United Kingdom	7.8	EU	74.9

Principal imports[a][b]

	$bn cif		$bn cif
Machinery & transport		Metals & products	9.5
equipment	32.0	Energy & products	9.3
Chemicals	14.9	Textiles & clothing	7.7
Agric. products &		Precious stones & jewellery	7.4
foodstuffs	10.7	Total incl. others	**125.2**

Main origins of imports

	% of total		% of total
Germany	23.9	Italy	4.5
Netherlands	17.5	United States	4.4
France	16.5	Japan	2.2
United Kingdom	7.7	EU	73.5

Balance of payments[a], reserves and aid, $bn

Visible exports fob	103.8	Capital balance	-11.7
Visible imports fob	99.9	Overall balance	-2.1
Trade balance	3.9	Change in reserves	-2.4
Invisibles inflows	120.5	Level of reserves	
Invisibles outflows	-109.3	end Dec.	12.6
Net transfers	-2.6	No. months import cover	1.5
Current account balance	12.6	Aid given	0.8
– as % of GDP	5.5	– as % of GDP	0.39

Family life

No. of households	3.6m	Divorces per 1,000 pop.	2.1
Av. no. per household	2.7	Cost of living, Sept. 1994	
Marriages per 1,000 pop.	5.8	New York = 100	112

a Including Luxembourg.
b 1992.
c Energy trade data are distorted by transitory and oil refining activities.

BRAZIL

Area	8,511,965 sq km	Currency	Real (R)
Capital	Brasilia		

People

Population	156.4m	Life expectancy: men	66 yrs
Pop. per sq km	18	women	70 yrs
Av. ann. growth		Adult literacy	82.1%
in pop. 1985–93	1.9%	Fertility rate (per woman)	2.7
Pop. under 15	32.2%		
Pop. over 65	5.2%		*per 1,000 pop.*
No. of men per 100 women	99	Crude birth rate	22.7
Human Development Index	76	Crude death rate	7.2

The economy

GDP	R14bn	GDP per head	$3,018
GDP	$472bn	GDP per head in purchasing	
Av. ann. growth in real		power parity (USA=100)	24
GDP 1985–93	1.9%		

Origins of GDP[a]		Components of GDP[b]	
	% of total		*% of total*
Agriculture	10.8	Private consumption	62.4
Industry, of which:	33.8	Public consumption	15.2
manufacturing	25.0	Investment	19.1
Services	55.4	Exports	9.7
		Imports	-6.3

Structure of manufacturing

	% of total		*% of total*
Agric. & food processing	15	Other	52
Textiles & clothing	11	Av. ann. increase in industrial	
Machinery & transport	22	output 1980–92	1.4%

Energy

	'000 TCE		
Total output	82,711	% output exported	5.7
Total consumption	124,759	% consumption imported	46.6
Consumption per head,			
kg coal equivalent	810		

Inflation and finance

Consumer price		*av. ann. increase 1988–92*	
inflation 1994	2,443%	Narrow money (M1)	...
Av. ann. inflation 1988–93	1,461%	Broad money	...

Exchange rates

	end 1994		*end June 1994*
R per $	0.85	Effective rates,	*1990 = 100*
R per SDR	1.24	– Nominal	...
R per Ecu	0.69	– Real	...

Principal exports

	$m fob		$m fob
Crude oil	676	Coffee	56
Cocoa	79	Cotton	54
		Total incl. others	**1,525**

Main export destinations

	% of total		% of total
France	19.0	Italy	11.0
Spain	16.0	Netherlands	7.0

Principal imports

	$m fob		$m fob
Manufactures	1,181	Fuel	21
Primary products	246	Total incl. others	**1,585**

Main origins of imports

	% of total		% of total
France	37.0	Japan	5.0
Belgium/Luxembourg	8.0	United States	5.0

Balance of payments[b], reserves and debt, $bn

Visible exports fob	1.1	Overall balance	0.03
Visible imports fob	-0.9	Change in reserves	0.04
Trade balance	0.2	Level of reserves	
Invisibles inflows	0.4	end Dec.	0.02
Invisibles outflows	-0.13	No. months import cover	0.3
Net transfers	0.04	Foreign debt	6.6
Current account balance	-0.7	– as % of GDP	71.8
– as % of GDP	-7.7	Debt service	0.44
Capital balance	0.9	Debt service ratio	21.8

Family life

No. of households	1.4m	Divorces per 1,000 pop.	...
Av. no. per household	5.2	Cost of living, Sept. 1994	
Marriages per 1,000 pop.	...	New York = 100	78

a 1985.
b 1992.

CANADA

Area[a]	9,922,385 sq km	Currency	Canadian dollar (C$)
Capital	Ottawa		

People

Population	27.8m	Life expectancy: men		75 yrs
Pop. per sq km	3		women	81 yrs
Av. ann. growth		Adult literacy		99.0%
in pop. 1985–93	1.3%	Fertility rate (per woman)		1.9
Pop. under 15	20.7%			
Pop. over 65	12.0%			*per 1,000 pop.*
No. of men per 100 women	97	Crude birth rate		14.1
Human Development Index	93	Crude death rate		7.7

The economy

GDP	C$742bn	GDP per head	$20,664
GDP	$575bn	GDP per head in purchasing	
Av. ann. growth in real		power parity (USA=100)	87
GDP 1985–93	1.9%		

Origins of GDP		Components of GDP	
	% of total		*% of total*
Agriculture	3.1	Private consumption	60.7
Industry, of which:	30.7	Public consumption	20.2
manufacturing	22.1	Investment	18.5
Services	66.2	Exports	33.3
		Imports	-32.5

Structure of manufacturing

	% of total		*% of total*
Agric. & food processing	15	Other	54
Textiles & clothing	5	Av. ann. increase in industrial	
Machinery & transport	26	output 1980–92	2.4%

Energy

	'000 TCE		
Total output	416,238	% output exported	44.3
Total consumption	300,073	% consumption imported	18.2
Consumption per head,			
kg coal equivalent	10,965		

Inflation and finance

Consumer price		*av. ann. increase 1989–93*	
inflation 1994	0.2%	Narrow money (M1)	4.7%
Av. ann. inflation 1989–94	3.1%	Broad money	9.4%

Exchange rates

	end 1994		*end June 1994*
C$ per $	1.40	Effective rates	*1990 = 100*
C$ per SDR	2.05	– nominal	83.2
C$ per Ecu	1.73	– real	82.8

Principal exports

	C$bn fob		C$bn fob
Motor vehicles & other		Forest products	31.2
transport equipment	58.0	Energy products	21.7
Machinery & industrial		Agric. products &	
equipment	43.0	foodstuffs	17.6
Industrial supplies	39.2	Total incl. others	**164.6**

Main export destinations

	% of total		% of total
United States	80.3	Germany	1.5
Japan	4.4	South Korea	0.9
United Kingdom	1.6		

Principal imports

	C$bn cif		C$bn cif
Machinery & industrial		Consumer goods	23.5
equipment	65.6	Agric. products & foodstuffs	12.6
Motor vehicles & other		Energy products	7.1
transport equipment	47.8		
Industrial supplies	38.7	Total incl. others	**151.7**

Main origins of imports

	% of total		% of total
United States	73.0	Germany	2.3
Japan	4.9	South Korea	1.3
United Kingdom	2.6		

Balance of payments, reserves and aid, $bn

Visible exports fob	144.0	Capital balance	29.2
Visible imports fob	136.4	Overall balance	0.5
Trade balance	7.6	Change in reserves	-0.3
Invisibles inflows	24.7	Level of reserves	
Invisibles outflows	-56.3	end Dec.	12.8
Net transfers	0.2	No. months import cover	1.1
Current account balance	-23.9	Aid given	2.37
– as % of GDP	-4.2	– as % of GDP	0.45

Family life

No. of households	10.0m	Divorces per 1,000 pop.	2.9
Av. no. per household	2.7	Cost of living, Sept. 1994	
Marriages per 1,000 pop.	7.1	New York = 100	84

a Including freshwater.

CHILE

Area	751,625 sq km	Currency	Chilean peso (peso)
Capital	Santiago		

People

Population	13.8m	Life expectancy: men		71 yrs
Pop. per sq km	18		women	78 yrs
Av. ann. growth		Adult literacy		93.8%
in pop. 1985–93	1.6%	Fertility rate (per woman)		2.4
Pop. under 15	30.4%			
Pop. over 65	6.4%			*per 1,000 pop.*
No. of men per 100 women	98	Crude birth rate		20.0
Human Development Index	85	Crude death rate		5.8

The economy

GDP	16,983bn pesos	GDP per head	$3,074
GDP	$42bn	GDP per head in purchasing	
Av. ann. growth in real		power parity (USA=100)	32
GDP 1985–93	6.9%		

Origins of GDP[a]		Components of GDP[a]	
	% of total		*% of total*
Agriculture	8.6	Private consumption	65.5
Industry, of which:	36.0	Public consumption	8.6
manufacturing	20.8	Investment	23.0
Services	55.4	Exports	33.5
		Imports	-30.6

Structure of manufacturing

	% of total		*% of total*
Agric. & food processing	25	Other	62
Textiles & clothing	8	Av. ann. increase in industrial	
Metal products & machinery	5	output 1980–91	3.6%

Energy

	'000 TCE		
Total output	8,074	% output exported	0.4
Total consumption	17,745	% consumption imported	55.2
Consumption per head,			
kg coal equivalent	1,305		

Inflation and finance

		av. ann. increase 1989–92	
Consumer price			
inflation 1994	11.4%	Narrow money (M1)	28.6%
Av. ann. inflation 1989–94	17.3%	Broad money	25.9%

Exchange rates

	end 1994		*end June 1994*
Peso per $	402.9	Effective rates	*1990 = 100*
Peso per SDR	588.2	– nominal	232.9
Peso per Ecu	497.4	– real	111.6

Principal exports[a]

	$bn fob		$bn fob
Industrial products incl.		Agric. products &	
other mining prods.	4.7	foodstuffs	1.2
Copper	3.9	Total incl. others	**10.0**

Main export destinations

	% of total		% of total
Japan	16.7	Taiwan	5.0
United States	16.1	South Korea	4.6
Germany	5.8	Brazil	4.4
United Kingdom	5.8		

Principal imports[a]

	$bn cif		$bn cif
Industrial supplies	5.4	Consumer goods	1.9
Capital goods	2.8	Total incl. others	**10.1**

Main origins of imports

	% of total		% of total
United States	20.0	Germany	6.5
Brazil	10.2	Nigeria	3.3
Japan	10.1	France	2.9
Argentina	6.6		

Balance of payments, reserves and debt, $bn

Visible exports fob	9.2	Overall balance	2.5
Visible imports fob	-10.2	Change in reserves	0.6
Trade balance	-1.0	Level of reserves	
Invisibles inflows	3.1	end Dec.	9.7
Invisibles outflows	-4.6	No. months import cover	11.4
Net transfers	0.4	Foreign debt	20.6
Current account balance	-2.1	– as % of GDP	49.0
– as % of GDP	-4.9	Debt service	2.88
Capital balance	2.2	Debt service ratio	23.4

Family life

No. of households	3.3m	Divorces per 1,000 pop.	0.5
Av. no. per household	4.1	Cost of living, Sept. 1994	
Marriages per 1,000 pop.	6.9	New York = 100	68

a 1992.

CHINA

Area	9,597,000 sq km	Currency	Yuan
Capital	Beijing		

People

Population	1,175.4m	Life expectancy: men	68 yrs
Pop. per sq km	123	women	72 yrs
Av. ann. growth		Adult literacy	80.0%
in pop. 1985–93	1.4%	Fertility rate (per woman)	2.0
Pop. under 15	27.3%		
Pop. over 65	6.3%		per 1,000 pop.
No. of men per 100 women	106	Crude birth rate	17.3
Human Development Index	64	Crude death rate	7.1

The economy

GDP	Yuan3,348bn	GDP per head	$494
GDP	$581bn	GDP per head in purchasing	
Av. ann. growth in real		power parity (USA=100)	13
GDP 1985–93	9.2%		

Origins of GDP[a]		Components of GDP[b]	
	% of total		% of total
Agriculture	29.2	Private consumption	52.0
Industry, of which:	49.4	Public consumption	9.0
manufacturing	...	Investment	36.0
Services	21.4	Exports	20.0
		Imports	-17.0

Structure of manufacturing

	% of total		% of total
Agric. & food processing	15	Other	46
Textiles & clothing	14	Av. ann. increase in industrial	
Metal products & machinery	25	output 1980–92	11.1%

Energy

	'000 TCE		
Total output	1,036,818	% output exported	5.6
Total consumption	972,660	% consumption imported	3.3
Consumption per head,			
kg coal equivalent	833		

Inflation and finance

Consumer price		av. ann. increase 1989–93	
inflation 1994	21.8%	Narrow money (M1)	20.9%
Av. ann. inflation 1989–94	11.5%	Broad money	25.1%

Exchange rates

	end 1994		end June 1994
		Effective rates	1990 = 100
Yuan per $	8.45	Effective rates	1990 = 100
Yuan per SDR	12.33	– nominal	...
Yuan per Ecu	10.43	– real	...

Principal exports

	$bn fob		$bn fob
Textiles	26.1	Footwear	5.3
Garments	16.5	Chemicals	4.4
Machinery & transport		Food	4.4
equipment	13.9	Total incl. others	**91.8**

Main export destinations

	% of total		% of total
Hong Kong[c]	24.6	Germany	4.4
United States	18.5	South Korea	3.2
Japan	17.2	Russia	2.9

Principal imports

	$bn fob		$bn fob
Machinery	35.8	Plastics	5.6
Iron & Steel	12.1	Fuels	2.3
Textiles	9.7	Garments	0.5
Chemicals	5.6	Total incl. others	**104.0**

Main origins of imports

	% of total		% of total
Japan	22.4	Germany	5.8
Taiwan	12.9	South Korea	5.2
United States	10.3	Russia	4.8
Hong Kong[c]	10.2		

Balance of payments[a], reserves and debt, $bn

Visible exports fob	69.6	Overall balance	-2.1
Visible imports fob	-64.4	Change in reserves	14.6
Trade balance	5.2	Level of reserves	
Invisibles inflows	14.8	end Dec.	23.0
Invisibles outflows	-9.8	No. months import cover	4.3
Net transfers	1.2	Foreign debt	83.8
Current account balance	6.4	- as % of GDP	21.4
- as % of GDP	1.4	Debt service	10.1
Capital balance	1.8	Debt service ratio	10.7

Family life

No. of households	220.1m	Divorces per 1,000 pop.	...
Av. no. per household	4.4	Cost of living, Sept. 1994	
Marriages per 1,000 pop.	...	New York = 100	94

a 1992.
b 1991.
c Including Macau.

COLOMBIA

Area	1,138,915 sq km	Currency	Colombian peso (peso)
Capital	Bogota		

People

Population	35.7m	Life expectancy: men		53 yrs
Pop. per sq km	31	women		73 yrs
Av. ann. growth		Adult literacy		87.4%
in pop. 1985–93	2.4%	Fertility rate (per woman)		2.5
Pop. under 15	32.9%			
Pop. over 65	4.5%		*per 1,000 pop.*	
No. of men per 100 women	98	Crude birth rate		22.0
Human Development Index	81	Crude death rate		5.8

The economy

GDP	43,153bn pesos	GDP per head	$1,405
GDP	$50bn	GDP per head in purchasing	
Av. ann. growth in real		power parity (USA=100)	25
GDP 1985–93	4.2%		

Origins of GDP		Components of GDP	
	% of total		*% of total*
Agriculture	20.5	Private consumption	70.2
Industry, of which:	28.0	Public consumption	13.0
manufacturing	21.0	Investment	22.8
Services	51.5	Exports	23.1
		Imports	-29.1

Structure of manufacturing

	% of total		*% of total*
Agric. & food processing	30	Other	46
Textiles & clothing	16	Av. ann. increase in industrial	
Machinery & transport	8	output 1980–92	4.7%

Energy

	'000 TCE		
Total output	61,887	% output exported	53.1
Total consumption	28,558	% consumption imported	9.2
Consumption per head,			
kg coal equivalent	854		

Inflation and finance

Consumer price		*av. ann. increase 1991–93*	
inflation 1994	22.9%	Narrow money (M1)	35.6
Av. ann. inflation 1989–94	26.3%	Broad money	34.2

Exchange rates

	end 1994		*end June 1994*
Peso per $	831	Effective rates	*1990 = 100*
Peso per SDR	1,214	– nominal	149.3
Peso per Ecu	1,026	– real	133.0

Principal exports

	$bn fob		$bn fob
Petroleum & products	1.3	Gold	0.3
Coffee	1.1	Ferro-nickel	0.1
Coal	0.6	Total incl. others	**7.4**

Main export destinations

	% of total		% of total
United States	39.9	Peru	2.9
Venezuela	9.8	EU	22.2
Puerto Rico	3.3		

Principal imports

	$bn fob		$bn fob
Industrial supplies	3.8	Consumer goods	1.7
Capital goods	3.6	Total incl. others	**9.1**

Main origins of imports

	% of total		% of total
United States	33.3	EU	17.4
Japan	11.1	Andean group[a]	12.9
Argentina	3.8		

Balance of payments[b], reserves and debt, $bn

Visible exports fob	7.3	Overall balance	1.1
Visible imports fob	-6.0	Change in reserves	1.2
Trade balance	1.3	Level of reserves	
Invisibles inflows	2.4	end Dec.	7.6
Invisibles outflows	-4.5	No. months import cover	15.2
Net transfers	1.7	Foreign debt	17.2
Current account balance	0.9	– as % of GDP	33.4
– as % of GDP	2.0	Debt service	3.2
Capital balance	-0.9	Debt service ratio	29.2

Family life

No. of households	5.3m	Divorces per 1,000 pop.	...
Av. no. per household	5.2	Cost of living, Sept. 1994	
Marriages per 1,000 pop.	2.4	New York = 100	71

a   Bolivia, Colombia, Ecuador, Peru, Venezuela.
b   1992.

CÔTE D'IVOIRE

Area	322,465 sq km	Currency	CFA franc (CFAfr)
Capital	Abidjan/Yamoussoukro		

People

Population	13.4m	Life expectancy: men		49 yrs
Pop. per sq km	42	women		51 yrs
Av. ann. growth		Adult literacy		55.8%
in pop. 1985–93	3.8%	Fertility rate (per woman)		6.9
Pop. under 15	49.0%			
Pop. over 65	2.6%		*per 1,000 pop.*	
No. of men per 100 women	103	Crude birth rate		47.6
Human Development Index	37	Crude death rate		15.3

The economy

GDP	CFAfr2,265bn	GDP per head	$629
GDP	$8bn	GDP per head in purchasing	
Av. ann. growth in real		power parity (USA=100)	7
GDP 1985–93	-0.7%		

Origins of GDP[a]		Components of GDP[a]	
	% of total		*% of total*
Agriculture	33.7	Private consumption	67.9
Industry, of which:	28.8	Public consumption	18.2
manufacturing	...	Investment	8.9
Services	37.5	Exports	33.6
		Imports	-28.6

Structure of manufacturing

	% of total		*% of total*
Agric. & food processing	...	Other	...
Textiles & clothing	...	Av. ann. increase in industrial	
Metal products & machinery	...	output 1980–92	4.4%

Energy

	'000 TCE		
Total output	595	% output exported	64.4
Total consumption	2,697	% consumption imported	107.9
Consumption per head,			
kg coal equivalent	209		

Inflation and finance

		av. ann. change 1989–93	
Consumer price			
inflation 1993	2.8%	Narrow money (M1)	-5.0%
Av. ann. inflation 1989–93	1.6%	Broad money	-3.4%

Exchange rates

	end 1994		*end June 1994*
CFAfr per $	534.6	Effective rates	*1990 = 100*
CFAfr per SDR	780.4	– nominal	91.4
CFAfr per Ecu	660.0	– real	63.6

Principal exports

	$m fob		$m fob
Cocoa beans & products	909	Raw cotton	108
Sawn timber	241		
Coffee & products	215	Total incl. others	**2,734**

Main export destinations[a]

	% of total		% of total
France	15.8	Netherlands	7.1
Germany	8.3	Italy	6.8

Principal imports

	$m cif		$m cif
Crude oil	459	Fresh fish	106
Machinery & equipment	123		
Pharmaceuticals	117	Total incl. others	**1,662**

Main origins of imports[a]

	% of total		% of total
France	30.7	United States	4.4
Nigeria	25.9	Italy	3.8

Balance of payments, reserves and debt, $bn

Visible exports fob	2.7	Overall balance	0.03
Visible imports fob	-1.7	Change in reserves	0.02
Trade balance	1.0	Level of reserves	
Invisibles inflows	0.6	end Dec.	0.04
Invisibles outflows	-2.6	No. months import cover	0.3
Net transfers	-0.2	Foreign debt	19.1
Current account balance	-1.2	– as % of GDP	243.9
– as % of GDP	-14.6	Debt service	1.0
Capital balance	1.2	Debt service ratio	30.0

Family life

No. of households	1.8m	Divorces per 1,000 pop.	...
Av. no. per household	6.0	Cost of living, Sept. 1994	
Marriages per 1,000 pop.	...	New York = 100	97

a 1992.

CZECH REPUBLIC

Area	78,835 sq km	Currency	Koruna (Kc)
Capital	Prague		

People

Population	10.3m	Life expectancy: men		68 yrs
Pop. per sq km	131	women		75 yrs
Av. ann. growth		Adult literacy[a]		99.0%
in pop. 1985–93	nil	Fertility rate (per woman)		1.8
Pop. under 15[a]	20.9%			
Pop. over 65[a]	12.1%		*per 1,000 pop.*	
No. of men per 100 women[a]	95	Crude birth rate		13.8
Human Development Index[a]	87	Crude death rate		12.9

The economy

GDP	Kcs816bn	GDP per head	$2,732
GDP	$28bn	GDP per head in purchasing	
Av. ann. growth in real		power parity (USA=100)	30[a]
GDP 1985–92[a]	-2.5%		

Origins of GDP		Components of GDP	
	% of total		*% of total*
Agriculture	4.1	Private consumption[c]	54.2
Industry, of which:	45.4	Public consumption	25.7
manufacturing	...	Investment	23.3
Services	50.5	Net exports	3.1
		Imports	...

Structure of manufacturing

	% of total		*% of total*
Agric. & food processing	10	Other	44
Textiles & clothing	11	Av. ann. increase in industrial	
Metal products & machinery	35	output 1980–92	0.4%

Energy

	'000 TCE		
Total output	49,796	% output exported	20.9
Total consumption	58,373	% consumption imported	34.1
Consumption per head,			
kg coal equivalent	5,610		

Inflation and finance

Consumer price		*av. ann. increase 1989–92*	
inflation 1994	10.0%	Narrow money (M1)	8.3%
Av. ann. inflation 1992–94	13.9%	Broad money	11.7%

Exchange rates

	end 1994		*end June 1994*
Kc per $	28.05	Effective rates	*1990 = 100*
Kc per SDR	40.95	– nominal	...
Kc per Ecu	34.63	– real	...

Principal exports[abc]

	$bn fob		$bn fob
Manufactured goods	3.8	Chemicals	0.8
Machinery & industrial		Food products	0.5
equipment	1.3	Total incl. others	**7.4**

Main export destinations[ab]

	% of total		% of total
Germany	30.6	EU	49.4
Ex-Soviet Union	10.9	Other Eastern Europe	13.7

Principal imports[abc]

	$bn fob		$bn fob
Machinery & industrial		Raw materials	0.4
equipment	5.9	Agric. products & foodstuffs	0.4
Chemicals & products	1.0	Total incl. others	**7.8**

Main origins of imports[ab]

	% of total		% of total
Ex-Soviet Union	24.6	EU	42.1
Germany	24.6	Other Eastern Europe	6.7

Balance of payments[ab], reserves[a] and debt[a], $bn

Visible exports fob	11.5	Overall balance	-0.4
Visible imports fob	-13.3	Change in reserves	-2.3
Trade balance	-1.8	Level of reserves	
Invisibles inflows	4.8	end Dec.	3.9
Invisibles outflows	-3.1	No. months import cover	3.5
Net transfers	0.1	Foreign debt	8.7
Current account balance	-0.03	– as % of GDP	27.5
– as % of GDP	-0.1	Debt service	1.3
Capital balance	-0.2	Debt service ratio	9.5

Family life[a]

No. of households	5.4m	Divorces per 1,000 pop.	2.4
Av. no. per household	2.8	Cost of living, Sept. 1994	
Marriages per 1,000 pop.	7.2	New York = 100	57

a Ex-Czechoslovakia.
b 1992.
c Western countries.

DENMARK

Area	43,075 sq km	Currency	Danish krone (DKr)
Capital	Copenhagen		

People

Population	5.2m	Life expectancy: men		73 yrs
Pop. per sq km	121		women	79 yrs
Av. ann. growth		Adult literacy		99.0%
in pop. 1985–93	0.2	Fertility rate (per woman)		1.7
Pop. under 15	17.1%			
Pop. over 65	15.4%			*per 1,000 pop.*
No. of men per 100 women	98	Crude birth rate		12.0
Human Development Index	91	Crude death rate		11.8

The economy

GDP	DKr888bn	GDP per head	$26,514
GDP	$137bn	GDP per head in purchasing	
Av. ann. growth in real		power parity (USA=100)	81
GDP 1985–93	1.3%		

Origins of GDP		Components of GDP	
	% of total		*% of total*
Agriculture	3.8	Private consumption	52.4
Industry, of which:	26.9	Public consumption	26.3
manufacturing	19.7	Investment	13.5
Services	69.0	Exports	34.8
		Imports	-27.0

Structure of manufacturing

	% of total		*% of total*
Agric. & food processing	23	Other	50
Textiles & clothing	4	Av. ann. increase in industrial	
Machinery & transport	23	output 1980–92	2.7%

Energy

	'000 TCE		
Total output	16,551	% output exported	87.4
Total consumption	24,010	% consumption imported	102.3
Consumption per head,			
kg coal equivalent	4,655		

Inflation and finance

Consumer price		*av. ann. increase 1989–93*	
inflation 1994	2.0%	Narrow money (M1)	5.6%
Av. ann. inflation 1989–94	2.5%	Broad money	5.4%

Exchange rates

	end 1994		*end June 1994*
DKr per $	6.08	Effective rates	*1990 = 100*
DKr per SDR	8.88	– nominal	106.4
DKr per Ecu	7.51	– real	101.9

Principal exports

	$bn fob		$bn fob
Machinery & electrical products	8.3	Energy & products	1.3
Agric. products & foodstuffs	5.0	Total incl. others	**37.4**

Main export destinations

	% of total		% of total
Germany	23.8	France	5.4
Sweden	10.0	Norway	6.9
United Kingdom	8.8	EU	54.3

Principal imports

	$bn cif		$bn cif
Consumer goods	8.1	Fuels	1.8
Capital goods	3.1	Agricultural products	1.2
Building & construction	2.1	Total incl. others	**29.4**

Main origins of imports

	% of total		% of total
Germany	22.7	Netherlands	6.4
Sweden	10.9	EU	52.3
United Kingdom	7.5		

Balance of payments, reserves and aid, $bn

Visible exports fob	37.4	Capital balance	-6.8
Visible imports fob	-29.4	Overall balance	-0.6
Trade balance	8.0	Change in reserves	-0.8
Invisibles inflows	35.6	Level of reserves	
Invisibles outflows	-37.5	end Dec.	10.4
Net transfers	-0.6	No. months import cover	4.2
Current account balance	5.5	Aid given	1.34
– as % of GDP	4.0	– as % of GDP	1.03

Family life

No. of households	2.3m	Divorces per 1,000 pop.	2.5
Av. no. per household	2.2	Cost of living, Sept. 1994	
Marriages per 1,000 pop.	6.3	New York = 100	118

EGYPT

Area	1,000,250 sq km	Currency	Egyptian pound (£E)
Capital	Cairo		

People

Population	55.8m	Life expectancy: men	65 yrs
Pop. per sq km	56	women	67 yrs
Av. ann. growth		Adult literacy	50.0%
in pop. 1985–93	2.3%	Fertility rate (per woman)	3.4
Pop. under 15	37.9%		
Pop. over 65	4.2%		*per 1,000 pop.*
No. of men per 100 women	103	Crude birth rate	26.4
Human Development Index	55	Crude death rate	7.1

The economy

GDP	£E125bn	GDP per head	$658
GDP	$37bn	GDP per head in purchasing	
Av. ann. growth in real		power parity (USA=100)	16
GDP 1985–93	3.0%		

Origins of GDP		**Components of GDP**	
	% of total		*% of total*
Agriculture	16.6	Private consumption	73.9
Industry, of which:	32.9	Public consumption	10.8
manufacturing	...	Investment	18.6
Services	50.5	Exports	28.9
		Imports	-32.2

Structure of manufacturing

	% of total		*% of total*
Agric. & food processing	25	Other	51
Textiles & clothing	17	Av. ann. increase in industrial	
Machinery & transport	7	output 1980–92	3.9%

Energy

	'000 TCE		
Total output	80,888	% output exported	47.0
Total consumption	38,612	% consumption imported	4.7
Consumption per head,			
kg coal equivalent	704		

Inflation and finance

			av. ann. increase 1989–93
Consumer price			
inflation 1993	12.1%	Narrow money (M1)	10.7%
Av. ann. inflation 1989–93	16.7%	Broad money	19.8%

Exchange rates

	end 1994		*end June 1994*
£E per $	3.39	Effective rates	*1990 = 100*
£E per SDR	4.95	– nominal	...
£E per Ecu	4.16	– real	...

Principal exports[b]

	$m fob		$m fob
Petroleum & products	1,803	Other agric. products	161
Cotton yarn & textiles	450	Raw cotton	37
Industrial goods	364	Total incl. others	**3,417**

Main export destinations

	% of total		% of total
Italy	17.8	France	5.7
United States	12.9	United Kingdom	5.5
India	8.4	Saudi Arabia	4.6

Principal imports[b]

	$m cif		$m cif
Machinery & transport equipment	2,547	Raw materials	1,267
		Chemicals & rubber	1,107
Agric. products & foodstuffs	1,877	Wood, paper & textiles	1,100
		Total incl. others	**10,732**

Main origins of imports

	% of total		% of total
United States	21.4	France	8.0
Germany	10.0	Japan	5.8
Italy	9.3	United Kingdom	3.9

Balance of payments, reserves and debt, $bn

Visible exports fob	3.2	Overall balance	2.8
Visible imports fob	-9.9	Change in reserves	2.1
Trade balance	-6.7	Level of reserves	
Invisibles inflows	9.3	end Dec.	13.0
Invisibles outflows	-7.3	No. months import cover	15.8
Net transfers	7.7	Foreign debt	40.6
Current account balance	2.3	– as % of GDP	104.8
– as % of GDP	6.3	Debt service	2.4
Capital balance	-1.5	Debt service ratio	15.2

Family life

No. of households	9.7m	Divorces per 1,000 pop.	1.4
Av. no. per household	4.9	Cost of living, Sept. 1994	
Marriages per 1,000 pop.	8.4	New York = 100	88

a 1991.
b Year ending June 30, 1993.

FINLAND

Area	337,030 sq km	Currency	Markka (Fmk)
Capital	Helsinki		

People

Population	5.1m	Life expectancy: men	73 yrs
Pop. per sq km	15	women	80 yrs
Av. ann. growth		Adult literacy	99%
in pop. 1985–93	0.4%	Fertility rate (per woman)	1.9
Pop. under 15	18.9%		
Pop. over 65	14.1%		*per 1,000 pop.*
No. of men per 100 women	95	Crude birth rate	12.5
Human Development Index	91	Crude death rate	10.2

The economy

GDP	Fmk548bn	GDP per head	$18,978
GDP	$96bn	GDP per head in purchasing	
Av. ann. growth in real		power parity (USA=100)	73
GDP 1985–93	0.5%		

Origins of GDP		Components of GDP	
	% of total		*% of total*
Agriculture	6.5	Private consumption	52.5
Industry, of which:	35.4	Public consumption	22.8
manufacturing	28.7	Investment	18.3
Services	58.2	Exports	31.5
		Imports	-21.5

Structure of manufacturing

	% of total		*% of total*
Agric. & food processing	16	Other	59
Textiles & clothing	3	Av. ann. increase in industrial	
Machinery & transport	22	output 1980–92	2.4%

Energy

	'000 TCE		
Total output	10,974	% output exported[a]	48.7
Total consumption	32,885	% consumption imported[a]	78.3
Consumption per head,			
kg coal equivalent	6,566		

Inflation and finance

Consumer price		*av. ann. increase 1989–93*	
inflation 1994	1.1%	Narrow money (M1)	31.9%
Av. ann. inflation 1989–94	3.8%	Broad money	4.4%

Exchange rates

	end 1994		*end June 1994*
Fmk per $	4.74	Effective rates	*1990 = 100*
Fmk per SDR	6.92	– nominal	77.9
Fmk per Ecu	5.85	– real	66.9

Principal exports

	$bn fob		$bn fob
Metals & engineering		Chemicals	2.5
equipment	8.4	Wood & products	1.9
Paper & products	6.5	Total incl. others	**23.4**

Main export destinations

	% of total		% of total
Germany	13.2	France	5.3
Sweden	11.1	Netherlands	5.0
United Kingdom	10.5	Russia	4.5
United States	7.8	EU	46.9

Principal imports

	$bn cif		$bn cif
Raw materials	9.6	Energy & products	1.9
Consumer goods	3.7		
Capital goods	2.7	Total incl. others	**18.0**

Main origins of imports

	% of total		% of total
Germany	16.4	Japan	5.8
Sweden	10.2	Norway	4.9
United Kingdom	8.9	EU	47.2
Russia	7.6	Efta	19.0
United States	7.3		

Balance of payments, reserves and aid, $bn

Visible exports fob	23.1	Capital balance	0.1
Visible imports fob	-16.7	Overall balance	0.3
Trade balance	6.4	Change in reserves	0.2
Invisibles inflows	6.0	Level of reserves	
Invisibles outflows	-12.8	end Dec.	5.5
Net transfers	-0.6	No. months import cover	4.0
Current account balance	-1.0	Aid given	0.355
– as % of GDP	-1.0	– as % of GDP	0.45

Family life

No. of households	2.0m	Divorces per 1,000 pop.	2.5
Av. no. per household	2.5	Cost of living, Sept. 1994	
Marriages per 1,000 pop.	4.6	New York = 100	108

a Energy trade data are distorted by transitory and oil refinery activities.

FRANCE

Area	543,965 sq km	Currency	Franc (FFr)
Capital	Paris		

People

Population	57.7m	Life expectancy: men	74 yrs
Pop. per sq km	105	women	81 yrs
Av. ann. growth		Adult literacy	99.0%
in pop. 1985–93	0.6%	Fertility rate (per woman)	1.7
Pop. under 15	19.8%		
Pop. over 65	14.9%		*per 1,000 pop.*
No. of men per 100 women	95	Crude birth rate	12.4
Human Development Index	93	Crude death rate	9.6

The economy

GDP	FFr7,300bn	GDP per head	$22,363
GDP	$1,289bn	GDP per head in purchasing	
Av. ann. growth in real		power parity (USA=100)	83
GDP, 1985–93	2.1%		

Origins of GDP		Components of GDP	
	% of total		*% of total*
Agriculture	2.5	Private consumption	60.9
Industry, of which:	30.0	Public consumption	19.3
manufacturing	24.5	Investment	17.5
Services	67.5	Exports	22.6
		Imports	-20.4

Structure of manufacturing

	% of total		*% of total*
Agric. & food processing	13	Other	51
Textiles & clothing	6	Av. ann. increase in industrial	
Metal products & machinery	30	output 1980–92	1.1%

Energy

	'000 TCE		
Total output	152,243	% output exported	17.7
Total consumption	310,854	% consumption imported	65.4
Consumption per head,			
kg coal equivalent	5,434		

Inflation and finance

Consumer price		*av. ann. increase 1989–93*	
inflation 1994	1.7%	Narrow money (M1)	1.6%
Av. ann. inflation 1989–94	2.7%	Broad money	2.2%

Exchange rates

	end 1994		*end June 1994*
FFr per $	5.35	Effective rates	*1990 = 100*
FFr per SDR	7.80	– nominal	106.5
FFr per Ecu	6.60	– real	104.4

Principal exports

	$bn fob		$bn fob
Capital equipment	56.2	Chemicals	31.0
Agric. products		Motor vehicles & other	
& foodstuffs	34.7	transport equipment	26.9
Non-durable consumer		Steel & metals	17.6
goods	32.5	Total incl. others	**209.5**

Main export destinations

	% of total		% of total
Germany	17.3	United States	7.1
Italy	9.4	Spain	6.6
United Kingdom	9.4	Netherlands	4.8
Belgium/Luxembourg	8.6	EU	59.7

Principal imports

	$bn cif		$bn cif
Capital equipment	48.5	Motor vehicles & other	
Non-durable consumer		transport equipment	21.8
goods	35.0	Energy products	17.7
Chemicals	30.9	Steel & metals	16.5
Agric. products			
& foodstuffs	24.6	Total incl. others	**201.9**

Main origins of imports

	% of total		% of total
Germany	17.6	United Kingdom	8.1
Italy	9.9	Spain	5.4
Belgium/Luxembourg	8.9	Netherlands	5.1
United States	8.7	EU	58.5

Balance of payments, reserves and aid, $bn

Visible exports fob	195.1	Capital balance	-12.9
Visible imports fob	-188.1	Overall balance	-5.0
Trade balance	7.0	Change in reserves	1.4
Invisibles inflows	187.5	Level of reserves	
Invisibles outflows	-178.2	end Dec.	26.6
Net transfers	-6.1	No. months import cover	1.7
Current account balance	10.2	Aid given[a]	7.9
– as % of GDP	0.8	– as % of GDP	0.63

Family life

No. of households	21.5m	Divorces per 1,000 pop.	1.9
Av. no. per household	2.6	Cost of living, Sept. 1994	
Marriages per 1,000 pop.	4.8	New York = 100	128

a Including aid to French overseas territories.

GERMANY

Area	356,840 sq km	Currency	Deutschemark (DM)
Capital	Berlin		

People

Population	80.8m	Life expectancy: men	74 yrs
Pop. per sq km	226	women	80 yrs
Av. ann. growth		Adult literacy	99.0%
in pop. 1985–93	0.6%	Fertility rate (per woman)	1.3
Pop. under 15	17.1%		
Pop. over 65	14.8%		*per 1,000 pop.*
No. of men per 100 women	95	Crude birth rate	9.2
Human Development Index	92	Crude death rate	10.9

The economy

GDP	DM3,146bn	GDP per head	$22,561
GDP	$1,903bn	GDP per head in purchasing	
Av. ann. growth in real		power parity (USA=100)	89
GDP 1985–93[a]	2.8%		

Origins of GDP[a]		Components of GDP[a]	
	% of total		*% of total*
Agriculture	1.2	Private consumption	55.3
Industry, of which:	35.3	Public consumption	18.0
manufacturing	...	Investment	19.2
Services	63.7	Exports	36.5
		Imports	-29.0

Structure of manufacturing[a]

	% of total		*% of total*
Agric. & food processing	10	Other	45
Textiles & clothing	4	Av. ann. increase in industrial	
Machinery & transport	41	output 1980–92	1.1

Energy

	'000 TCE		
Total output	228,610	% output exported	11.5
Total consumption	472,726	% consumption imported	61.4
Consumption per head,			
kg coal equivalent	5,890		

Inflation[a] and finance

		av. ann. increase 1989–93	
Consumer price			
inflation 1994	3.0%	Narrow money (M1)	10.5%
Av. ann. inflation 1989–94	3.4%	Broad money	9.0%

Exchange rates

	end 1994		*end June 1994*
DM per $	1.55	Effective rates	*1990 = 100*
DM per SDR	2.26	– nominal	107.2
DM per Ecu	1.91	– real	108.2

ONG KONG

	1,062 sq km	Currency	Hong Kong dollar (HK$)
al	Victoria		

ple

ılation	5.9m	Life expectancy: men	76 yrs
per sq km	5,677	women	82 yrs
ın. growth		Adult literacy	90.0%
op. 1985–93	0.9%	Fertility rate (per woman)	1.2
ınder 15	19.1%		
ıver 65	10.1%		per 1,000 pop.
f men per 100 women	107	Crude birth rate	9.8
n Development Index	88	Crude death rate	6.3

economy

	HK$819bn	GDP per head	$17,842
	$105bn	GDP per head in purchasing	
ın. growth in real		power parity (USA=100)	84
1985–93	6.8%		

ıs of GDP

	% of total	Components of GDP	% of total
ılture	0.2	Private consumption	57.4
try, of which:	21.0	Public consumption	8.1
ıufacturing	13.7	Investment	27.7
ces	78.8	Exports	140.8
		Imports	-133.9

cture of manufacturing

	% of total		% of total
& food processing	9	Other	34
es & clothing	36	Av. ann. increase in industrial	
ınery & transport	21	output 1980–89	6.5%

ıgy

	'000 TCE		
ıutput	nil	% output exported	nil
onsumption	13,252	% consumption imported	174.4
ımption per head,			
ɔal equivalent	2,285		

ion and finance

		av. ann. increase 1988–92
ner price		
ion 1994	8.1%	Narrow money (M1) ...
ı. inflation 1989–94	9.6%	Broad money ...

ange rates

	end 1994		end June 1994
r $	7.74	Effective rates	1990 = 100
r SDR	11.30	– nominal	...
r Ecu	9.52	– real	...

Principal exports

	$bn fob		$bn fob
Non-electrical machinery	74.8	Food, drink & tobacco	20.4
Road vehicles & aircraft	70.9	Iron & steel	12.1
Chemicals	53.7		
Electrical machinery			
& appliances	43.0	Total incl. others	**422.8**

Main export destinations

	% of total		% of total
France	12.2	Italy	7.6
United Kingdom	8.0	United States	7.4
Netherlands	7.7	Belgium/Luxembourg	6.8
Italy	7.6	EU	49.8

Principal imports[a]

	$bn cif		$bn cif
Road vehicles & aircraft	44.1	Non-electrical machinery	34.8
Chemicals	40.3	Food, drink & tobacco	34.6
Electrical machinery &		Textiles & clothing	29.2
appliances	35.3	Total incl. others	**377.2**

Main origins of imports

	% of total		% of total
France	11.5	Belgium/Luxembourg	6.0
Netherlands	8.8	United States	5.3
Italy	8.5	EU	48.2
United Kingdom	6.3		

Balance of payments, reserves and aid, $bn

Visible exports fob	363.4	Capital balance	35.4
Visible imports fob	-318.8	Overall balance	-15.5
Trade balance	44.6	Change in reserves	-14.2
Invisibles inflows	151.8	Level of reserves	
Invisibles outflows	-185.1	end Dec.	82.2
Net transfers	-31.2	No. months import cover	3.1
Current account balance	-20.0	Aid given	7.0
– as % of GDP	-1.0	– as % of GDP	0.37

Family life

No. of households	32.7m	Divorces per 1,000 pop.	1.7
Av. no. per household	2.3	Cost of living, Sept. 1994	
Marriages per 1,000 pop.	5.7	New York = 100	111

a Western Germany.

GREECE

Area	131,985 sq km	Currency	Drachma (Dr)
Capital	Athens		

People

Population	10.4m	Life expectancy: men	76 yrs
Pop. per sq km	79	women	81 yrs
Av. ann. growth		Adult literacy	93.8%
in pop. 1985–93	0.5%	Fertility rate (per woman)	1.4
Pop. under 15	17.3%		
Pop. over 65	15.4%		per 1,000 pop.
No. of men per 100 women	97	Crude birth rate	9.8
Human Development Index	87	Crude death rate	10.1

The economy

GDP	Dr17,652bn	GDP per head	$7,389
GDP	$77bn	GDP per head in purchasing	
Av. ann. growth in real		power parity (USA=100)	35
GDP 1985–93	1.5%		

Origins of GDP

	% of total	Components of GDP	% of total
Agriculture	13.7	Private consumption	71.8
Industry, of which:	35.0	Public consumption	19.8
manufacturing	25.8	Investment	18.1
Services	51.3	Exports	23.2
		Imports	-33.1

Structure of manufacturing

	% of total		% of total
Agric. & food processing	25	Other	43
Textiles & clothing	20	Av. ann. increase in industrial	
Metal products & machinery	12	output 1980–92	1.2%

Energy

	'000 TCE		
Total output	11,251	% output exported[a]	62.2
Total consumption	32,997	% consumption imported[a]	98.2
Consumption per head,			
kg coal equivalent	3,241		

Inflation and finance

		av. ann. increase 1989–93	
Consumer price			
inflation 1994	10.9%	Narrow money (M1)	17.7%
Av. ann. inflation 1989–94	15.6%	Broad money[b]	12.7%

Exchange rates

	end 1994		end June 1994
Dr per $	236	Effective rates	1990 = 100
Dr per SDR	346	– nominal	289.0
Dr per Ecu	291	– real	288.7

Principal exports[b]

	$bn fob		
Manufactured products	3.1	Raw materials & ind	
Food & beverages	1.5	supplies	
Petroleum products	0.6	Tobacco	
Minerals	0.3	Total incl. others	

Main export destinations

	% of total		
Germany	23.0	United Kingdom	
Italy	18.0	United States	
France	7.2	EU	

Principal imports[b]

	$bn cif		
Manufactured consumer		Petroleum	
goods	8.0	Chemicals & product	
Machinery equipment	3.5	Iron & steel	
Foodstuffs	2.8	Total incl. others	

Main origins of imports

	% of total		
Germany	20.2	Netherlands	
Italy	14.2	Japan	
France	7.8	EU	

Balance of payments, reserves and debt, $bn

Visible exports fob	5.0	Overall balance	
Visible imports fob	-15.6	Change in reserves	
Trade balance	-10.6	Level of reserves	
Invisibles inflows	9.2	end Dec.	
Invisibles outflows	-5.9	No. months import	
Net transfers	6.5	Foreign debt	
Current account balance	-0.7	– as % of GDP	
– as % of GDP	-1.0	Debt service	
Capital balance	1.4	Debt service ratio	

Family life

No. of households	3.0m	Divorces per 1,00	
Av. no. per household	3.1	Cost of living, Se	
Marriages per 1,000 pop.	6.1	New York = 100	

a   Energy trade figures are distorted by transitory and oil refir
b   1992.

Principal exports[b]

	$bn fob		$bn fob
Clothing	9.3	Telecomms equipment	1.6
Textiles	2.1		
Watches & clocks	1.7	Total incl. others	**28.8**

Main export destinations[c]

	% of total		% of total
China	32.3	Japan	5.1
United States	23.0	United Kingdom	3.4
Germany	5.2		

Principal imports

	$bn cif		$bn cif
Consumer goods	58.8	Agric. products & foodstuffs	5.8
Raw materials & semi-		Fuels	2.4
manufactured products	45.9		
Capital goods	25.8	Total incl. others	**138.7**

Main origins of imports

	% of total		% of total
China	37.5	United States	7.4
Japan	16.6	Singapore	4.5
Taiwan	8.8	South Korea	4.5

Balance of payments, reserves and debt, $bn

Visible exports fob	135.2	Overall balance	...
Visible imports cif	139.1	Change in reserves	...
Trade balance	-3.8	Level of reserves	
Invisibles inflows	...	end Dec.	...
Invisibles outflows	...	No. months import cover	...
Net transfers	...	Foreign debt	15.2
Current account balance	9.2	– as % of GDP	13.7
– as % of GDP	8.8	Debt service	1.7
Capital balance	...	Debt service ratio	1.1

Family life

No. of households	1.6m	Divorces per 1,000 pop.	1.0
Av. no. per household	3.4	Cost of living, Sept. 1994	
Marriages per 1,000 pop.	7.4	New York = 100	113

a 1992.
b Domestic.
c Including re-exports.

HUNGARY

Area	93,030 sq km	Currency	Forint (Ft)
Capital	Budapest		

People

Population	10.3m	Life expectancy: men	65 yrs
Pop. per sq km	111	women	74 yrs
Av. ann. growth		Adult literacy	99.0%
in pop. 1985–93	-0.5%	Fertility rate (per woman)	1.7
Pop. under 15	18.5%		
Pop. over 65	13.9%		*per 1,000 pop.*
No. of men per 100 women	93	Crude birth rate	12.4
Human Development Index	86	Crude death rate	14.5

The economy

GDP	Ft3,126bn	GDP per head	$3,332
GDP	$34bn	GDP per head in purchasing	
Av. ann. growth in real		power parity (USA=100)	28
GDP 1985–93	-1.5%		

Origins of GDP[a]		Components of GDP[a]	
	% of total		*% of total*
Agriculture	5.6	Private consumption	72.3
Industry, of which:	28.4	Public consumption	13.1
manufacturing	23.1	Investment	22.6
Services	66.0	Exports	27.3
		Imports	-35.2

Structure of manufacturing

	% of total		*% of total*
Agric. & food processing	10	Other	56
Textiles & clothing	8	Av. ann. increase in industrial	
Machinery & transport	26	output 1980–92	-2.5%

Energy

	'000 TCE		
Total output	19,585	% output exported	5.7
Total consumption	35,103	% consumption imported	51.3
Consumption per head,			
kg coal equivalent	3,339		

Inflation and finance

Consumer price		*av. ann. increase 1989–91*	
inflation 1994	18.8%	Narrow money (M1)	16.2%
Av. ann. inflation 1989–94	23.9%	Broad money	24.1%

Exchange rates

	end 1994		*end June 1994*
			1990 = 100
Ft per $	110.7	Effective rates	
Ft per SDR	161.6	– nominal	75.6
Ft per Ecu	136.7	– real	137.4

Principal exports

	$bn fob		$bn fob
Raw materials	3.2	Capital equipment	1.2
Consumer goods	2.3	Fuels & electricity	0.3
Food products	1.9	Total incl. others	**8.9**

Main export destinations

	% of total		% of total
Germany	26.6	Eastern Europe	26.3
Ex-Soviet Union	15.2	Efta	13.8
EU	46.5		

Principal imports

	$bn cif		$bn cif
Raw materials	4.2	Fuel & electricity	1.6
Capital equipment	3.3	Food products	0.7
Consumer goods	2.7	Total incl. others	**12.5**

Main origins of imports

	% of total		% of total
Ex-Soviet Union	21.8	Eastern Europe	29.6
Germany	21.6	Efta	17.4
EU	40.2		

Balance of payments, reserves and debt, $bn

Visible exports fob	8.1	Overall balance	2.5
Visible imports fob	-12.1	Change in reserves	2.3
Trade balance	-4.0	Level of reserves	
Invisibles inflows	3.3	end Dec.	6.8
Invisibles outflows	-4.3	No. months import cover	6.7
Net transfers	0.7	Foreign debt	24.8
Current account balance	-4.3	– as % of GDP	67.1
– as % of GDP	-12.4	Debt service	4.4
Capital balance	3.5	Debt service ratio	40.8

Family life

No. of households	3.9m	Divorces per 1,000 pop.	2.4
Av. no. per household	2.7	Cost of living, Sept. 1994	
Marriages per 1,000 pop.	5.4	New York = 100	58

a 1990.

INDIA

Area	3,165,830 sq km	Currency	Indian rupee (Rs)
Capital	New Delhi		

People

Population	900.5m	Life expectancy: men	63 yrs
Pop. per sq km	274	women	63 yrs
Av. ann. growth		Adult literacy	49.8%
in pop. 1985–93	2.1%	Fertility rate (per woman)	3.4
Pop. under 15	34.8%		
Pop. over 65	4.9%		*per 1,000 pop.*
No. of men per 100 women	107	Crude birth rate	26.6
Human Development Index	31	Crude death rate	8.9

The economy

GDP	Rs8,020bn	GDP per head	$292
GDP	$263bn	GDP per head in purchasing	
Av. ann. growth in real		power parity (USA=100)	5
GDP 1985–93	4.8%		

Origins of GDP[a]		Components of GDP[a]	
	% of total		*% of total*
Agriculture	32.3	Private consumption	67.1
Industry, of which:	26.9	Public consumption	12.2
manufacturing	...	Investment	24.0
Services	40.9	Exports	9.6
		Imports	-12.9

Structure of manufacturing

	% of total		*% of total*
Agric. & food processing	13	Other	48
Textiles & clothing	12	Av. ann. increase in industrial	
Machinery & transport	27	output 1980–92	6.4%

Energy

	'000 TCE		
Total output	270,071	% output exported	0.2
Total consumption	307,796	% consumption imported	18.9
Consumption per head,			
kg coal equivalent	350		

Inflation and finance

Consumer price		*av. ann. increase 1989–93*	
inflation 1994	7.5%	Narrow money (M1)	16.7%
Av. ann. inflation 1989–94	9.1%	Broad money	16.9%

Exchange rates

	end 1994		*end June 1994*
Rs per $	31.38	Effective rates	*1990 = 100*
Rs per SDR	45.81	– nominal	...
Rs per Ecu	38.74	– real	...

Principal exports

	$bn fob		$bn fob
Gems & jewellery	4.1	Textiles	1.9
Clothing	2.7	Leather goods	0.9
Engineering products	2.1	Total incl. others	**18.1**

Main export destinations[b]

	% of total		% of total
United States	16.4	Germany	7.1
Ex-Soviet Union	9.2	United Kingdom	6.4
Japan	9.2	EU	27.0

Principal imports

	$bn cif		$bn cif
Capital goods	6.0	Chemicals	0.8
Crude oil & products	5.9	Iron & steel	0.8
Uncut gems & jewellery	2.7	Total incl. others	**23.9**

Main origins of imports[b]

	% of total		% of total
United States	10.3	United Kingdom	6.2
Germany	8.0	EU	29.2
Japan	7.1		

Balance of payments[c], reserves and debt, $bn

Visible exports fob	18.3	Overall balance	-1.9
Visible imports fob	-23.4	Change in reserves	-1.8
Trade balance	-5.1	Level of reserves	
Invisibles inflows	5.1	end Dec.	10.8
Invisibles outflows	-9.8	No. months import cover	...
Net transfers	2.8	Foreign debt	91.8
Current account balance[d]	-7.0	– as % of GDP	37.3
– as % of GDP[d]	-2.7	Debt service	8.9
Capital balance	7.6	Debt service ratio	28.4

Family life

No. of households	118.6m	Divorces per 1,000 pop.	...
Av. no. per household	5.5	Cost of living, Sept. 1994	
Marriages per 1,000 pop.	...	New York = 100	45

a Year ending March 31, 1993.
b Year ending March 31, 1992.
c 1990.
d 1992 estimates.

INDONESIA

Area	1,919,445 sq km	Currency	Rupiah (Rp)
Capital	Jakarta		

People

Population	187.2m	Life expectancy: men	63 yrs
Pop. per sq km	98	women	67 yrs
Av. ann. growth		Adult literacy	84.4%
in pop. 1985–93	1.8%	Fertility rate (per woman)	2.6
Pop. under 15	33.4%		
Pop. over 65	4.4%		*per 1,000 pop.*
No. of men per 100 women	99	Crude birth rate	23.1
Human Development Index	59	Crude death rate	7.6

The economy

GDP	Rp285,933bn	GDP per head	$732
GDP	$137bn	GDP per head in purchasing	
Av. ann. growth in real		power parity (USA=100)	12
GDP 1985–93	6.4%		

Origins of GDP

	% of total
Agriculture	18.5
Industry, of which:	38.5
manufacturing	22.3
Services	43.0

Components of GDP

	% of total
Private consumption	52.4
Public consumption	9.9
Investment	35.3
Exports	28.3
Imports	-25.8

Structure of manufacturing

	% of total		% of total
Agric. & food processing	24	Other	48
Textiles & clothing	16	Av. ann. increase in industrial	
Machinery & transport	12	output 1980–92	6.1%

Energy

	'000 TCE		
Total output	196,784	% output exported	63.6
Total consumption	73,205	% consumption imported	22.3
Consumption per head,			
kg coal equivalent	383		

Inflation and finance

		av. ann. increase 1989–92	
Consumer price			
inflation 1994	8.5%	Narrow money (M1)	20.1%
Av. ann. inflation 1989–94	9.0%	Broad money	29.9%

Exchange rates

	end 1994		end June 1994
Rp per $	2,200	Effective rates	1990 = 100
Rp per SDR	3,212	– nominal	...
Rp per Ecu	2,716	– real	...

Principal exports

	$bn fob		$bn fob
Petroleum & products	6.1	Rubber & products	2.7
Textiles & clothing	6.0	Shrimp	0.9
Timber	5.5		
Natural gas	3.7	Total incl. others	**36.8**

Main export destinations

	% of total		% of total
Japan	30.3	Taiwan	3.9
United States	14.2	China	3.4
Singapore	9.2	Germany	3.2
South Korea	6.2		

Principal imports

	$bn cif		$bn cif
Machinery & transport equipment	12.2	Fuels	2.2
		Food, drink & tobacco	1.3
Chemicals	4.0		
Raw materials	2.4	Total incl. others	**28.3**

Main origins of imports

	% of total		% of total
Japan	22.1	Singapore	6.3
United States	11.5	Australia	4.9
South Korea	7.4	Taiwan	4.6
Germany	7.3		

Balance of payments, reserves and debt, $bn

Visible exports fob	36.6	Overall balance	0.6
Visible imports fob	-28.4	Change in reserves	0.9
Trade balance	10.2	Level of reserves	
Invisibles inflows	4.9	end Dec.	11.4
Invisibles outflows	-15.8	No. months import cover	4.8
Net transfers	0.6	Foreign debt	89.5
Current account balance	-2.0	– as % of GDP	65.9
– as % of GDP	-1.5	Debt service	13.3
Capital balance	5.1	Debt service ratio	32.6

Family life

No. of households	39.7m	Divorces per 1,000 pop.	0.8
Av. no. per household	4.5	Cost of living, Sept. 1994	
Marriages per 1,000 pop.	7.4	New York = 100	90

IRAN

Area	1,648,000 sq km	Currency	Rial (IR)
Capital	Tehran		

People

Population	61.4m	Life expectancy: men	69 yrs
Pop. per sq km	37	women	70 yrs
Av. ann. growth		Adult literacy	56.0%
in pop. 1985–93	3.6%	Fertility rate (per woman)	4.5
Pop. under 15	45.9%		
Pop. over 65	3.8%		per 1,000 pop.
No. of men per 100 women	104	Crude birth rate	32.5
Human Development Index	67	Crude death rate	5.8

The economy

GDP	IR59,585bn	GDP per head	$765
GDP	$47bn	GDP per head in purchasing	
Av. ann. growth in real		power parity (USA=100)	21
GDP 1985–93	1.1%		

Origins of GDP[a]		Components of GDP	
	% of total		% of total
Agriculture	17.8	Private consumption	55.0
Industry, of which:	35.2	Public consumption	14.5
manufacturing	...	Investment	29.1
Services	47.0	Exports	24.1
		Imports	-22.8

Structure of manufacturing

	% of total		% of total
Agric. & food processing	16	Other	47
Textiles & clothing	21	Av. ann. increase in industrial	
Metal products & machinery	16	output 1980–92	4.4%

Energy

	'000 TCE		
Total output	285,675	% output exported	64.9
Total consumption	102,287	% consumption imported	10.7
Consumption per head,			
kg coal equivalent	1,661		

Inflation and finance

Consumer price		av. ann. increase 1989–93	
inflation 1993	20.3%	Narrow money (M1)	19.1%
Av. ann. inflation 1989–93	17.9%	Broad money	23.3%

Exchange rates

	end 1994		end June 1994
IR per $	1,736	Effective rates	1990 = 100
IR per SDR	2,534	– nominal	...
IR per Ecu	2,143	– real	...

Principal exports[b]

	$bn fob		$bn fob
Crude oil	14.2		
Others	1.8	Total incl. others	**16.0**

Main export destinations

	% of total		% of total
Japan	14.8	South Korea	6.7
France	8.8	Germany	4.9
Italy	8.4	Singapore	4.0
Netherlands	7.2	Belgium/Luxembourg	3.5

Principal imports[b]

	$bn cif		$bn cif
Manufactures	17.8		
Raw materials	3.8	Total incl. others	**21.7**

Main origins of imports

	% of total		% of total
Germany	17.5	United Kingdom	5.3
Japan	10.3	France	5.1
Italy	9.1	United States	4.3
UAE	7.0	Turkey	3.4

Balance of payments[c], reserves and debt, $bn

Visible exports fob	19.9	Overall balance	-0.2
Visible imports fob	-23.3	Change in reserves	-0.2
Trade balance	-3.4	Level of reserves	
Invisibles inflows	0.9	end Dec.	...
Invisibles outflows	-5.9	No. months import cover	...
Net transfers	2.0	Foreign debt	20.6
Current account balance	-6.5	– as % of GDP[d]	11.4
– as % of GDP	-5.0	Debt service	1.3
Capital balance	4.9	Debt service ratio	7.2

Family life

No. of households	10.8m	Divorces per 1,000 pop.	0.7
Av. no. per household	5.2	Cost of living, Sept. 1994	
Marriages per 1,000 pop.	7.5	New York = 100	47

a Iranian year ending March 20, 1991.
b 1991.
c Iranian year ending March 20, 1992.
d 1992.

IRAQ

Area	438,445 sq km	Currency	Iraqi dinar (ID)
Capital	Baghdad		

People

Population	19.8m	Life expectancy: men		67 yrs
Pop. per sq km	45	women		70 yrs
Av. ann. growth		Adult literacy		62.5%
in pop. 1985–93	3.2%	Fertility rate (per woman)		5.3
Pop. under 15	43.7%			
Pop. over 65	3.0%			*per 1,000 pop.*
No. of men per 100 women	104	Crude birth rate		35.8
Human Development Index	61	Crude death rate		5.9

The economy

GDP[a]	ID5.6bn	GDP per head[a]	$911
GDP[a]	$18bn	GDP per head in purchasing	
Av. ann. growth in real		power parity (USA=100)[a]	16
GDP 1985–93	-8.0%		

Origins of GDP[b]		Components of GDP[c]	
	% of total		*% of total*
Agriculture	5.1	Private consumption	52.7
Industry, of which:	72.9	Public consumption	30.0
manufacturing	11.6	Investment	21.9
Services	22.0	Exports	24.6
		Imports	-29.1

Structure of manufacturing

	% of total		*% of total*
Agric. & food processing	...	Other	...
Textiles & clothing	...	Av. ann. increase in industrial	
Machinery & transport	...	output 1980–92	4.4

Energy

	'000 TCE		
Total output	41,005	% output exported	16.5
Total consumption	24,055	% consumption imported	0.0
Consumption per head,			
kg coal equivalent	1,247		

Inflation and finance[a]

Consumer price		*av. ann. increase 1988–92*	
inflation 1993	75%	Narrow money (M1)	...
Av. ann. inflation 1989–93	46.7%	Broad money	...

Exchange rates

	end 1994		*end June 1994*
ID per $	0.31	Effective rates	*1990 = 100*
ID per SDR	0.45	– nominal	101.1
ID per Ecu	0.38	– real	...

Principal exports[abe]

	$bn fob		$bn fob
Crude oil	14.5	Total incl. others	**14.6**

Main export destinations[ad]

	% of total		% of total
United States	28.5	Netherlands	7.4
Brazil	9.9	Spain	4.6
Turkey	9.8	France	3.5
Japan	7.8		

Principal imports[a]

	$bn cif		$bn cif
Civilian goods	5.0		
Military goods	2.7	Total incl. others	**7.7**

Main origins of imports[ad]

	% of total		% of total
Germany	13.3	United Kingdom	8.4
United States	10.7	Japan	4.5
Turkey	9.2	Italy	4.5
France	8.7	Brazil	3.1

Balance of payments[be], reserves and debt[e], $bn

Visible exports fob	9.5	Overall balance	...
Visible imports fob	5.1	Change in reserves	...
Trade balance	4.4	Level of reserves	
Invisibles inflows	...	end Dec.	...
Invisibles outflows	...	No. months import cover	...
Net transfers	...	Foreign debt	82.9
Current account balance	-0.9	– as % of GDP	...
– as % of GDP	...	Debt service	161
Capital balance	...	Debt service ratio	...

Family life

No. of households	2.1m	Divorces per 1,000 pop.	0.1
Av. no. per household	7.1	Cost of living, Sept. 1994	
Marriages per 1,000 pop.	8.5	New York = 100	...

a Estimate.
b 1989.
c 1985.
d 1988.
e Trade, balance of payments and debt data for Iraq are estimates based on limited and inconsistent information.

IRELAND

Area	68,895 sq km	Currency	Punt (I£)
Capital	Dublin		

People

Population	3.6m	Life expectancy: men	73 yrs
Pop. per sq km	51	women	79 yrs
Av. ann. growth		Adult literacy	99.0%
in pop. 1985–93	nil	Fertility rate (per woman)	2.1
Pop. under 15	24.7%		
Pop. over 65	11.6%		*per 1,000 pop.*
No. of men per 100 women	100	Crude birth rate	15.1
Human Development Index	89	Crude death rate	8.8

The economy

GDP	I£31bn	GDP per head	$12,579
GDP	$45bn	GDP per head in purchasing	
Av. ann. growth in real		power parity (USA=100)	52
GDP 1985–93	4.5%		

Origins of GDP		Components of GDP	
	% of total		*% of total*
Agriculture	9.0	Private consumption	56.0
Industry, of which:	37.0	Public consumption	16.0
manufacturing	...	Investment	14.0
Services	54.0	Exports	68.0
		Imports	-54.0

Structure of manufacturing

	% of total		*% of total*
Agric. & food processing	27	Other	42
Textiles & clothing	4	Av. ann. increase in industrial	
Machinery & transport	27	output 1980–89	-4.3%

Energy

	'000 TCE		
Total output	4,778	% output exported	23.8
Total consumption	13,934	% consumption imported	76.6
Consumption per head,			
kg coal equivalent	3,997		

Inflation and finance

Consumer price		*av. ann. increase 1989–93*	
inflation 1994	2.3%	Narrow money (M1)	5.2%
Av. ann. inflation 1989–94	2.9%	Broad money	12.4%

Exchange rates

	end 1994		*end June 1994*
I£ per $	0.65	Effective rates	*1990 = 100*
I£ per SDR	0.94	– nominal	96.9
I£ per Ecu	0.80	– real	...

Principal exports

	$bn fob		$bn fob
Machinery & transport equipment	8.4	Chemicals	5.6
		Other products	4.0
Agric. products & foodstuffs	5.7	Total incl. others	**28.9**

Main export destinations

	% of total		% of total
United Kingdom	28.4	Netherlands	5.7
Germany	13.3	Belgium/Luxembourg	4.0
France	9.1	Japan	3.7
United States	9.1	EU	68.3

Principal imports

	$bn cif		$bn cif
Machinery & transport equipment	8.0	Chemicals	2.7
Manufactured goods	5.4	Total incl. others	**21.7**

Main origins of imports

	% of total		% of total
United Kingdom	36.2	France	3.9
United States	17.1	Netherlands	3.1
Germany	7.2	Italy	2.0
Japan	6.5	EU	56.3

Balance of payments, reserves and aid, $bn

Visible exports fob	28.7	Capital balance	-3.8
Visible imports fob	-20.6	Overall balance	2.7
Trade balance	8.1	Change in reserves	2.6
Invisibles inflows	5.9	Level of reserves	
Invisibles outflows	-13.0	end Dec.	5.9
Net transfers	2.8	No. months import cover	3.4
Current account balance	3.8	Aid given	0.08
– as % of GDP	8.6	– as % of GDP	0.20

Family life

No. of households	0.9m	Divorces per 1,000 pop.	...
Av. no. per household	3.6	Cost of living, Sept. 1994	
Marriages per 1,000 pop.	4.6	New York = 100	101

ISRAEL

Area	20,770 sq km	Currency	New Shekel (NIS)
Capital	Jerusalem		

People

Population	5.3m	Life expectancy: men		75 yrs
Pop. per sq km	255	women		79 yrs
Av. ann. growth		Adult literacy		95.0%
in pop. 1985–93	2.9%	Fertility rate (per woman)		2.7
Pop. under 15	28.8%			
Pop. over 65	9.7%		*per 1,000 pop.*	
No. of men per 100 women	98	Crude birth rate		19.6
Human Development Index	90	Crude death rate		6.5

The economy

GDP	NIS207bn	GDP per head	$13,762
GDP	$73bn	GDP per head in purchasing	
Av. ann. growth in real		power parity (USA=100)	61
GDP 1985–93	4.5%		

Origins of NDP		Components of GDP	
	% of total		*% of total*
Agriculture	2.6	Private consumption	63.1
Industry, of which:	30.4	Public consumption	28.8
manufacturing	21.5	Investment	23.8
Services	67.0	Exports	33.6
		Imports	-49.3

Structure of manufacturing

	% of total		*% of total*
Agric. & food processing	14	Other	46
Textiles & clothing	9	Av. ann. increase in industrial	
Machinery & transport	31	output 1980–90	...

Energy

	'000 TCE		
Total output	47	% output exported[a]	3,931.9
Total consumption	16,768	% consumption imported[a]	130.3
Consumption per head,			
kg coal equivalent	3,268		

Inflation and finance

Consumer price		*av. ann. increase 1989–93*	
inflation 1994	14.3%	Narrow money (M1)	26.1%
Av. ann. inflation 1989–94	15.5%	Broad money	21.2%

Exchange rates

	end 1994		*end June 1994*
NIS per $	3.02	Effective rates	*1990 = 100*
NIS per SDR	4.41	– nominal	...
NIS per Ecu	3.73	– real	...

Principal exports[b]

	$bn fob		$bn fob
Metal, machinery & electronics	5.1	Textiles & clothing	0.9
		Agric. products & foodstuffs	0.6
Diamonds	3.0		
Chemicals	1.9	Total incl. others	**12.4**

Main export destinations[b]

	% of total		% of total
United States	30.9	Germany	5.3
United Kingdom	5.5	Japan	5.2
Belgium/Luxembourg	5.4	France	3.9

Principal imports[b]

	$bn cif		$bn cif
Investment goods	3.6	Energy & products	1.7
Diamonds	3.4	Durable consumer products	1.0
Non-durable consumer products	2.5	Total incl. others	**18.6**

Main origins of imports[b]

	% of total		% of total
United States	17.7	United Kingdom	8.6
Belgium/Luxembourg	12.2	Switzerland	7.4
Germany	10.4	Italy	7.3

Balance of payments, reserves and debt, $bn

Visible exports fob	14.8	Overall balance	1.5
Visible imports fob	-20.4	Change in reserves	1.4
Trade balance	-5.6	Level of reserves	
Invisibles inflows	7.3	end Dec.	6.4
Invisibles outflows	-9.9	No. months import cover	3.8
Net transfers	6.7	Foreign debt	26.5
Current account balance	-1.4	– as % of GDP	40.7
– as % of GDP	-1.9	Debt service	3.2
Capital balance	0.5	Debt service ratio	14.4

Family life

No. of households	1.1m	Divorces per 1,000 pop.	1.3
Av. no. per household	3.5	Cost of living, Sept. 1994	
Marriages per 1,000 pop.	6.5	New York = 100	103

a Energy trade data are distorted by transitory and oil refining activities.
b 1992.

ITALY

Area	301,245 sq km	Currency	Lira (L)
Capital	Rome		

People

Population	57.8m	Life expectancy: men	75 yrs
Pop. per sq km	192	women	81 yrs
Av. ann. growth		Adult literacy	97.4%
in pop. 1985–93	0.2%	Fertility rate (per woman)	1.3
Pop. under 15	15.4%		
Pop. over 65	15.6%		*per 1,000 pop.*
No. of men per 100 women	95	Crude birth rate	9.6
Human Development Index	89	Crude death rate	9.9

The economy

GDP	L1,786,150bn	GDP per head	$19,623
GDP	$1,135bn	GDP per head in purchasing	
Av. ann. growth in real		power parity (USA=100)	77
GDP 1985–93	2.0%		

Origins of GDP		Components of GDP	
	% of total		*% of total*
Agriculture	2.9	Private consumption	62.4
Industry, of which:	31.7	Public consumption	17.9
manufacturing	26.1	Investment	16.9
Services	65.4	Exports	21.4
		Imports	-18.6

Structure of manufacturing

	% of total		*% of total*
Agric. & food processing	8	Other	45
Textiles & clothing	13	Av. ann. increase in industrial	
Machinery & transport	34	output 1980–92	2.2%

Energy

	'000 TCE		
Total output	40,046	% output exported	73.1
Total consumption	232,326	% consumption imported	96.6
Consumption per head,			
kg coal equivalent	4,019		

Inflation and finance

Consumer price		*av. ann. increase 1989–93*	
inflation 1994	3.9%	Narrow money (M1)	7.4%
Av. ann. inflation 1989–94	5.4%	Broad money	8.3%

Exchange rates

	end 1994		*end June 1994*
L per $	1,630	Effective rates	*1990 = 100*
L per SDR	2,379	– nominal	77.3
L per Ecu	2,012	– real	80.6

Principal exports

	$bn fob		$bn fob
Engineering	58.5	Chemicals	13.3
Textiles & clothing	29.1		
Transport equipment	15.2	Total incl. others	**168.4**

Main export destinations

	% of total		% of total
Germany	19.5	Spain	4.3
France	13.1	Switzerland	3.9
United States	7.7	EU	53.3
United Kingdom	6.4		

Principal imports

	$bn cif		$bn cif
Engineering	32.6	Energy	17.9
Agriculture & food	22.3	Transport equipment	16.2
Chemicals	19.9	Total incl. others	**135.9**

Main origins of imports

	% of total		% of total
Germany	19.4	United States	5.3
France	13.6	Switzerland	5.1
United Kingdom	5.8	EU	55.4
Netherlands	5.7		

Balance of payments, reserves and aid, $bn

Visible exports fob	168.5	Capital balance	5.9
Visible imports fob	-136.2	Overall balance	-3.1
Trade balance	32.3	Change in reserves	-0.1
Invisibles inflows	87.9	Level of reserves	
Invisibles outflows	-103.6	end Dec.	30.8
Net transfers	-5.4	No. months import cover	2.7
Current account balance	11.2	Aid given	3.04
– as % of GDP	1.0	– as % of GDP	0.31

Family life

No. of households	19.8m	Divorces per 1,000 pop.	0.5
Av. no. per household	2.8	Cost of living, Sept. 1994	
Marriages per 1,000 pop.	5.3	New York = 100	92

JAPAN

Area	369,700 sq km	Currency	Yen (¥)
Capital	Tokyo		

People

Population	124.9m	Life expectancy:	men	77 yrs
Pop. per sq km	331		women	83 yrs
Av. ann. growth		Adult literacy		99.0%
in pop. 1985–93	0.4%	Fertility rate (per woman)		1.5
Pop. under 15	16.8%			
Pop. over 65	13.9%			*per 1,000 pop.*
No. of men per 100 women	97	Crude birth rate		10.5
Human Development Index	93	Crude death rate		8.3

The economy

GDP	¥436,682bn	GDP per head	$31,451
GDP	$3,927bn	GDP per head in purchasing	
Av. ann. growth in real		power parity (USA=100)	88
GDP 1985–93	3.5%		

Origins of NDP[a]		Components of GDP	
	% of total		*% of total*
Agriculture	2.2	Private consumption	58.1
Industry, of which:	41.1	Public consumption	9.6
manufacturing	27.9	Investment	29.7
Services	61.1	Exports	9.4
		Imports	-7.1

Structure of manufacturing

	% of total		*% of total*
Agric. & food processing	9	Other	46
Textiles & clothing	5	Av. ann. increase in industrial	
Machinery & transport	40	output 1980–92	5.1%

Energy

	'000 TCE		
Total output	107,111	% output exported[b]	8.8
Total consumption	589,432	% consumption imported[b]	89.9
Consumption per head,			
kg coal equivalent	4,735		

Inflation and finance

Consumer price		*av. ann. increase 1989–93*	
inflation 1994	0.7%	Narrow money (M1)	4.9%
Av. ann. inflation 1989–94	2.1%	Broad money	5.7%

Exchange rates

	end 1994		*end June 1994*
¥ per $	99.7	Effective rates	*1990 = 100*
¥ per SDR	145.6	– nominal	151.0
¥ per Ecu	123.1	– real	138.5

Principal exports

	$bn fob		$bn fob
Motor vehicles	58.4	Iron & steel products	14.5
Office machinery	27.6		
Chemicals	20.2		
Scientific & optical equipment	14.3	Total incl. others	**351.3**

Main export destinations

	% of total		% of total
United States	29.2	South Korea	5.3
Hong Kong	6.3	Germany	5.0
Taiwan	6.1	China	4.8

Principal imports

	$bn cif		$bn cif
Energy	48.8	Textiles	16.6
Agric. products & foodstuffs	39.4	Wood	10.2
Chemicals	18.0	Total incl. others	**209.8**

Main origins of imports

	% of total		% of total
United States	23.0	Australia	5.1
China	8.5	South Korea	4.9
Indonesia	5.2	Germany	4.1

Balance of payments, reserves and aid, $bn

Visible exports fob	351.3	Capital balance	-131.3
Visible imports fob	-209.7	Overall balance	27.7
Trade balance	141.6	Change in reserves	26.9
Invisibles inflows	203.7	Level of reserves	
Invisibles outflows	-207.6	end Dec.	99.7
Net transfers	-6.1	No. months import cover	5.7
Current account balance	131.5	Aid given	11.26
– as % of GDP	3.3	– as % of GDP	0.26

Family life

No. of households	40.7m	Divorces per 1,000 pop.	1.4
Av. no. per household	3.0	Cost of living, Sept. 1994	
Marriages per 1,000 pop.	6.0	New York = 100	221

a 1992.
b Energy trade data are distorted by transitory and oil refining activities.

KENYA

Area	582,645 sq km	Currency	Kenyan shilling (KSh)
Capital	Nairobi		

People

Population	25.4m	Life expectancy: men		53 yrs
Pop. per sq km	44		women	55 yrs
Av. ann. growth		Adult literacy		70.5%
in pop. 1985–93	3.0%	Fertility rate (per woman)		5.8%
Pop. under 15	47.4%			
Pop. over 65	2.9%			*per 1,000 pop.*
No. of men per 100 women	100	Crude birth rate		42.8
Human Development Index	43	Crude death rate		11.8

The economy

GDP	KSh389bn	GDP per head	$266
GDP	$6.7bn	GDP per head in purchasing	6
Av. ann. growth in real		power parity (USA=100)	
GDP 1985–93	3.9%		

Origins of GDP		Components of GDP	
	% of total		*% of total*
Agriculture	28.9	Private consumption	65.9
Industry, of which:	33.7	Public consumption	13.1
manufacturing	10.4	Investment	16.0
Services	37.4	Exports	41.8
		Imports	-36.8

Structure of manufacturing

	% of total		*% of total*
Agric. & food processing	40	Other	41
Textiles & clothing	9	Av. ann. increase in industrial	
Machinery & transport	10	output 1980–92	3.9%

Energy

	'000 TCE		
Total output	677	% output exported[a]	137.8
Total consumption	111	% consumption imported[a]	3,127.0
Consumption per head,			
kg coal equivalent	2,851		

Inflation and finance

Consumer price		*av. ann. increase 1989–93*	
inflation 1994	22.0%	Narrow money (M1)	22.4%
Av. ann. inflation 1989–94	23.8%	Broad money	21.4%

Exchange rates

	end 1994		*end June 1994*
KSh per $	44.84	Effective rates	1990 = 100
KSh per SDR	65.46	– nominal	...
KSh per Ecu	55.36	– real	...

Principal exports

	$m fob		$m fob
Tea	322	Petroleum products	116
Coffee	190		
Horticultural products	135	Total incl. others	**1,268**

Main export destinations

	% of total		% of total
United Kingdom	16.0	Tanzania	7.4
Uganda	8.9	Germany	7.3

Principal imports

	$m cif		$m cif
Petroleum & products	424	Motor vehicles & chassis	95
Industrial machinery	225		
Iron & steel	104	Total incl. others	**1,744**

Main origins of imports

	% of total		% of total
UAE	15.0	Japan	7.6
United Kingdom	11.9	Germany	7.1

Balance of payments, reserves and debt, $bn

Visible exports fob	1.2	Overall balance	0.5
Visible imports fob	-1.5	Change in reserves	0.4
Trade balance	-0.3	Level of reserves	
Invisibles inflows	1.1	end Dec.	0.4
Invisibles outflows	-0.9	No. months import cover	3.2
Net transfers	0.2	Foreign debt	7.0
Current account balance	0.2	– as % of GDP	135.2
– as % of GDP	2.3	Debt service	0.7
Capital balance	-0.4	Debt service ratio	28.0

Family life

No. of households	3.0m	Divorces per 1,000 pop.	...
Av. no. per household	5.1	Cost of living, Sept. 1994	
Marriages per 1,000 pop.	...	New York = 100	64

a Energy trade data are distorted by transitory and oil refining activities.

MALAYSIA

Area	332,965 sq km	Currency	Malaysian dollar/ringgit
Capital	Kuala Lumpur		(M$)

People

Population	19.0m	Life expectancy: men		70 yrs
Pop. per sq km	58		women	74 yrs
Av. ann. growth		Adult literacy		80.0%
in pop. 1985–93	2.4%	Fertility rate (per woman)		3.2
Pop. under 15	37.9%			
Pop. over 65	3.9%			*per 1,000 pop.*
No. of men per 100 women	102	Crude birth rate		25.2
Human Development Index	79	Crude death rate		4.8

The economy

GDP	M$154bn	GDP per head	$3,156
GDP	$60bn	GDP per head in purchasing	
Av. ann. growth in real		power parity (USA=100)	33
GDP 1985–93	7.4%		

Origins of GDP		Components of GDP	
	% of total		*% of total*
Agriculture	15.8	Private consumption	49.3
Industry, of which:	42.0	Public consumption	12.6
manufacturing	30.1	Investment	33.2
Services	42.2	Exports	80.3
		Imports	-75.4

Structure of manufacturing

	% of total		*% of total*
Agric. & food processing	11	Other	48
Textiles & clothing	6	Av. ann. increase in industrial	
Machinery & transport	35	output 1980–92	8.0%

Energy

	'000 TCE		
Total output	72,780	% output exported	73.0
Total consumption	33,842	% consumption imported	43.2
Consumption per head,			
kg coal equivalent	1,801		

Inflation and finance

Consumer price		*av. ann. increase 1989–93*	
inflation 1994	3.7%	Narrow money (M1)	20.7%
Av. ann. inflation 1989–94	3.6%	Broad money	19.5%

Exchange rates

	end 1994		*end June 1994*
M$ per $	2.56	Effective rates	*1990 = 100*
M$ per SDR	3.73	– nominal	96.8
M$ per Ecu	3.16	– real	97.7

Principal exports

	$bn fob		$bn fob
Electronic components	21.4	Palm oil	2.3
Petroleum & products	3.4	Textiles	2.1
Timber & products	2.9	Total incl. others	**46.0**

Main export destinations

	% of total		% of total
Singapore	21.7	United Kingdom	4.2
United States	20.3	Germany	3.7
Japan	13.0	Thailand	3.6

Principal imports

	$bn cif		$bn cif
Manufacturing supplies	15.7	Agric. products & foodstuffs	1.6
Machinery & transport		Durables & consumer goods	1.6
equipment	7.9		
Metal products	2.8	Total incl. others	**42.6**

Main origins of imports

	% of total		% of total
Japan	27.4	Taiwan	5.4
United States	16.9	Germany	3.8
Singapore	15.2	United Kingdom	3.1

Balance of payments, reserves and debt, $bn

Visible exports fob	45.9	Overall balance	11.4
Visible imports fob	-42.5	Change in reserves	9.2
Trade balance	3.4	Level of reserves	
Invisibles inflows	7.4	end Dec.	27.4
Invisibles outflows	-13.0	No. months import cover	7.7
Net transfers	0.1	Foreign debt	23.3
Current account balance	-2.1	as % of GDP	37.8
– as % of GDP	-3.5	Debt service	4.2
Capital balance	-1.9	Debt service ratio	7.9

Family life

No. households	2.5m	Divorces per 1,000 pop.	...
Av. no. per household	5.2	Cost of living, Sept. 1994	
Marriages per 1,000 pop.	3.2	New York = 100	79

MEXICO

Area	1,972,545 sq km	Currency	Mexican peso (PS)
Capital	Mexico City		

People

Population	86.7m	Life expectancy: men	69 yrs
Pop. per sq km	44	women	75 yrs
Av. ann. growth		Adult literacy	88.6%
in pop. 1985–93	1.8%	Fertility rate (per woman)	2.8
Pop. under 15	36.0%		
Pop. over 65	4.0%		*per 1,000 pop.*
No. of men per 100 women	99	Crude birth rate	24.8
Human Development Index	80	Crude death rate	5.1

The economy

GDP	1,013bn New pesos	GDP per head	$3,748
GDP	$325bn	GDP per head in purchasing	32
Av. ann. growth in real		power parity (USA=100)	
GDP 1985–93	1.6%		

Origins of GDP		Components of GDP	
	% of total		*% of total*
Agriculture	7.4	Private consumption	66.7
Industry, of which:	32.8	Public consumption	11.0
manufacturing	22.4	Investment	20.7
Services	59.8	Exports	18.8
		Imports	-17.5

Structure of manufacturing

	% of total		*% of total*
Agric. & food processing	24	Other	51
Machinery & transport	9	Av. ann. increase in industrial	
Textiles & clothing	16	output 1980–92	1.6%

Energy

	'000 TCE		
Total output	271,005	% output exported	39.8
Total consumption	166,736	% consumption imported	9.0
Consumption per head,			
kg coal equivalent	1,891		

Inflation and finance

Consumer price		*av. ann. increase 1989–93*	
inflation 1994	6.9%	Narrow money (M1)	49.2%
Av. ann. inflation 1989–94	16.7%	Broad money	38.3%

Exchange rates

	end 1994		*end June 1994*
PS per $	5.33	Effective rates	1990 = 100
PS per SDR	7.77	– nominal	...
PS per Ecu	6.58	– real	...

Principal exports

	$bn fob		$bn fob
Manufactured products	42.5	Agric. products & foodstuffs	2.5
Petroleum & products	6.4	Total incl. others	**51.8**

Main export destinations

	% of total		% of total
United States	83.0	Japan	1.3
Canada	3.0	France	0.8
Spain	1.7		

Principal imports

	$bn cif		$bn cif
Industrial supplies	46.5	Consumer goods	7.8
Capital goods	11.0	Total incl. others	**65.4**

Main origins of imports

	% of total		% of total
United States	71.1	Canada	1.8
Japan	5.2	Brazil	1.8
Germany	4.3		

Balance of payments, reserves and debt, $bn

Visible exports fob	30.0	Overall balance	7.2
Visible imports fob	-48.9	Change in reserves	7.3
Trade balance	-18.9	Level of reserves	
Invisibles inflows	17.5	end Dec.	25.1
Invisibles outflows	-24.7	No. months import cover	6.2
Net transfers	2.7	Foreign debt	118.0
Current account balance	-23.4	– as % of GDP	35.5
– as % of GDP	-7.2	Debt service	20.9
Capital balance	24.8	Debt service ratio	32.7

Family life

No. of households	16.2m	Divorces per 1,000 pop.	0.6
Av. no. per household	5.0	Cost of living, Sept. 1994	
Marriages per 1,000 pop.	7.3	New York = 100	81

MOROCCO

Area	458,730 sq km	Currency	Dirham (Dh)
Capital	Rabat		

People

Population	26.7m	Life expectancy: men	64 yrs
Pop. per sq km	60	women	68 yrs
Av. ann. growth		Adult literacy	52.5%
in pop. 1985–93	2.4%	Fertility rate (per woman)	3.1
Pop. under 15	38.7%		
Pop. over 65	3.9%		*per 1,000 pop.*
No. of men per 100 women	100	Crude birth rate	25.5
Human Development Index	55	Crude death rate	7.1

The economy

GDP	Dh260bn	GDP per head	$1,035
GDP	$28bn	GDP per head in purchasing	
Av. ann. growth in real		power parity (USA=100)	15
GDP 1985–93	2.9%		

Origins of GDP		Components of GDP	
	% of total		*% of total*
Agriculture	14.3	Private consumption	66.0
Industry, of which:	32.4	Public consumption	18.2
manufacturing	18.0	Investment	21.2
Services	53.3	Exports	22.5
		Imports	-27.9

Structure of manufacturing

	% of total		*% of total*
Agric. & food processing	32	Other	35
Textiles & clothing	23	Av. ann. increase in industrial	
Machinery & transport	10	output 1980–92	3.0%

Energy

	'000 TCE		
Total output	744	% output exported	0.0
Total consumption	10,661	% consumption imported	111.6
Consumption per head,			
kg coal equivalent	405		

Inflation and finance

Consumer price		*av. ann. increase 1989–93*	
inflation 1993	5.2%	Narrow money (M1)	11.6%
Av. ann. inflation 1989–93	5.8%	Broad money	12.3%

Exchange rates

	end 1994		*end June 1994*
Dh per $	8.96	Effective rates	*1990 = 100*
Dh per SDR	13.08	– nominal	118.5
Dh per Ecu	11.06	– real	106.6

Principal exports

	$bn fob		$bn fob
Consumer goods	1.1	Mineral ores	0.4
Agricultural products & foodstuffs	1.0	Capital goods	0.2
Semi-finished goods	0.9	Total incl. others	**3.7**

Main export destinations

	% of total		% of total
France	34.7	Italy	5.6
Germany	9.9	Japan	4.9
Spain	7.8		

Principal imports

	$bn cif		$bn cif
Industrial equipment	1.8	Energy & fuels	1.0
Semi-manufactured goods	1.5	Consumer goods	0.7
Agric. products & foodstuffs	1.0	Total incl. others	**6.1**

Main origins of imports

	% of total		% of total
France	29.9	United States	7.7
Spain	9.2	Italy	6.7
Germany	8.0		

Balance of payments, reserves and debt, $bn

Visible exports fob	3.7	Overall balance	0.1
Visible imports fob	-6.1	Change in reserves	0.2
Trade balance	-2.4	Level of reserves	
Invisibles inflows	2.6	end Dec.	3.7
Invisibles outflows	-3.0	No. months import cover	7.3
Net transfers	2.3	Foreign debt	21.4
Current account balance	-0.5	– as % of GDP	81.7
– as % of GDP	-1.9	Debt service	2.6
Capital balance	0.9	Debt service ratio	30.7

Family life

No. of households	3.4m	Divorces per 1,000 pop.	...
Av. no. per household	5.9	Cost of living, Sept. 1994	
Marriages per 1,000 pop.	...	New York = 100	75

NETHERLANDS

Area[a]	41,160 sq km	Currency	Guilder (G)
Capital	Amsterdam		

People

Population	15.3m	Life expectancy: men	75 yrs
Pop. per sq km	403	women	81 yrs
Av. ann. growth		Adult literacy	99.0%
in pop. 1985–93	0.7%	Fertility rate (per woman)	1.6
Pop. under 15	18.7%		
Pop. over 65	13.0%		*per 1,000 pop.*
No. of men per 100 women	98	Crude birth rate	12.3
Human Development Index	92	Crude death rate	8.8

The economy

GDP	Fl587bn	GDP per head	$20,707
GDP	$316bn	GDP per head in purchasing	
Av. ann. growth in real		power parity (USA=100)	76
GDP 1985–93	2.4%		

Origins of GDP[b]		Components of GDP[b]	
	% of total		*% of total*
Agriculture	4.0	Private consumption	60.1
Industry, of which:	30.0	Public consumption	14.3
manufacturing	23.9	Investment	20.5
Services	66.0	Exports	52.4
		Imports	-47.3

Structure of manufacturing

	% of total		*% of total*
Agric. & food processing	16	Other	57
Textiles & clothing	3	Av. ann. increase in industrial	
Machinery & transport	24	output 1980–89	1.1%

Energy

	'000 TCE		
Total output	104,532	% output exported[c]	108.9
Total consumption	107,951	% consumption imported[c]	121.0
Consumption per head,			
kg coal equivalent	7,122		

Inflation and finance

Consumer price		*av. ann. increase 1989–93*	
inflation 1994	2.8%	Narrow money (M1)	5.6%
Av. ann. inflation 1989–94	2.7%	Broad money	6.7%

Exchange rates

	end 1994		*end June 1994*
Fl per $	1.74	Effective rates	*1990 = 100*
Fl per SDR	2.53	– nominal	105.9
Fl per Ecu	2.15	– real	107.8

Principal exports

	$bn fob		$bn fob
Machinery & transport equipment	37.3	Fuels	11.7
		Raw materials, oils & fats	8.5
Agric. products & foodstuffs	27.0		
Chemicals & plastics	20.9	Total incl. others	**138.8**

Main export destinations

	% of total		% of total
Germany	29.1	United Kingdom	9.4
Belgium/Luxembourg	12.7	Italy	5.7
France	10.6	EU	77.1

Principal imports

	$bn cif		$bn cif
Machinery & transport equipment	43.7	Fuels	11.1
		Raw materials, oils & fats	6.4
Agric. products & foodstuffs	14.8		
Chemicals & plastics	13.5	Total incl. others	**126.3**

Main origins of imports

	% of total		% of total
Germany	23.6	United States	8.0
Belgium/Luxembourg	11.7	France	7.5
United Kingdom	10.4	EU	61.3

Balance of payments, reserves and aid, $bn

Visible exports fob	120.5	Capital balance	-16.7
Visible imports fob	-107.4	Overall balance	6.6
Trade balance	13.1	Change in reserves	6.0
Invisibles inflows	64.9	Level of reserves	
Invisibles outflows	-62.8	end Dec.	33.0
Net transfers	-5.1	No. months import cover	3.7
Current account balance	10.0	Aid given	2.53
– as % of GDP	3.2	– as % of GDP	0.82

Family life

No. of households	5.9m	Divorces per 1,000 pop.	1.8
Av. no. per household	2.5	Cost of living, Sept. 1994	
Marriages per 1,000 pop.	6.4	New York = 100	110

a   Includes water.
b   1992.
c   Energy trade data are distorted due to transitory and oil refining activities.

NEW ZEALAND

Area	265,150 sq km	Currency New Zealand dollar (NZ$)	
Capital	Wellington		

People

Population	3.5m	Life expectancy: men	73 yrs
Pop. per sq km	13	women	79 yrs
Av. ann. growth		Adult literacy	99.0%
in pop. 1985–93	0.8%	Fertility rate (per woman)	2.1
Pop. under 15	23.0%		
Pop. over 65	11.2%		*per 1,000 pop.*
No. of men per 100 women	98	Crude birth rate	16.0
Human Development Index	91	Crude death rate	8.2

The economy

GDP	NZ$83bn	GDP per head	$12,912
GDP	$45bn	GDP per head in purchasing	
Av. ann. growth in real		power parity (USA=100)	63
GDP 1985–93	0.4%		

Origins of GDP[a]		**Components of GDP**[b]	
	% of total		*% of total*
Agriculture	7.9	Private consumption	59.7
Industry, of which:	25.8	Public consumption	15.4
manufacturing	17.4	Investment	20.9
Services	66.3	Exports	30.6
		Imports	-27.7

Structure of manufacturing

	% of total		*% of total*
Agric. & food processing	27	Other	51
Textiles & clothing	8	Av. ann. increase in industrial	
Machinery & transport	14	output 1980–92	1.3%

Energy

	'000 TCE		
Total output	17,407	% output exported	11.3
Total consumption	20,507	% consumption imported	24.8
Consumption per head,			
kg coal equivalent	5,935		

Inflation and finance

Consumer price		*av. ann. increase 1989–93*	
inflation 1994	1.8%	Narrow money (M1)	13.1%
Av. ann. inflation 1989–94	3.1%	Broad money	21.7%

Exchange rates

	end 1994		*end June 1994*
NZ$ per $	1.57	Effective rates	*1990 = 100*
NZ$ per SDR	2.27	– nominal	99.2
NZ$ per Ecu	1.94	– real	93.8

Principal exports

	$bn fob		$bn fob
Meat	1.8	Wool	0.5
Dairy produce	1.6	Fruit & vegetables	0.4
Forest products	0.9		
Fish	0.6	Total incl. others	**10.5**

Main export destinations

	% of total		% of total
Australia	19.9	United States	11.6
Japan	14.6	United Kingdom	6.1

Principal imports

	$bn cif		$bn cif
Machinery & mechanical		Mineral fuels	0.6
appliances	1.5	Plastic & products	0.5
Vehicles & aircraft	1.1	Total incl. others	**8.7**

Main origins of imports

	% of total		% of total
Australia	21.3	Japan	16.2
United States	17.8	United Kingdom	5.8

Balance of payments, reserves and aid, $bn

Visible exports fob	10.5	Capital balance	-1.0
Visible imports fob	-8.7	Overall balance	-0.1
Trade balance	1.8	Change in reserves	0.3
Invisibles inflows	2.9	Level of reserves	
Invisibles outflows	-6.1	end Dec.	3.3
Net transfers	0.5	No. months import cover	4.6
Current account balance	-0.9	Aid given	0.10
– as % of GDP	-2.1	– as % of GDP	0.25

Family life

No. of households	1.2m	Divorces per 1,000 pop.	2.7
Av. no. per household	2.8	Cost of living, Sept. 1994	
Marriages per 1,000 pop.	6.8	New York = 100	83

a Year ending March 31, 1991.
b Year ending March 31, 1994.

NIGERIA

Area	923,850 sq km	Currency	Naira (N)
Capital	Abuja		

People

Population	104.9m	Life expectancy: men	51 yrs
Pop. per sq km	114	women	54 yrs
Av. ann. growth		Adult literacy	52.0%
in pop. 1985–93	2.9%	Fertility rate (per woman)	6.0
Pop. under 15	46.9%		
Pop. over 65	2.6%		*per 1,000 pop.*
No. of men per 100 women	98	Crude birth rate	42.3
Human Development Index	35	Crude death rate	13.9

The economy

GDP	N728bn	GDP per head	$315
GDP	$33bn	GDP per head in purchasing	
Av. ann. growth in real		power parity (USA=100)	6
GDP 1985–93	4.7%		

Origins of GDP		**Components of GDP**	
	% of total		*% of total*
Agriculture	35.0	Private consumption	70.5
Industry, of which:	21.2	Public consumption	10.0
manufacturing	8.5	Investment	12.8
Services	43.8	Exports	29.2
		Imports	-22.5

Structure of manufacturing

	% of total		*% of total*
Agric. & food processing	...	Other	...
Textiles & clothing	...	Av. ann. increase in industrial	
Machinery & transport	...	output 1980–92	0.2%

Energy

	'000 TCE		
Total output	137,819	% output exported	83.1
Total consumption	23,897	% consumption imported	11.3
Consumption per head,			
kg coal equivalent	207		

Inflation and finance

Consumer price		*av. ann. increase 1989–91*	
inflation 1994	150%	Narrow money (M1)	36.9%
Av. ann. inflation 1989–94	47.7%	Broad money	28.7%

Exchange rates

	end 1994		*end June 1994*
N per $	22.00	Effective rates	*1990 = 100*
N per SDR	32.11	– nominal	54.9
N per Ecu	27.16	– real	131.0

Principal exports

	$bn fob		$bn fob
Petroleum	9.7		
Cocoa beans & products	0.1	Total incl. others	**10.6**

Main export destinations

	% of total		% of total
United States	44.1	France	5.9
Germany	6.8	India	5.9
Spain	6.0		

Principal imports

	$bn cif		$bn cif
Machinery & transport equipment	3.2	Agric products & foodstuffs	0.6
Manufactured goods	1.8		
Chemicals	1.3	Total incl. others	7.5

Main origins of imports

	% of total		% of total
United Kingdom	14.0	France	8.3
United States	13.1	Japan	7.3
Germany	10.1		

Balance of payments[a], reserves and debt, $bn

Visible exports fob	11.8	Overall balance	-3.7
Visible imports fob	-7.2	Change in reserves	-3.5
Trade balance	4.6	Level of reserves	
Invisibles inflows	1.2	end Dec.	1.4
Invisibles outflows	-4.3	No. months import cover	2.3
Net transfers	0.8	Foreign debt	32.5
Current account balance	2.3	– as % of GDP	100.7
– as % of GDP	6.9	Debt service	1.8
Capital balance	-2.1	Debt service ratio	29.4

Family life

No. households	...	Divorces per 1,000 pop.	...
Av. no. per household	...	Cost of living, Sept. 1994	
Marriages per 1,000 pop.	...	New York = 100	119

a 1992.

NORWAY

Area	323,895 sq km	Currency	Norwegian krone (Nkr)
Capital	Oslo		

People

Population	4.3m	Life expectancy: men		74 yrs
Pop. per sq km	13	women		81 yrs
Av. ann. growth		Adult literacy		99.0%
in pop. 1985–93	0.5%	Fertility rate (per woman)		2.0
Pop. under 15	19.7%			
Pop. over 65	15.9%			*per 1,000 pop.*
No. of men per 100 women	98	Crude birth rate		14.2
Human Development Index	93	Crude death rate		10.8

The economy

GDP	Nkr809bn	GDP per head	$26,340
GDP	$114bn	GDP per head in purchasing	
Av. ann. growth in real		power parity (USA=100)	78
GDP 1985–93	1.9%		

Origins of GDP[a]		Components of GDP	
	% of total		*% of total*
Agriculture	2.8	Private consumption	51.8
Industry, of which:	32.7	Public consumption	22.1
manufacturing	13.5	Investment	18.5
Services	64.5	Exports	43.4
		Imports	-35.8

Structure of manufacturing

	% of total		*% of total*
Agric. & food processing	22	Other	50
Textiles & clothing	2	Av. ann. increase in industrial	
Machinery & transport	26	output 1980–92	5.3%

Energy

	'000 TCE		
Total output	206,215	% output exported	86.8
Total consumption	28,814	% consumption imported	19.0
Consumption per head,			
kg coal equivalent	6,713		

Inflation and finance

			av. ann. increase 1989–93
Consumer price			
inflation 1994	1.4%	Narrow money (M1)	12.1%
Av. ann. inflation 1989–94	3.0%	Broad money	6.3%

Exchange rates

	end 1994		*end June 1994*
Nkr per $	6.76	Effective rates	*1990 = 100*
Nkr per SDR	9.87	– nominal	97.0
Nkr per Ecu	8.35	– real	96.1

Principal exports[a]

	$bn fob		$bn fob
Oil, gas & products	17.6	Fish & fish products	2.3
Non-ferrous metals	2.4	Iron & steel	2.2
Machinery incl.		Ships & oil platforms	1.9
electricals	2.4	Total incl. others	**35.2**

Main export destinations

	% of total		% of total
United Kingdom	24.6	Netherlands	8.5
Germany	13.0	France	7.9
Sweden	8.7		

Principal imports[a]

	$bn cif		$bn cif
Machinery incl.		Clothing	1.4
electricals	6.3	Iron & steel	1.2
Transport equipment		Ships & oil platforms	0.9
excl.ships	2.4		
Food, drink & tobacco	1.6	Total incl. others	**27.8**

Main origins of imports

	% of total		% of total
Sweden	14.1	United States	8.1
Germany	13.5	Denmark	7.4
United Kingdom	9.1		

Balance of payments, reserves and aid, $bn

Visible exports fob	32.0	Capital balance	-0.8
Visible imports fob	-24.0	Overall balance	7.7
Trade balance	8.0	Change in reserves	-1.3
Invisibles inflows	15.3	Level of reserves	
Invisibles outflows	-19.4	end Dec.	19.7
Net transfers	-1.4	No. months import cover	9.9
Current account balance	2.5	Aid given	1.01
– as % of GDP	2.2	– as % of GDP	1.01

Family life

No. households	1.8m	Divorces per 1,000 pop.	2.4
Av. no. per household	2.4	Cost of living, Sept. 1994	
Marriages per 1,000 pop.	4.7	New York = 100	137

a 1992.

PAKISTAN

Area	803,940 sq km	Currency	Pakistan rupee (PRs)
Capital	Islamabad		

People

Population	122.8m	Life expectancy: men		63 yrs
Pop. per sq km	154	women		65 yrs
Av. ann. growth		Adult literacy		36.4%
in pop. 1985–93	3.1%	Fertility rate (per woman)		5.6
Pop. under 15	43.6%			
Pop. over 65	2.9%			*per 1,000 pop.*
No. of men per 100 women	108	Crude birth rate		37.3
Human Development Index	39	Crude death rate		7.8

The economy

GDP	PRs1,490bn	GDP per head	$434
GDP	$53bn	GDP per head in purchasing	
Av. ann. growth in real		power parity (USA=100)	9
GDP 1985–93	5.5%		

Origins of GDP[a]		Components of GDP[a]	
	% of total		*% of total*
Agriculture	24.1	Private consumption	72.1
Industry, of which:	28.2	Public consumption	13.0
manufacturing	18.2	Investment	20.7
Services	47.7	Exports	16.2
		Imports	-22.0

Structure of manufacturing

	% of total		*% of total*
Agric. & food processing	29	Other	45
Textiles & clothing	19	Av. ann. increase in industrial	
Machinery & transport	7	output 1980–92	7.3%

Energy

	'000 TCE		
Total output	26,267	% output exported	2.5
Total consumption	37,248	% consumption imported	36.3
Consumption per head,			
kg coal equivalent	299		

Inflation and finance

			av. ann. increase 1989–93
Consumer price			
inflation 1994	12.5%	Narrow money (M1)	15.1%
Av. ann. inflation 1989–94	10.0%	Broad money	16.0%

Exchange rates

	end 1994		*end June 1994*
PRs per $	30.76	Effective rates	*1990 = 100*
PRs per SDR	44.90	– nominal	...
PRs per Ecu	37.98	– real	...

Principal exports[b]

	$bn fob		$bn fob
Cotton yarn	1.2	Raw cotton	0.4
Clothing	0.8	Rice	0.4
Cotton fabrics	0.7	Total incl. others	**6.2**

Main export destinations[b]

	% of total		% of total
United States	10.8	United Kingdom	7.3
Germany	8.9	Hong Kong	6.3
Japan	8.3	South Korea	3.9

Principal imports[b]

	$bn cif		$bn cif
Petroleum & products	1.7	Transport equipment	0.4
Non-electrical machinery	1.4		
Chemicals	0.7	Total incl. others	**7.6**

Main origins of imports[b]

	% of total		% of total
Japan	13.0	Saudi Arabia	6.3
United States	11.8	United Kingdom	4.9
Germany	7.3	UAE	3.0

Balance of payments, reserves and debt, $bn

Visible exports fob	6.7	Overall balance	0.4
Visible imports fob	-9.3	Change in reserves	0.4
Trade balance	-2.6	Level of reserves	
Invisibles inflows	1.6	end Dec.	1.3
Invisibles outflows	-4.2	No. months import cover	1.7
Net transfers	2.3	Foreign debt	26.1
Current account balance[c]	-2.9	– as % of GDP	49.7
– as % of GDP[c]	-5.5	Debt service	2.5
Capital balance	3.0	Debt service ratio	24.7

Family life

No. households	12.6m	Divorces per 1,000 pop.	...
Av. no. per household	6.7	Cost of living, Sept. 1994	
Marriages per 1,000 pop.	...	New York = 100	54

a Fiscal year ending June 30, 1993.
b Fiscal year ending June 30, 1991.
c 1992 estimates.

PERU

Area	1,285,215 sq km	Currency	Nuevo Sol (New Sol)
Capital	Lima		

People

Population	22.8m	Life expectancy: men	66 yrs
Pop. per sq km	18	women	69 yrs
Av. ann. growth		Adult literacy[a]	86.2%
in pop. 1985–93	2.1%	Fertility rate (per woman)	3.1
Pop. under 15	35.5%		
Pop. over 65	4.1%		per 1,000 pop.
No. of men per 100 women	101	Crude birth rate	25.7
Human Development Index	64	Crude death rate	6.5

The economy

GDP	New Soles 67.6bn	GDP per head	$1,493
GDP	$34bn	GDP per head in purchasing	
Av. ann. growth in real		power parity (USA=100)	14
GDP 1985–93	-0.2%		

Origins of GDP[b]		Components of GDP	
	% of total		% of total
Agriculture	13.6	Private consumption	78.1
Industry, of which:	39.4	Public consumption	6.5
manufacturing	22.3	Investment	18.5
Services	47.0	Exports	10.6
		Imports	-13.7

Structure of manufacturing

	% of total		% of total
Agric. & food processing	23	Other	53
Textiles & clothing	14	Av. ann. increase in industrial	
Machinery & transport	10	output 1980–92	-0.5%

Energy

	'000 TCE		
Total output	10,828	% output exported	28.9
Total consumption	10,870	% consumption imported	31.9
Consumption per head,			
kg coal equivalent	484		

Inflation and finance

Consumer price		av. ann. increase 1989–92	
inflation 1994	21%	Narrow money (M1)	866%
Av. ann. inflation 1989–94	490%	Broad money	1,028%

Exchange rates

	end 1994		end June 1994
New Soles per $	2.18	Effective rates	1990 = 100
New Soles per SDR	3.18	– nominal	...
New Soles per Ecu	2.70	– real	...

Principal exports

	$bn fob		$bn fob
Non-traditional products	1.1	Gold	0.2
Copper	0.7	Petroleum & products	0.2
Fishmeal	0.5		
Zinc	0.3	Total incl. others	**3.5**

Main export destinations

	% of total		% of total
United States	20.9	Germany	6.2
Japan	9.2	Italy	4.8
United Kingdom	8.5		

Principal imports

	$bn fob		$bn fob
Industrial supplies	1.8	Consumer goods	0.9
Capital goods	1.1	Total incl. others	**4.0**

Main origins of imports

	% of total		% of total
United States	27.6	Argentina	6.4
Japan	7.6	Brazil	6.2

Balance of payments, reserves and debt, $bn

Visible exports fob	3.5	Overall balance	0.4
Visible imports fob	-4.0	Change in reserves	0.4
Trade balance	-0.5	Level of reserves	
Invisibles inflows	1.0	end Dec.	3.5
Invisibles outflows	-2.7	No. months import cover	10.5
Net transfers	0.4	Foreign debt	20.3
Current account balance	-1.8	– as % of GDP	51.6
– as % of GDP	-5.3	Debt service	2.8
Capital balance	0.7	Debt service ratio	63.7

Family life

No. of households	4.2m	Divorces per 1,000 pop.	...
Av. no. per household	5.1	Cost of living, Sept. 1994	
Marriages per 1,000 pop.	6.0	New York = 100	70

a Excluding indigenous jungle population.
b 1991.

PHILIPPINES

Area	300,000 sq km	Currency	Philippine peso (P)
Capital	Manila		

People

Population	65.8m	Life expectancy: men	67 yrs
Pop. per sq km	219	women	70 yrs
Av. ann. growth		Adult literacy	90.4%
in pop. 1985–93	2.3%	Fertility rate (per woman)	3.6
Pop. under 15	38.4%		
Pop. over 65	3.3%		*per 1,000 pop.*
No. of men per 100 women	103	Crude birth rate	28.0
Human Development Index	62	Crude death rate	5.7

The economy

GDP	P1,492bn	GDP per head	$830
GDP	$55bn	GDP per head in purchasing	
Av. ann. growth in real		power parity (USA=100)	11
GDP 1985–93	3.1%		

Origins of GDP[a]		Components of GDP	
	% of total		*% of total*
Agriculture	22.5	Private consumption	76.2
Industry, of which:	34.9	Public consumption	8.1
manufacturing	25.3	Investment	24.2
Services	42.6	Exports	31.1
		Imports	-39.2

Structure of manufacturing

	% of total		*% of total*
Agric. & food processing	36	Other	45
Textiles & clothing	11	Av. ann. increase in industrial	
Machinery & transport	8	output 1980–92	-0.2%

Energy

	'000 TCE		
Total output	9,232	% output exported	6.2
Total consumption	26,346	% consumption imported	83.2
Consumption per head,			
kg coal equivalent	404		

Inflation and finance

Consumer price		*av. ann. increase 1989–93*	
inflation 1994	9.1%	Narrow money (M1)	17.9%
Av. ann. inflation 1989–94	11.7%	Broad money	22.7%

Exchange rates

	end 1994		*end June 1994*
P per $	24.42	Effective rates	*1990 = 100*
P per SDR	38.15	– nominal	83.6
P per Ecu	30.15	– real	112.1

Principal exports[a]

	$bn fob		$bn fob
Electrical & electronic		Copper	0.4
equipment	2.7	Fish & products	0.3
Clothing	2.1		
Coconut products	0.6	Total incl. others	**9.8**

Main export destinations

	% of total		% of total
United States	38.3	Hong Kong	4.8
Japan	16.3	United Kingdom	4.5
Germany	5.1	Singapore	3.4

Principal imports[a]

	$bn cif		$bn cif
Raw materials		Crude oil	1.6
& intermediaries	6.7		
Capital goods	4.0	Total incl. others	**14.5**

Main origins of imports

	% of total		% of total
Japan	22.8	Hong Kong	5.4
United States	19.8	South Korea	4.6
Singapore	5.7	Saudi Arabia	4.3
Taiwan	5.7		

Balance of payments, reserves and debt, $bn

Visible exports fob	11.4	Overall balance	0.3
Visible imports fob	-17.6	Change in reserves	0.7
Trade balance	-6.2	Level of reserves	
Invisibles inflows	7.5	end Dec.	4.8
Invisibles outflows	-5.3	No. months import cover	3.3
Net transfers	0.7	Foreign debt	35.3
Current account balance	-3.3	– as % of GDP	63.7
– as % of GDP	-6.0	Debt service	4.8
Capital balance	3.0	Debt service ratio	24.9

Family life

No. of households	11.4m	Divorces per 1,000 pop.	...
Av. no. per household	5.3	Cost of living, Sept. 1994	
Marriages per 1,000 pop.	6.0	New York = 100	65

a 1992.

POLAND

Area	312,685 sq km	Currency	Zloty (Zl)
Capital	Warsaw		

People

Population	38.5m	Life expectancy: men	67 yrs
Pop. per sq km	124	women	76 yrs
Av. ann. growth		Adult literacy	99.0%
in pop. 1985–93	0.4%	Fertility rate (per woman)	1.9
Pop. under 15	23.5%		
Pop. over 65	10.9%		*per 1,000 pop.*
No. of men per 100 women	95	Crude birth rate	13.5
Human Development Index	82	Crude death rate	10.7

The economy

GDP	Zl1,576,005bn	GDP per head	$2,271
GDP	$87bn	GDP per head in purchasing	
Av. ann. growth in real		power parity (USA=100)	20
GDP 1985–93	-0.5%		

Origins of GDP[a]		Components of GDP[a]	
	% of total		*% of total*
Agriculture	7.3	Private consumption	57.1
Industry, of which:	50.8	Public consumption	20.8
manufacturing	...	Accumulation	22.1
Services	41.9	Exports	...
		Imports	...

Structure of manufacturing

	% of total		*% of total*
Agric. & food processing	21	Other	44
Textiles & clothing	9	Av. ann. increase in industrial	
Machinery & transport	26	output 1980–90	...

Energy

	'000 TCE		
Total output	128,842	% output exported	16.1
Total consumption	133,828	% consumption imported	22.0
Consumption per head,			
kg coal equivalent	3,484		

Inflation and finance

Consumer price		*av. ann. increase 1989–93*	
inflation 1994	32.0%	Narrow money (M1)	113.8%
Av. ann. inflation 1989–94	117.1%	Broad money	125.8%

Exchange rates

	end 1994		*end June 1994*
Zl per $	24,372	Effective rates	*1990 = 100*
Zl per SDR	35,579	– nominal	59.7
Zl per Ecu	36,089	– real	165.2

Principal exports[a]

	$bn fob		$bn fob
Machinery	3.2	Copper	0.8
Chemicals	1.6	Steel	0.7
Food & agric. products	1.3	Total incl. others	**13.2**

Main export destinations

	% of total		% of total
Germany	36.3	United Kingdom	4.3
Netherlands	5.9	France	4.2
Ex-Soviet Union	7.6	United States	2.9
Italy	5.2		

Principal imports[a]

	$bn fob		$bn fob
Machinery	5.7	Light industry	0.7
Chemicals	2.8	Metals	0.7
Oil	2.7		
Food & agric. products	1.4	Total incl. others	**16.1**

Main origins of imports

	% of total		% of total
Germany	28.0	United States	5.1
Ex-Soviet Union	9.1	Netherlands	4.7
Italy	7.8	France	4.2
United Kingdom	5.8		

Balance of payments, reserves and debt, $bn

Visible exports fob	13.6	Overall balance	-0.1
Visible imports fob	-17.1	Change in reserves	0.1
Trade balance	-3.5	Level of reserves	
Invisibles inflows	4.8	end Dec.	4.1
Invisibles outflows	-7.8	No. months import cover	2.9
Net transfers	2.9	Foreign debt	45.3
Current account balance	-5.8	– as % of GDP	52.7
– as % of GDP	-6.6	Debt service	1.7
Capital balance	3.8	Debt service ratio	10.6

Family life

No. of households	12.0m	Divorces per 1,000 pop.	0.8
Av. no. per household	3.1	Cost of living, Sept. 1994	
Marriages per 1,000 pop.	5.7	New York = 100	63

a 1992.

PORTUGAL

Area	91,630 sq km	Currency	Escudo (Esc)
Capital	Lisbon		

People

Population	9.9m	Life expectancy: men	72 yrs
Pop. per sq km	107	women	79 yrs
Av. ann. growth		Adult literacy	86.2%
in pop. 1985–93	-0.6%	Fertility rate (per woman)	1.6
Pop. under 15	18.5%		
Pop. over 65	14.2%		*per 1,000 pop.*
No. of men per 100 women	93	Crude birth rate	11.8
Human Development Index	84	Crude death rate	10.5

The economy

GDP	Esc12,542bn	GDP per head	$7,893
GDP	$78bn	GDP per head in purchasing	
Av. ann. growth in real		power parity (USA=100)	43
GDP 1985–93	3.0%		

Origins of GDP		Components of GDP	
	% of total		*% of total*
Agriculture	5.0	Private consumption	66.9
Industry, of which:	38.8	Public consumption	18.9
manufacturing	28.6	Investment	26.7
Services	56.2	Exports	23.3
		Imports	-35.8

Structure of manufacturing

	% of total		*% of total*
Agric. & food processing	18	Other	49
Textiles & clothing	19	Av. ann. increase in industrial	
Machinery & transport	14	output 1980–90	...

Energy

	'000 TCE		
Total output	759	% output exported[a]	586.0
Total consumption	20,827	% consumption imported[a]	130.0
Consumption per head,			
kg coal equivalent	2,111		

Inflation and finance

Consumer price		*av. ann. increase 1989–93*	
inflation 1994	5.2%	Narrow money (M1)	14.6%
Av. ann. inflation 1989–94	9.6%	Broad money	17.5%

Exchange rates

	end 1994		*end June 1994*
Esc per $	159.1	Effective rates	*1990 = 100*
Esc per SDR	232.3	– nominal	91.7
Esc per Ecu	196.4	– real	109.0

Principal exports

	$bn fob		$bn fob
Textiles & clothing	5.9	Food products	1.1
Machinery & transport equipment	3.2	Chemicals & plastics	0.9
Forestry products	1.6	Total incl. others	**15.4**

Main export destinations

	% of total		% of total
Germany	19.7	Netherlands	5.2
France	15.3	United States	4.3
Spain	14.4	EU	75.5
United Kingdom	11.4	Efta	7.8

Principal imports

	$bn cif		$bn cif
Machinery & transport equipment	8.7	Textiles & clothing	2.6
		Energy & fuels	2.1
Food products	3.3		
Chemicals & plastics	2.9	Total incl. others	**24.3**

Main origins of imports

	% of total		% of total
Spain	17.8	United Kingdom	7.5
Germany	15.0	Netherlands	4.9
France	13.0	EU	72.1
Italy	8.7	Opec	6.1

Balance of payments, reserves and debt, $bn

Visible exports fob	15.4	Overall balance	-2.8
Visible imports fob	-22.3	Change in reserves	-3.3
Trade balance	-6.9	Level of reserves	
Invisibles inflows	9.1	end Dec.	16.6
Invisibles outflows	-8.0	No. months import cover	8.9
Net transfers	6.7	Foreign debt	36.9
Current account balance	0.9	– as % of GDP	49.8
– as % of GDP	1.2	Debt service	5.6
Capital balance	-0.8	Debt service ratio	18.4

Family life

No. of households	3.4m	Divorces per 1,000 pop.	1.1
Av. no. per household	2.9	Cost of living, Sept. 1994	
Marriages per 1,000 pop.	7.3	New York = 100	87

a Energy trade data are distorted by transitory and oil refining activities.

ROMANIA

Area	237,500 sq km	Currency	Leu (L)
Capital	Bucharest		

People

Population	22.8m	Life expectancy: men	67 yrs
Pop. per sq km	99	women	73 yrs
Av. ann. growth		Adult literacy	96.9%
in pop. 1985–93	nil	Fertility rate (per woman)	1.5
Pop. under 15	22.3%		
Pop. over 65	11.3%		*per 1,000 pop.*
No. of men per 100 women	98	Crude birth rate	11.6
Human Development Index	73	Crude death rate	11.5

The economy

GDP	L19,001bn	GDP per head	$1,117
GDP	$25bn	GDP per head in purchasing	
Av. ann. growth in real		power parity (USA=100)	16
GDP 1985–93	-4.8%		

Origins of GDP		Components of GDP	
	% of total		*% of total*
Agriculture	23.7	Private consumption	63.7
Industry, of which:	44.4	Public consumption	14.6
manufacturing	...	Investment	27.5
Services	31.9	Net exports of goods &	
		services	-5.8

Structure of manufacturing

	% of total		*% of total*
Agric. & food processing	14	Other	46
Textiles & clothing	18	Av. ann. increase in industrial	
Machinery & transport	22	output 1980–92	-2.6%

Energy

	'000 TCE		
Total output	46,161	% output exported	7.1
Total consumption	63,035	% consumption imported	36.5
Consumption per head,			
kg coal equivalent	2,702		

Inflation and finance

Consumer price		*av. ann. increase 1989–93*	
inflation 1994	137%	Narrow money (M1)	55.1%
Av. ann. inflation 1989–94	112%	Broad money	51.9%

Exchange rates

	end 1994		*end June 1994*
L per $	1,767.0	Effective rates	1990 = 100
L per SDR	2,579.6	– nominal	...
L per Ecu	2,181.5	– real	...

Principal exports

	$bn fob		$bn fob
Basic metals & products	1.0	Oil products	0.6
Textiles & footwear	1.0		
Machinery & equipment	0.8	Total incl. others	**4.9**

Main export destinations

	% of total		% of total
Germany	13.9	Turkey	5.9
China	9.1	Netherlands	4.6
Italy	7.9	France	4.5

Principal imports

	$bn cif		$bn cif
Fuels, minerals & metals	1.7	Chemicals	0.7
Machinery & equipment	1.3		
Food products	0.8	Total incl. others	**6.0**

Main origins of imports

	% of total		% of total
Germany	15.9	France	8.3
Russia	12.7	Iran	8.3
Italy	9.5		

Balance of payments, reserves and debt, $bn

Visible exports fob	4.9	Overall balance	-0.1
Visible imports fob	-6.0	Change in reserves	0.2
Trade balance	-1.1	Level of reserves	
Invisibles inflows	0.9	end Dec.	1.1
Invisibles outflows	-1.1	No. months import cover	2.2
Net transfers	0.2	Foreign debt	4.5
Current account balance	-1.2	– as % of GDP	18.1
– as % of GDP	-4.6	Debt service	0.4
Capital balance	1.0	Debt service ratio	6.2

Family life

No. of households	7.3m	Divorces per 1,000 pop.	1.3
Av. no. per household	3.1	Cost of living, Sept. 1994	
Marriages per 1,000 pop.	7.5	New York = 100	56

RUSSIA[a]

Area	17,078,005 sq km	Currency	Rouble (Rb)
Capital	Moscow		

People

Population	148.5m	Life expectancy: men	62 yrs
Pop. per sq km	9	women	74 yrs
Av. ann. growth		Adult literacy	98.7%
in pop. 1985–93	0.4%	Fertility rate (per woman)	1.5
Pop. under 15	22.8%		
Pop. over 65	10.0%		*per 1,000 pop.*
No. of men per 100 women[b]	88	Crude birth rate	10.8
Human Development Index	86	Crude death rate	13.0

The economy

GDP	Rb324,420bn	GDP per head	$2,346
GDP	$348bn	GDP per head in purchasing	
Av. ann. growth in real		power parity (USA=100)	31
GDP 1987–93	-6.7%		

Origins of NMP[c]		Components of GDP[c]	
	% of total		*% of total*
Agriculture	13.4	Private consumption	44.4
Industry, of which:	59.5	Public consumption	16.7
manufacturing	...	Investment	42.9
Services	26.8	Foreign trade balance	0.3

Structure of manufacturing

	% of total		*% of total*
Agric. & food processing	...	Other	...
Textiles & clothing	...	Av. ann. increase in industrial	
Machinery & transport	...	output 1980–88	3.9%

Energy

	'000 TCE		
Total output	1,603,528	% output exported	30.0
Total consumption	1,096,235	% consumption imported	5.5
Consumption per head,			
kg coal equivalent	7,357		

Inflation and finance

Consumer price		*av. ann. increase 1988–92*	
inflation 1994	307%	Narrow money (M1)	...
Av. ann. inflation 1991–94	177.9%	Broad money	...

Exchange rates

	end 1994		*end June 1994*
Rb per $	3,550	Effective rates	1990 = 100
Rb per SDR	5,183	– nominal	...
Rb per Ecu	4,366	– real	...

Principal exports[e]

	$ bn		$ bn
Fuels & raw materials	31.0	Timber & paper	1.9
Machinery & equipment	2.9	Food	1.8
Chemicals & rubber	2.7	Total incl. others	**44.3**

Main export destinations[e]

	% of total		% of total
Western countries	65.2	Developing countries	11.9
Former Comecon[f]	14.4	Others	8.5

Principal imports[e]

	$ bn		$ bn
Machinery & equipment	11.2	Fuels & raw materials	2.4
Food products	7.3	Chemicals & rubber	2.0
Textiles	5.4	Total incl. others	**33.0**

Main origins of imports[e]

	% of total		% of total
Western countries	67.4	Former Comecon[f]	9.0
Developing countries	14.1	Others	9.5

Balance of payments, reserves and debt, $bn

Visible exports fob	44.3	Overall balance	...
Visible imports fob	-33.0	Change in reserves	...
Trade balance	11.3	Level of reserves	
Invisibles inflows	...	end Dec.	
Invisibles outflows	...	No. months import cover	...
Net transfers	...	Foreign debt	83.1
Current account balance	6.2	– as % of GDP	...
– as % of GDP	3.6	Debt service	2.3
Capital balance	...	Debt service ratio	...

Family life

No. of households	40.5m	Divorces per 1,000 pop.	4.0
Av. no. per household	2.9	Cost of living, Sept.1994	
Marriages per 1,000 pop.	8.6	New York = 100	114

a For selected data on Ukraine and other ex-Soviet republics, see pages 202–203.
b 1990.
c 1991.
d Moscow Interbank Currency Exchange rate.
e Outside ex-Soviet Union only.
f The Council for Mutual Economic Assistance whose members included the Soviet Union and the countries of Eastern Europe was the communist world's version of the European Economic Community. It dissolved in 1991.

SAUDI ARABIA

Area	2,400,900 sq km	Currency	Riyal (SR)
Capital	Riyadh		

People

Population	17.4m	Life expectancy: men	70 yrs
Pop. per sq km	8	women	73 yrs
Av. ann. growth		Adult literacy	64.1%
in pop. 1985–93	4.4%	Fertility rate (per woman)	5.9
Pop. under 15	42.0%		
Pop. over 65	2.7%		*per 1,000 pop.*
No. of men per 100 women	124	Crude birth rate	34.7
Human Development Index	74	Crude death rate	4.2

The economy

GDP	SR453bn	GDP per head	$6,958
GDP	$121bn	GDP per head in purchasing	
Av. ann. growth in real		power parity (USA=100)	49
GDP 1985–93	4.1%		

Origins of GDP[a]		Components of GDP[b]	
	% of total		*% of total*
Agriculture	7.3	Private consumption	38.3
Industry, of which:	45.5	Public consumption	36.6
manufacturing	8.1	Investment	24.4
Services	44.2	Exports	39.5
		Imports	-38.9

Structure of manufacturing

	% of total		*% of total*
Agric. & food processing	7	Other	88
Textiles & clothing	1	Av. ann. increase in industrial	
Machinery & transport	4	output 1980–92	-2.9%

Energy

	'000 TCE		
Total output	674,087	% output exported	79.5
Total consumption	97,082	% consumption imported	0.0
Consumption per head,			
kg coal equivalent	6,097		

Inflation and finance

Consumer price		*av. ann. increase 1989–93*	
inflation 1994	1.0%	Narrow money (M1)	6.1%
Av. ann. inflation 1989–94	1.7%	Broad money	4.3%

Exchange rates

	end 1994		*end June 1994*
SR per $	3.75	Effective rates	*1990 = 100*
SR per SDR	5.47	– nominal	97.3
SR per Ecu	4.63	– real	91.9

Principal exports[c]

	$bn fob		$bn fob
Crude oil & refined		Petrochemicals	2.4
petroleum	43.7	Total incl. others	**48.2**

Main export destinations

	% of total		% of total
Japan	17.1	Singapore	5.7
United States	16.2	France	5.2
South Korea	8.2	United Kingdom	3.7

Principal imports[c]

	$bn cif		$bn cif
Transport equipment	7.0	Agric. products & foodstuffs	3.6
Consumer goods	5.2	Building materials	3.3
Machinery & equipment	4.6	Total incl. others	**29.1**

Main origins of imports

	% of total		% of total
United States	20.6	Germany	7.2
Japan	12.7	Italy	6.3
United Kingdom	8.5	France	4.3

Balance of payments, reserves and debt, $bn

Visible exports fob	44.9	Overall balance	1.5
Visible imports fob	-25.9	Change in reserves	1.5
Trade balance	19.0	Level of reserves	
Invisibles inflows	9.7	end Dec.	7.7
Invisibles outflows	-26.3	No. months import cover	3.6
Net transfers	-16.7	Foreign debt	20.0
Current account balance	-14.2	– as % of GDP	16.0
– as % of GDP	-11.8	Debt service	2.4
Capital balance	14.2	Debt service ratio	4.5

Family life

No. of households	...	Divorces per 1,000 pop.	...
Av. no. per household	...	Cost of living, Sept. 1994	
Marriages per 1,000 pop.	...	New York = 100	75

a   1989.
b   1992.
c   1991.

SINGAPORE

Area	616 sq km	Currency	Singapore dollar (S$)
Capital	Singapore		

People

Population	2.9m	Life expectancy: men	74 yrs
Pop. per sq km	4,617	women	79 yrs
Av. ann. growth		Adult literacy	92.0%
in pop. 1985–93	1.9%	Fertility rate (per woman)	1.7
Pop. under 15	22.7%		
Pop. over 65	6.4%		*per 1,000 pop.*
No. of men per 100 women	103	Crude birth rate	13.9
Human Development Index	84	Crude death rate	5.7

The economy

GDP	S$89bn	GDP per head	$19,293
GDP	$55bn	GDP per head in purchasing	
Av. ann. growth in real		power parity (USA=100)	67
GDP 1985–93	7.8%		

Origins of GDP		Components of GDP	
	% of total		*% of total*
Agriculture	0.2	Private consumption	42.7
Industry, of which:	36.6	Public consumption	9.3
manufacturing	27.5	Investment	43.8
Services	62.1	Exports less imports	3.5

Structure of manufacturing

	% of total		*% of total*
Agric. & food processing	4	Other	41
Textiles & clothing	3	Av. ann. increase in industrial	
Machinery & transport	52	output 1980–92	6.0%

Energy

	'000 TCE		
Total output	...	% output exported	...
Total consumption	23,545	% consumption imported[a]	404.2
Consumption per head,			
kg coal equivalent	8,503		

Inflation and finance

Consumer price		*av. ann. increase 1989–93*	
inflation 1994	3.6%	Narrow money (M1)	12.4%
Av. ann. inflation 1989–94	2.9%	Broad money	15.2%

Exchange rates

	end 1994		*end June 1994*
S$ per $	1.46	Effective rates	*1990 = 100*
S$ per SDR	2.13	– nominal	111.5
S$ per Ecu	1.80	– real	...

Principal exports

	$bn fob		$bn fob
Machinery & equipment	43.3	Agric. products & foodstuffs	1.8
Minerals & fuels	9.1	Crude materials	1.3
Chemicals	4.8		
Manufactured products	4.8	Total incl. others	**74.2**

Main export destinations

	% of total		% of total
United States	20.3	Thailand	5.7
Malaysia	14.2	Germany	3.9
Hong Kong	8.6	United Kingdom	2.9
Japan	7.4		

Principal imports

	$bn cif		$bn cif
Machinery & equipment	44.7	Agric. products & foodstuffs	3.1
Manufactured products	9.9	Crude minerals	1.2
Mineral fuels	9.3		
Chemicals	6.0	Total incl. others	**85.5**

Main origins of imports

	% of total		% of total
Japan	21.9	Taiwan	3.9
Malaysia	16.5	Saudi Arabia	3.9
United States	16.2	South Korea	3.2
Thailand	4.1		

Balance of payments, reserves and debt, $bn

Visible exports fob	72.0	Overall balance	7.6
Visible imports fob	-80.0	Change in reserves	8.5
Trade balance	-8.0	Level of reserves	
Invisibles inflows	30.0	end Dec.	48.4
Invisibles outflows	-19.2	No. months import cover	7.3
Net transfers	-0.7	Foreign debt	5.5
Current account balance	2.0	– as % of GDP	10.0
– as % of GDP	3.7	Debt service	0.6
Capital balance	1.9	Debt service ratio	0.6

Family life

No. of households	0.6m	Divorces per 1,000 pop.	1.3
Av. no. per household	4.6	Cost of living, Sept. 1994	
Marriages per 1,000 pop.	9.3	New York = 100	113

a Energy trade data are distorted by transitory and oil refining activities.

SLOVAKIA

Area	49,035 sq km	Currency	Koruna (Kc)
Capital	Bratislava		

People

Population	5.4m	Life expectancy: men	67 yrs
Pop. per sq km	108	women	75 yrs
Av. ann. growth		Adult literacy	...
in pop. 1985–93	0.4%	Fertility rate (per woman)	1.9
Pop. under 15	...		
Pop. over 65	...		*per 1,000 pop.*
No. of men per 100 women	...	Crude birth rate	14.8
Human Development Index[a]	87	Crude death rate	10.6

The economy

GDP	Kc308bn	GDP per head	$1,896
GDP	$10bn	GDP per head in purchasing	
Av. ann. growth in real		power parity (USA=100)	...
GDP 1992–93	-4.1%		

Origins of GDP[b]		Components of GDP	
	% of total		*% of total*
Agriculture	5.7	Private consumption	...
Industry, of which:	60.1	Public consumption	...
manufacturing	52.7	Investment	...
Services	34.2	Exports	...
		Imports	...

Structure of manufacturing

	% of total		*% of total*
Agric. & food processing	...	Other	...
Textiles & clothing	...	Av. ann. increase in industrial	
Machinery & transport	...	output 1980–92	...

Energy

	'000 TCE		
Total output	6,643	% output exported	0.0
Total consumption	22,648	% consumption imported[a]	79.1
Consumption per head,			
kg coal equivalent	4,253		

Inflation and finance

Consumer price		*av. ann. increase 1989–93*	
inflation 1993	23.2%	Narrow money (M1)	...
Av. ann. inflation 1991–93	29.7%	Broad money	...

Exchange rates

	end 1994		*end June 1994*
Kc per $	31.07	Effective rates	*1990 = 100*
Kc per SDR	45.36	– nominal	...
Kc per Ecu	38.22	– real	...

Principal exports[acd]

	$bn fob		$bn fob
Manufactured goods	3.8	Chemicals	0.8
Machinery & industrial		Food products	0.5
equipment	1.3	Total incl. others	**7.4**

Main export destinations[ac]

	% of total		% of total
Germany	30.6	EU	49.4
Ex-Soviet Union	10.9	Other Eastern Europe	13.7

Principal imports[acd]

	$bn fob		$bn fob
Machinery & industrial		Raw materials	0.4
equipment	5.9	Agric. products & foodstuffs	0.4
Chemicals & products	1.0	Total incl. others	**7.8**

Main origins of imports[ac]

	% of total		% of total
Ex-Soviet Union	24.6	EU	42.1
Germany	24.6	Other Eastern Europe	6.7

Balance of payments[ac], reserves and debt, $bn

Visible exports fob	11.5	Overall balance	-0.4
Visible imports fob	-13.3	Change in reserves	-2.3
Trade balance	-1.8	Level of reserves	
Invisibles inflows	4.8	end Dec.	3.9
Invisibles outflows	-3.1	No. months import cover	3.5
Net transfers	0.1	Foreign debt	3.3
Current account balance	-0.03	– as % of GDP	32.3
– as % of GDP	-0.1	Debt service	0.6
Capital balance	-0.2	Debt service ratio	8.2

Family life

No. of households	...	Divorces per 1,000 pop.	...
Av. no. per household	...	Cost of living, Sept. 1994	
Marriages per 1,000 pop.	...	New York = 100	...

a Ex-Czechoslovakia.
b 1991.
c 1992.
d Western countries.

SOUTH AFRICA

Area	1,184,825 sq km	Currency	Rand (R)
Capital	Pretoria		

People

Population	40.7m	Life expectancy: men	62 yrs
Pop. per sq km	33	women	68 yrs
Av. ann. growth		Adult literacy	80.0%
in pop. 1985–93	2.4%	Fertility rate (per woman)	3.8
Pop. under 15	37.5%		
Pop. over 65	4.0%		*per 1,000 pop.*
No. of men per 100 women	99	Crude birth rate	29.5
Human Development Index	65	Crude death rate	7.5

The economy

GDP	R385bn	GDP per head	$2,902
GDP	$118bn	GDP per head in purchasing	
Av. ann. growth in real		power parity (USA=100)	18
GDP 1985–93	0.8%		

Origins of GDP		Components of GDP	
	% of total		*% of total*
Agriculture	14.0	Private consumption	61.8
Industry, of which:	37.2	Public consumption	21.1
manufacturing	24.6	Investment	12.8
Services	48.8	Exports	24.6
		Imports	-20.3

Structure of manufacturing

	% of total		*% of total*
Agric. & food processing	16	Other	59
Textiles & clothing	8	Av. ann. increase in industrial	
Machinery & transport	17	output 1980–92	-0.1%

Energy

	'000 TCE		
Total output	134,314	% output exported	32.3
Total consumption	112,694	% consumption imported	20.6
Consumption per head,			
kg coal equivalent	2,488		

Inflation and finance

Consumer price		*av. ann. increase 1989–90*	
inflation 1994	9.0%	Narrow money (M1)	13.3%
Av. ann. inflation 1989–94	12.8%	Broad money	28.1%

Exchange rates

	end 1994		*end June 1994*
R per $	3.54	Effective rates	*1990 = 100*
R per SDR	5.17	– nominal	70.8
R per Ecu	4.37	– real	97.4

Principal exports[a]

	$bn fob		$bn fob
Gold	7.1	Platinum[b]	1.0
Base metals	3.2	Agric. products & foodstuffs	0.7
Mineral products	2.5	Total incl. others	**23.7**

Main export destinations

	% of total		% of total
Italy	5.9	Germany	4.4
United States	5.7	United Kingdom	4.4
Japan	5.6		

Principal imports[a]

	$bn cif		$bn cif
Machinery & equipment	4.7	Oil[b]	1.5
Transport equipment	2.2	Base metals	0.8
Chemicals	1.8	Total incl. others	**17.5**

Main origins of imports

	% of total		% of total
Germany	13.4	United Kingdom	8.7
United States	11.3	Italy	3.4
Japan	10.4		

Balance of payments, reserves and debt, $bn

Visible exports fob	23.9	Overall balance	-1.8
Visible imports fob	-18.0	Change in reserves	-1.8
Trade balance	5.9	Level of reserves	
Invisibles inflows	4.4	end Dec.	1.2
Invisibles outflows	-8.6	No. months import cover	0.8
Net transfers	0.1	Foreign debt	17.3
Current account balance	1.8	– as % of GDP	14.7
– as % of GDP	1.5	Debt service	2.9
Capital balance	2.6	Debt service ratio	10.1

Family life

No. of households	...	Divorces per 1,000 pop.	0.4
Av. no. per household	...	Cost of living, Sept. 1994	
Marriages per 1,000 pop.	...	New York = 100	68

a   1991.
b   Estimate; no official figures published.

SOUTH KOREA

Area	98,445 sq km	Currency	Won (W)
Capital	Seoul		

People

Population	44.1m	Life expectancy: men	69 yrs
Pop. per sq km	448	women	76 yrs
Av. ann. growth		Adult literacy	96.8%
in pop. 1985–93	1.0%	Fertility rate (per woman)	1.8
Pop. under 15	23.4%		
Pop. over 65	5.4%		*per 1,000 pop.*
No. of men per 100 women	102	Crude birth rate	16.1
Human Development Index	86	Crude death rate	6.3

The economy

GDP	W271,302bn	GDP per head	$7,673
GDP	$338bn	GDP per head in purchasing	
Av. ann. growth in real		power parity (USA=100)	38
GDP 1985–93	8.9%		

Origins of GDP		Components of GDP	
	% of total		*% of total*
Agriculture	7.8	Private consumption	54.1
Industry, of which:	48.0	Public consumption	10.8
manufacturing	30.0	Investment	35.5
Services	44.2	Exports	29.4
		Imports	-29.0

Structure of manufacturing

	% of total		*% of total*
Agric. & food processing	11	Other	45
Textiles & clothing	11	Av. ann. increase in industrial	
Machinery & transport	33	output 1980–92	11.6%

Energy

	'000 TCE		
Total output	29,292	% output exported	60.9
Total consumption	140,781	% consumption imported	106.2
Consumption per head,			
kg coal equivalent	3,188		

Inflation and finance

Consumer price		*av. ann. increase 1989–93*	
inflation 1994	6.3%	Narrow money (M1)	21.8%
Av. ann. inflation 1989–94	6.8%	Broad money	19.3%

Exchange rates

	end 1994		*end June 1994*
W per $	789	Effective rates	*1990 = 100*
W per SDR	1,151	– nominal	...
W per Ecu	974	– real	...

Principal exports

	$bn fob		*$bn fob*
Machinery & transport		Clothing	6.2
equipment	37.0	Footwear	2.3
Textiles	6.4	Total incl. others	**82.2**

Main export destinations

	% of total		*% of total*
United States	22.1	Germany	4.4
Japan	14.1	Singapore	3.8
Hong Kong	7.8		

Principal imports

	$bn cif		*$bn cif*
Machinery & transport		Chemicals	8.2
equipment	28.4	Food & live animals	4.0
Mineral fuels & lubricants	15.1		
Raw materials	8.9	Total incl. others	**83.8**

Main origins of imports

	% of total		*% of total*
Japan	23.9	Saudi Arabia	4.5
United States	21.4	Australia	4.0
Germany	4.7		

Balance of payments, reserves and debt, $bn

Visible exports fob	81.0	Overall balance	3.0
Visible imports fob	-79.1	Change in reserves	3.1
Trade balance	1.9	Level of reserves	
Invisibles inflows	18.3	end Dec.	21.3
Invisibles outflows	-20.2	No. months import cover	3.2
Net transfers	0.5	Foreign debt	47.2
Current account balance	0.4	– as % of GDP	14.4
– as % of GDP	0.1	Debt service	9.2
Capital balance	0.3	Debt service ratio	9.2

Family life

No. of households	11.4m	Divorces per 1,000 pop.	0.9
Av. no. per household	3.8	Cost of living, Sept. 1994	
Marriages per 1,000 pop.	8.9	New York = 100	112

SPAIN

Area	504,880 sq km	Currency	Peseta (Pta)
Capital	Madrid		

People

Population	39.1m	Life expectancy: men		75 yrs
Pop. per sq km	78		women	81 yrs
Av. ann. growth		Adult literacy		98.0%
in pop. 1985–93	0.2%	Fertility rate (per woman)		1.2
Pop. under 15	17.1%			
Pop. over 65	14.7%			*per 1,000 pop.*
No. of men per 100 women	97	Crude birth rate		9.8
Human Development Index	89	Crude death rate		9.3

The economy

GDP	Pta67,957bn	GDP per head	$13,646
GDP	$534bn	GDP per head in purchasing	
Av. ann. growth in real		power parity (USA=100)	57
GDP 1985–93	3.0%		

Origins of GDP		**Components of GDP**	
	% of total		*% of total*
Agriculture	3.7	Private consumption	62.7
Industry, of which:	32.9	Public consumption	17.2
manufacturing	24.0	Investment	20.8
Services	63.4	Exports	19.8
		Imports	-20.5

Structure of manufacturing

	% of total		*% of total*
Agric. & food processing	18	Other	49
Textiles & clothing	8	Av. ann. increase in industrial	
Machinery & transport	25	output 1980–88	2.3%

Energy

	'000 TCE		
Total output	42,620	% output exported[a]	33.2
Total consumption	121,544	% consumption imported[a]	88.0
Consumption per head,			
kg coal equivalent	3,109		

Inflation and finance

Consumer price		*av. ann. increase 1989–93*	
inflation 1994	4.7%	Narrow money (M1)	10.9%
Av. ann. inflation 1989–94	5.8%	Broad money	11.5%

Exchange rates

	end 1994		*end June 1994*
Pta per $	131.7	Effective rates	*1990 = 100*
Pta per SDR	192.3	– nominal	80.9
Pta per Ecu	162.6	– real	88.2

Principal exports

	$bn fob		$bn fob
Raw materials &		Agric. products &	
intermediate products	25.8	foodstuffs	8.1
Non-food consumer goods	12.2	Energy products	1.7
Capital goods	8.5	Total incl. others	**62.7**

Main export destinations

	% of total		% of total
France	19.0	United States	4.7
Germany	15.0	EU	68.2
Italy	9.3	Latin America	5.7
United Kingdom	8.4	Opec	3.5

Principal imports

	$bn cif		$bn cif
Raw materials & intermediate		Energy products	8.7
products (excl. fuels)	36.7	Agric. products & foodstuffs	6.5
Non-foods consumer goods	21.9		
Capital goods	12.4	Total incl. others	**81.7**

Main origins of imports

	% of total		% of total
France	16.8	United States	6.8
Germany	15.6	EU	60.8
Italy	9.0	Opec	5.8
United Kingdom	7.6	Latin America	4.1

Balance of payments, reserves and aid, $bn

Visible exports fob	58.7	Capital balance	7.3
Visible imports fob	74.8	Overall balance	-4.8
Trade balance	-16.1	Change in reserves	-4.5
Invisibles inflows	39.0	Level of reserves	
Invisibles outflows	-33.7	end Dec.	41.8
Net transfers	4.5	No. months import cover	6.7
Current account balance	-6.3	Aid given	1.21
– as % of GDP	-1.2	– as % of GDP	0.25

Family life

No. of households	10.6m	Divorces per 1,000 pop.	0.6
Av. no. per household	3.5	Cost of living, Sept. 1994	
Marriages per 1,000 pop.	5.6	New York = 100	97

a   Energy trade data are distorted by transitory and oil refining activities.

SWEDEN

Area	449,790 sq km	Currency	Swedish krona (Skr)
Capital	Stockholm		

People

Population	8.7m	Life expectancy: men	76 yrs
Pop. per sq km	19	women	82 yrs
Av. ann. growth		Adult literacy	99.0%
in pop. 1985–93	0.6%	Fertility rate (per woman)	2.1
Pop. under 15	18.8%		
Pop. over 65	17.4%		*per 1,000 pop.*
No. of men per 100 women	98	Crude birth rate	13.6
Human Development Index	93	Crude death rate	10.9

The economy

GDP	Skr1,681bn	GDP per head	$24,833
GDP	$216bn	GDP per head in purchasing	
Av. ann. growth in real		power parity (USA=100)	79
GDP 1985–93	0.8%		

Origins of GDP		**Components of GDP**	
	% of total		*% of total*
Agriculture	3.1	Private consumption	54.7
Industry, of which:	29.7	Public consumption	27.7
manufacturing	23.8	Investment	13.7
Services	67.2	Exports	32.7
		Imports	-28.8

Structure of manufacturing

	% of total		*% of total*
Agric. & food processing	11	Other	55
Textiles & clothing	2	Av. ann. increase in industrial	
Machinery & transport	32	output 1980–92	2.3%

Energy

	'000 TCE		
Total output	32,846	% output exported	34.5
Total consumption	60,015	% consumption imported	64.1
Consumption per head,			
kg coal equivalent	6,937		

Inflation and finance

Consumer price		*av. ann. increase 1989–93*	
inflation 1994	2.2%	Narrow money (M1)	...
Av. ann. inflation 1989–94	5.8%	Broad money	4.6%

Exchange rates

	end 1994		*end June 1994*
Skr per $	7.46	Effective rates	*1990 = 100*
Skr per SDR	10.89	– nominal	80.9
Skr per Ecu	9.21	– real	72.4

Principal exports

	$bn fob		$bn fob
Machinery incl.		Transport equipment	7.6
electricals	14.0	Chemicals	5.0
Wood products, pulp &		Iron & steel	2.9
paper	8.1	Total incl. others	**49.9**

Main export destinations

	% of total		% of total
Germany	14.4	Denmark	6.6
United Kingdom	10.3	EU	53.2
United States	8.4	Efta	16.1
Norway	8.1		

Principal imports

	$bn cif		$bn cif
Machinery incl.		Transport equipment	3.7
electricals	11.7	Clothing, footwear & textiles	3.2
Chemicals	4.9		
Mineral fuels	3.9	Total incl. others	**42.6**

Main origins of imports

	% of total		% of total
Germany	17.9	Norway	6.5
United Kingdom	9.4	Finland	6.2
United States	9.1	EU	55.2
Denmark	7.3	Efta	16.0

Balance of payments, reserves and aid, $bn

Visible exports fob	49.3	Capital balance	6.8
Visible imports fob	-41.6	Overall balance	2.1
Trade balance	7.7	Change in reserves	-3.6
Invisibles inflows	20.6	Level of reserves	
Invisibles outflows	-28.4	end Dec.	19.3
Net transfers	-1.8	No. months import cover	5.6
Current account balance	-1.8	Aid given	1.77
– as % of GDP	-0.8	– as % of GDP	0.98

Family life

No. of households	3.8m	Divorces per 1,000 pop.	2.3
Av. no. per household	2.2	Cost of living, Sept. 1994	
Marriages per 1,000 pop.	4.3	New York = 100	112

SWITZERLAND

Area	41,285 sq km	Currency	Swiss franc (SFr)
Capital	Berne		

People

Population	7.0m	Life expectancy: men	75 yrs
Pop. per sq km	170	women	82 yrs
Av. ann. growth		Adult literacy	99.0%
in pop. 1985–93	1.0%	Fertility rate (per woman)	1.7
Pop. under 15	17.1%		
Pop. over 65	15.1%		*per 1,000 pop.*
No. of men per 100 women	96	Crude birth rate	12.3
Human Development Index	93	Crude death rate	9.0

The economy

GDP	SFr375bn	GDP per head	$36,399
GDP	$254bn	GDP per head in purchasing	
Av. ann. growth in real		power parity (USA=100)	98
GDP 1985–93	1.6%		

Origins of GDP[a]		Components of GDP	
	% of total		*% of total*
Agriculture	3.1	Private consumption	59.0
Industry, of which:	34.7	Public consumption	14.5
manufacturing	26.3	Investment	21.6
Services	62.2	Exports	36.4
		Imports	-31.4

Structure of manufacturing

	% of total		*% of total*
Agric. & food processing	...	Other	...
Textiles & clothing	...	Av. ann. increase in industrial	
Machinery & transport	...	output 1980–89[b]	1.8%

Energy

	'000 TCE		
Total output	12,907	% output exported	29.9
Total consumption	33,362	% consumption imported	75.5
Consumption per head,			
kg coal equivalent	4,877		

Inflation and finance

Consumer price			*av. ann. increase 1989–93*
inflation 1994	0.8%	Narrow money (M1)	0.2%
Av. ann. inflation 1989–94	3.8%	Broad money	3.5%

Exchange rates

	end 1994		*end June1994*
SFr per $	1.31	Effective rates	*1990 = 100*
SFr per SDR	1.91	– nominal	105.2
SFr per Ecu	1.62	– real	101.0

Principal exports

	$bn fob		$bn fob
Machinery	16.8	Metals & metal manufactures	5.0
Chemicals	15.1	Textiles & clothing	2.9
Precision instruments, watches & jewellery	13.8	Total incl. others	**63.1**

Main export destinations

	% of total		% of total
Germany	22.9	United Kingdom	6.6
France	9.1	Japan	3.5
United States	8.8	EU	56.7
Italy	7.8	Efta	6.3

Principal imports

	$bn cif		$bn cif
Machinery	12.1	Motor vehicles	5.7
Chemicals	8.0	Agric. products	5.3
Precision instruments, watches & jewellery	7.7	Metals & metals manufactures	4.9
Textiles & clothing	5.8	Total incl. others	**60.8**

Main origins of imports

	% of total		% of total
Germany	32.6	United States	6.2
France	10.9	EU	72.6
Italy	9.8	Efta	6.7
United Kingdom	7.2		

Balance of payments, reserves and aid, $bn

Visible exports fob	74.9	Capital balance	-17.9
Visible imports fob	-72.7	Overall balance	0.5
Trade balance	2.2	Change in reserves	-0.6
Invisibles inflows	45.0	Level of reserves	
Invisibles outflows	-27.7	end Dec.	36.6
Net transfers	-2.9	No. months import cover	6.0
Current account balance	16.7	Aid given	0.79
– as % of GDP	6.6	– as % of GDP	0.33

Family life

No. of households	2.5m	Divorces per 1,000 pop.	2.1
Av. no. per household	2.5	Cost of living, Sept. 1994	
Marriages per 1,000 pop.	6.6	New York = 100	140

a 1990.
b Based on index of manufacturing output.

TAIWAN

Area	35,990 sq km	Currency	Taiwan dollar (T$)
Capital	Taipei		

People

Population	20.8m	Life expectancy: men	...
Pop. per sq km[a]	578	women	...
Av. ann. growth		Adult literacy	...
in pop. 1985–93	1.1%	Fertility rate (per woman)	1.8
Pop. under 15	25.1%		
Pop. over 65	6.8%		*per 1,000 pop.*
No. of men per 100 women	106	Crude birth rate	15.5
Human Development Index	...	Crude death rate	5.3

The economy

GDP	T$5,702bn	GDP per head	$10,404
GDP	$216bn	GDP per head in purchasing	
Av. ann. growth in real		power parity (USA=100)	...
GDP 1985–93	6.7%		

Origins of GDP		**Components of GDP**	
	% of total		*% of total*
Agriculture	3.6	Private consumption	56.0
Industry, of which:	40.6	Public consumption	15.7
manufacturing	31.7	Investment	24.8
Services	55.8	Exports	43.5
		Imports	-41.7

Structure of manufacturing

	% of total		*% of total*
Agric. & food processing	...	Other	...
Textiles & clothing	...	Av. ann. increase in industrial	
Machinery & transport	...	output 1980–93	5.9%

Energy

	'000 TCE		
Total output	...	% output exported	3.3
Total consumption	...	% consumption imported	76.7
Consumption per head,			
kg coal equivalent	...		

Inflation and finance

Consumer price		*av. ann. increase 1989–93*	
inflation 1994	4.1%	Narrow money (M1)	7.5%
Av. ann. inflation 1989–94	4.0%	Broad money	15.7%

Exchange rates

	end 1994		*end June 1994*
T$ per $	26.29	Effective rates	*1990 = 100*
T$ per SDR	38.38	– nominal	...
T$ per Ecu	32.34	– real	...

Principal exports

	$bn fob		$bn fob
Machinery & electrical equipment	33.3	Vehicles & ships	4.7
		Footwear	3.3
Textiles & clothing	12.0	Toys & sporting goods	2.8
Base metals & manufactures	7.1		
Plastic & rubber articles	5.7	Total incl. others	**84.9**

Main export destinations

	% of total		% of total
United States	27.6	Singapore	3.4
Hong Kong	21.7	United Kingdom	2.6
Japan	10.6	Netherlands	2.5
Germany	4.1	Thailand	2.4

Principal imports

	$bn cif		$bn cif
Machinery & electrical equipment	24.1	Vehicles & ships	6.3
		Crude petroleum	3.0
Metals	9.9	Plastics & plastic products	2.0
Chemicals	7.6	Total incl. others	**77.1**

Main origins of imports

	% of total		% of total
Japan	30.1	Australia	2.7
United States	21.7	Malaysia	2.5
Germany	5.5	Singapore	2.4
South Korea	3.3	Hong Kong	2.2

Balance of payments, reserves and debt, $bn

Visible exports fob	84.2	Overall balance	1.5
Visible imports fob	-72.7	Change in reserves	-1.5
Trade balance	11.5	Level of reserves	
Invisibles inflows	19.8	end Dec.	84.2
Invisibles outflows	-24.4	No. months import cover	13.9
Net transfers	-0.1	Foreign debt	23.3
Current account balance	6.7	– as % of GDP	10.5
– as % of GDP	3.1	Debt service	1.7
Capital balance	-4.0	Debt service ratio	1.6

Family life

No. of households	...	Divorces per 1,000 pop.	...
Av. no. per household	...	Cost of living, Sept. 1994	
Marriages per 1,000 pop.	...	New York = 100	119

a 1992.

THAILAND

Area	514,000 sq km	Currency	Baht (Bt)
Capital	Bangkok		

People

Population	58.8m	Life expectancy: men	65 yrs
Pop. per sq km	114	women	72 yrs
Av. ann. growth		Adult literacy	93.8%
in pop. 1985–93	1.6%	Fertility rate (per woman)	2.1
Pop. under 15	29.2%		
Pop. over 65	4.5%		*per 1,000 pop.*
No. of men per 100 women	98	Crude birth rate	19.2
Human Development Index	80	Crude death rate	7.0

The economy

GDP	Bt3,038bn	GDP per head	$2,044
GDP	$120bn	GDP per head in purchasing	
Av. ann. growth in real		power parity (USA=100)	24
GDP 1985–93	9.1%		

Origins of GDP[a]		**Components of GDP**[a]	
	% of total		*% of total*
Agriculture[b]	13.4	Private consumption	55.1
Industry, of which:	37.7	Public consumption	10.1
manufacturing	28.8	Investment	40.1
Services	48.9	Exports	36.4
		Imports	-40.9

Structure of manufacturing

	% of total		*% of total*
Agric. & food processing	28	Other	34
Textiles & clothing	24	Av. ann. increase in industrial	
Machinery & transport	14	output 1980–92	10.1%

Energy

	'000 TCE		
Total output	21,661	% output exported	6.3
Total consumption	49,833	% consumption imported	62.8
Consumption per head,			
kg coal equivalent	888		

Inflation and finance

Consumer price		*av. ann. increase 1989–93*	
inflation 1994	5.1%	Narrow money (M1)	13.5%
Av. ann. inflation 1989–94	5.0%	Broad money	21.8%

Exchange rates

	end 1994		*end June 1994*
Bt per $	25.09	Effective rates	*1990 = 100*
Bt per SDR	36.63	– nominal	...
Bt per Ecu	30.98	– real	...

Principal exports

	$bn fob		$bn fob
Textiles & clothing	4.4	Precious stones	1.7
Computers & parts	2.4	Plastic products	1.6
Electrical appliances	2.2	Total incl. others	**37.0**

Main export destinations

	% of total		% of total
United States	21.7	Hong Kong	5.3
Japan	17.2	Germany	4.0
Singapore	12.1		

Principal imports

	$bn cif		$bn cif
Non-electrical machinery	6.9	Chemicals	3.5
Electrical machinery	4.8	Vehicles & parts	3.3
Energy & fuel	3.6	Total incl. others	**46.1**

Main origins of imports

	% of total		% of total
Japan	30.4	Germany	5.4
United States	11.5	Taiwan	5.1
Singapore	6.5		

Balance of payments[a], reserves and debt, $bn

Visible exports fob	32.1	Overall balance	2.9
Visible imports fob	-36.3	Change in reserves	2.7
Trade balance	-4.2	Level of reserves	
Invisibles inflows	10.2	end Dec.	24.6
Invisibles outflows	-13.0	No. months import cover	8.1
Net transfers	0.3	Foreign debt	45.8
Current account balance	-6.6	– as % of GDP	37.6
– as % of GDP	-5.5	Debt service	9.1
Capital balance	6.8	Debt service ratio	18.6

Family life

No. of households	12.2m	Divorces per 1,000 pop.	0.7
Av. no. per household	4.5	Cost of living, Sept. 1994	
Marriages per 1,000 pop.	7.1	New York = 100	79

a 1992.
b Includes mining.

TURKEY

Area	779,450 sq km	Currency	Turkish Lira (L)
Capital	Ankara		

People

Population	59.5m	Life expectancy: men		66 yrs
Pop. per sq km	76	women		71 yrs
Av. ann. growth		Adult literacy		81.9%
in pop. 1985–93	2.1%	Fertility rate (per woman)		3.0
Pop. under 15	33.7%			
Pop. over 65	4.8%			per 1,000 pop.
No. of men per 100 women	104	Crude birth rate		24.6
Human Development Index	74	Crude death rate		6.7

The economy

GDP	L1,384,060bn	GDP per head	$2,125
GDP	$126bn	GDP per head in purchasing	
Av. ann. growth in real		power parity (USA=100)	22
GDP 1985–93	5.1%		

Origins of GDP		Components of GDPª	
	% of total		% of total
Agriculture	15.1	Private consumption	70.0
Industry, of which:	34.0	Public consumption	7.5
manufacturing	26.6	Investment	26.2
Services	49.9	Exports	18.3
		Imports	-25.8

Structure of manufacturing

	% of total		% of total
Agric. & food processing	17	Other	52
Textiles & clothing	13	Av. ann. increase in industrial	
Machinery & transport	18	output 1980–92	5.8%

Energy

	'000 TCE		
Total output	25,341	% output exported	10.3
Total consumption	60,967	% consumption imported	69.7
Consumption per head,			
kg coal equivalent	1,045		

Inflation and finance

Consumer price		av. ann. increase 1989–93	
inflation 1994	106%	Narrow money (M1)	63.3%
Av. ann. inflation 1989–94	71.4%	Broad money	71.3%

Exchange rates

	end 1994		end June 1994
L per $	34,073	Effective rates	1990 = 100
L per SDR	49,998	– nominal	...
L per Ecu	42,065	– real	...

Principal exports

	$bn fob		$bn fob
Clothing	3.8	Synthetic fibres	0.5
Iron & steel	2.0	Leather	0.4
Other textiles & carpets	0.9	Total incl. others	**15.6**

Main export destinations

	% of total		% of total
Germany	23.8	France	5.0
United States	6.4	Italy	4.9
United Kingdom	5.4	EU	47.5

Principal imports

	$bn cif		$bn cif
Machinery	7.4	Chemicals	1.0
Metals	3.1	Plastics	0.8
Crude oil	2.6	Total incl. others	**29.8**

Main origins of imports

	% of total		% of total
Germany	15.4	Japan	5.5
United States	11.4	Russia	5.2
Italy	8.7	EU	44.0
France	6.6		

Balance of payments, reserves and debt, $bn

Visible exports fob	15.6	Overall balance	0.3
Visible imports fob	-29.8	Change in reserves	0.1
Trade balance	-14.2	Level of reserves	
Invisibles inflows	11.8	end Dec.	6.5
Invisibles outflows	-7.8	No. months import cover	2.6
Net transfers	3.8	Foreign debt	67.9
Current account balance	-6.4	– as % of GDP	55.3
– as % of GDP	-5.1	Debt service	8.6
Capital balance	8.7	Debt service ratio	28.3

Family life

No. of households	9.7m	Divorces per 1,000 pop.	0.5
Av. no. per household	5.2	Cost of living, Sept. 1994	
Marriages per 1,000 pop.	8.4	New York = 100	68

a 1992.

UKRAINE

Area	603,700 sq km	Currency	Coupons
Capital	Kiev		

People

Population	52.1m	Life expectancy: men	64 yrs
Pop. per sq km	86	women	74 yrs
Av. ann. growth		Adult literacy	95.0%
in pop. 1985–93	0.3%	Fertility rate (per woman)	1.6
No. of men per 100 women[b]	86		per 1,000 pop.
		Crude birth rate[a]	11.5
		Crude death rate[a]	13.6

The economy

GDP	$100bn	GDP per head	$1,912
Av. ann. growth in real		GDP per head in purchasing	
GDP 1988–93	-8.8%	power parity (USA=100)	23

Origins of NMP[b]		Components of NMP[b]	
	% of total		% of total
Agriculture	23.0	Private consumption	58.5
Industry	51.0	Public consumption	12.9
Construction	15.0	Net investment	23.8
Other	11.0	Net exports	4.7

Inflation and exchange rates

			end 1994
Consumer price			
inflation 1993	4,735%	Coupons per $	104,133
Av. ann. inflation 1991–93	965.8%	Coupons per Ecu	34,528

Principal exports[c]

	Rb bn		Rb bn
Machinery & metalworking	17.9	Chemicals & products	3.9
Ferrous metallurgy	7.6	Light industry	2.3
Food industry	6.7	Total incl. others	**45.7**

Main export destinations[cd]

	% of total		% of total
Other EU	14.6	Ex-Czechoslovakia	8.6
Germany	11.5	Other Eastern Europe	20.8
Bulgaria	9.3		

Principal imports[c]

	Rb bn		Rb bn
Machinery & metalworking	18.7	Food industry	4.0
Light industry	9.7	Oil & gas	3.9
Chemicals & products	5.7	Total incl. others	**53.8**

Main origins of imports[cd]

	% of total		% of total
Germany	17.7	Other EU	6.8
Poland	13.5	Other Eastern Europe	22.6
Ex-Czechoslovakia	9.9		

EX-SOVIET REPUBLICS

	Area '000 sq km	Population m	Population per sq km[a]	Capital	Currency
Armenia	29.8	3.73	125	Yerevan	Dram
Azerbaijan	86.6	7.44	86	Baku	Manat
Belarus	207.6	10.32	50	Minsk	Rouble
Estonia	45.1	1.55	34	Tallinn	Kroon
Georgia	69.7	5.46	78	Tbilisi	Coupon
Kazakhstan	2,717.3	17.17	6	Alma-Ata	Tenge
Kirgizstan	198.5	4.51	23	Bishkek	Som
Latvia	63.7	2.59	40	Riga	Lats
Lithuania	65.2	3.75	58	Vilnius	Litas
Moldova	33.7	4.36	129	Kishinev	Leu
Tajikistan	143.1	5.68	40	Dushanbe	Rouble
Turkmenistan	488.1	3.95	8	Ashkhabad	Manat
Uzbekistan	447.4	21.97	49	Tashkent	Som

People

	Av. ann. pop. growth 1985–93	Pop. under 15 %	Male life expect.[a] yrs	Birth rate[a]	Death rate[a]	Human Dev. Index
Armenia	1.4	28	70	18	6	80
Azerbaijan	1.4	31	68	19	6	73
Belarus	0.3	22	65	12	12	85
Estonia	0.1	22	64	11	13	87
Georgia	0.4	23	70	15	9	75
Kazakhstan	1.0	30	67	19	7	77
Kirgizstan	1.6	37	67	26	6	69
Latvia	-0.1	22	63	11	13	87
Lithuania	0.7	22	65	13	12	87
Moldova	0.5	31	64	16	11	71
Tajikistan	2.8	44	69	33	6	63
Turkmenistan	2.5	40	64	29	7	70
Uzbekistan	2.4	40	68	28	6	66

The economy

	GDP $bn	GDP Per head $	GDP PPP USA=100	Agric. as % of GDP	Exports[d] $m	Imports[d] $m	Foreign debt $m
Armenia	2.5	662	21	20.0	29	171	140.0
Azerbaijan	5.4	729	17	31.0	351	241	35.5
Belarus	29.3	2,838	31	21.3	838	996	960.7
Estonia	4.7	3,034	37	17.1	804	895	154.8
Georgia	3.1	562	17	26.8	222	461	568.1
Kazakhstan	26.4	1,543	20	28.5	1,271	358	1,639.6
Kirgizstan	3.8	832	15	28.4	100	106	308.3
Latvia	5.3	2,030	34	24.0	1,008	954	231.0
Lithuania	4.9	1,304	24	21.2	2,233	2,512	291.2
Moldova	5.2	1,183	16	33.5	174	210	289.0
Tajikistan	2.7	473	10	33.2	263	371	41.5
Turkmenistan	5.4	1,379	16	33.2	1,320	502	9.0
Uzbekistan	21.1	960	13	33.1	706	947	739.3

a 1995–2000.
b 1992.
c 1990.
d Outside ex-Soviet Union.

UNITED KINGDOM

Area	244,755 sq km	Currency	Pound (£)
Capital	London		

People

Population	58.0m	Life expectancy: men	74 yrs
Pop. per sq km	238	women	79 yrs
Av. ann. growth		Adult literacy	99.0%
in pop. 1985–93	0.3%	Fertility rate (per woman)	1.8
Pop. under 15	19.7%		
Pop. over 65	15.6%		*per 1,000 pop.*
No. of men per 100 women	96	Crude birth rate	12.9
Human Development Index	92	Crude death rate	10.9

The economy

GDP	£694bn	GDP per head	$17,965
GDP	$1,043bn	GDP per head in purchasing	
Av. ann. growth in real		power parity (USA=100)	74
GDP 1985–93	2.0%		

Origins of GDP		Components of GDP	
	% of total		*% of total*
Agriculture	1.8	Private consumption	64.4
Industry, of which:	31.7	Public consumption	21.9
manufacturing	21.6	Investment	15.0
Services	66.5	Exports	25.1
		Imports	-26.4

Structure of manufacturing

	% of total		*% of total*
Agric. & food processing	14	Other	50
Textiles & clothing	5	Av. ann. increase in industrial	
Machinery & transport	31	output 1980–92	1.3%

Energy

	'000 TCE		
Total output	307,730	% output exported	35.0
Total consumption	312,713	% consumption imported	39.5
Consumption per head,			
kg coal equivalent	5,400		

Inflation and finance

Consumer price		*av. ann. increase 1989–93*	
inflation 1994	2.5%	Narrow money (M1)	8.2%
Av. ann. inflation 1989–94	5.1%	Broad money	9.7%

Exchange rates

	end 1994		*end June 1994*
£ per $	0.64	Effective rates	*1990 = 100*
£ per SDR	0.93	– nominal	89.2
£ per Ecu	0.79	– real	94.0

Principal exports

	$bn fob		$bn fob
Finished manufactured products	96.2	Fuels	12.6
Semi-manufactured products	52.9	Basic materials	3.4
Agric. products & foodstuffs	13.6	Total incl. others	**181.2**

Main export destinations

	% of total		% of total
United States	12.9	Belgium/Luxembourg	5.4
Germany	11.9	Ireland	4.8
France	9.0	EU	48.0
Netherlands	6.2		

Principal imports

	$bn cif		$bn cif
Finished manufactured products	112.5	Fuels	10.6
Semi-manufactured products	53.0	Basic materials	7.7
Agric. products & foodstuffs	20.4	Total incl. others	**206.4**

Main origins of imports

	% of total		% of total
Germany	13.2	Netherlands	6.1
United States	12.0	Belgium/Luxembourg	4.5
France	9.0	EU	45.3
Japan	6.2		

Balance of payments, reserves and aid, $bn

Visible exports fob	181.2	Capital balance	18.2
Visible imports fob	-201.8	Overall balance	1.1
Trade balance	-20.6	Change in reserves	0.1
Invisibles inflows	164.0	Level of reserves	
Invisibles outflows	-152.2	end Dec.	37.7
Net transfers	-7.7	No. months import cover	2.2
Current account balance	-16.4	Aid given	2.91
– as % of GDP	-1.6	– as % of GDP	0.31

Family life

No. of households	20.0m	Divorces per 1,000 pop.	2.9
Av. no. per household	2.8	Cost of living, Sept. 1994	
Marriages per 1,000 pop.	6.5	New York = 100	110

UNITED STATES

Area	9,363,130 sq km	Currency	US dollar ($)
Capital	Washington DC		

People

Population	258.1m	Life expectancy: men	73 yrs
Pop. per sq km	27	women	80 yrs
Av. ann. growth		Adult literacy	99.0%
in pop. 1985–93	0.9%	Fertility rate (per woman)	2.1
Pop. under 15	21.9%		
Pop. over 65	12.6%		*per 1,000 pop.*
No. of men per 100 women	95	Crude birth rate	14.7
Human Development Index	93	Crude death rate	8.7

The economy

GDP	$6,388bn	GDP per head	$24,753
		GDP per head in purchasing	
Av. ann. growth in real		power parity (USA=100)	100
GDP 1985–93	2.3%		

Origins of GDP

	% of total		*% of total*
Agriculture	1.9	Private consumption	68.7
Industry, of which:	23.4	Public consumption	17.5
manufacturing	17.9	Investment	15.4
Services	74.9	Exports	10.6
		Imports	-12.2

Components of GDP

Structure of manufacturing

	% of total		*% of total*
Agric. & food processing	13	Other	51
Textiles & clothing	5	Av. ann. increase in industrial	
Machinery & transport	31	output 1980–92	2.9%

Energy

	'000 TCE		
Total output	2,291,464	% output exported	6.1
Total consumption	2,739,632	% consumption imported	23.1
Consumption per head,			
kg coal equivalent	10,737		

Inflation and finance

		av. ann. increase 1989–93	
Consumer price			
inflation 1994	2.6%	Narrow money (M1)	6.9%
Av. ann. inflation 1989–94	3.8%	Broad money	3.7%

Exchange rates

	end 1994		*end June 1994*
$ per SDR	1.46	Effective rates	*1990 = 100*
$ per Ecu	1.23	– nominal	98.2
		– real	98.9

ZAIRE

Area	2,345,410 sq km	Currency	Zaire (Z)
Capital	Kinshasa		

People

Population	41.0m	Life expectancy: men	50 yrs
Pop. per sq km	17	women	53 yrs
Av. ann. growth		Adult literacy	74.0%
in pop. 1985–93	3.3%	Fertility rate (per woman)	6.2
Pop. under 15	48.1%		
Pop. over 65	2.8%		*per 1,000 pop.*
No. of men per 100 women	98	Crude birth rate	44.8
Human Development Index	34	Crude death rate	13.9

The economy

GDP	Z36.9bn	GDP per head	$359
GDP	$14.7bn	GDP per head in purchasing	
Av. ann. growth in real		power parity (USA=100)	2
GDP 1985–93	-4.1%		

Origins of GDP[a]

	% of total		% of total
Agriculture	30.2	Private consumption	68.8
Industry, of which:	33.5	Public consumption	21.7
manufacturing	11.2	Investment	6.9
Services	36.3	Exports	21.6
		Imports	-19.0

Components of GDP[b]

Structure of manufacturing[c]

	% of total		% of total
Agric. & food processing	40	Other	36
Textiles & clothing	16	Av. ann. increase in industrial	
Machinery & transport	8	output 1980–90	2.3%

Energy

	'000 TCE		
Total output	2,831	% output exported	57.5
Total consumption	2,534	% consumption imported	61.7
Consumption per head,			
kg coal equivalent	64		

Inflation and finance

Consumer price		*av. ann. increase 1989–93*	
inflation 1993	1,986.9%	Narrow money (M1)	751%
Av. ann. inflation 1989–93	382.8%	Broad money	760%

Exchange rates

	end 1994		end June 1994
Z per $	3,250	Effective rates	1990 = 100
Z per SDR	4,745	– nominal	...
Z per Ecu	4,012	– real	72.4

Principal exports

	$bn fob		$bn fob
Other manufactures	237.5	Agric. products & foodstuffs	40.7
Machinery & transport			
equipment	164.3	Total incl. others	**456.9**

Main export destinations

	% of total		% of total
Canada	22.1	Germany	4.0
Japan	10.2	Taiwan	3.4
Mexico	9.6	EU	20.8
United Kingdom	5.6		

Principal imports

	$bn fob		$bn fob
Other manufactures	286.4	Agric. products & foodstuffs	27.9
Machinery & transport			
equipment	254.8	Total incl. others	**589.4**

Main origins of imports

	% of total		% of total
Canada	19.2	Germany	4.8
Japan	18.2	Taiwan	4.3
Mexico	6.9	EU	17.3
China	5.4		

Balance of payments, reserves and aid, $bn

Visible exports fob	456.9	Capital balance	82.8
Visible imports fob	-589.4	Overall balance	1.4
Trade balance	-132.5	Change in reserves	3.4
Invisibles inflows	298.6	Level of reserves	
Invisibles outflows	-237.9	end Dec.	74.9
Net transfers	-32.1	No. months import cover	1.5
Current account balance	-103.9	Aid given	9.72
– as % of GDP	-1.6	– as % of GDP	0.15

Family life

No. of households	95.6m	Divorces per 1,000 pop.	4.8
Av. no. per household	2.6	Cost of living, Sept. 1994	
Marriages per 1,000 pop.	9.3	New York = 100	100

VENEZUELA

Area	912,045 sq km	Currency	Bolivar (Bs)
Capital	Caracas		

People

Population	20.8m	Life expectancy: men	70 yrs
Pop. per sq km	23	women	76 yrs
Av. ann. growth		Adult literacy	89.0%
in pop. 1985–93	2.5%	Fertility rate (per woman)	3.0
Pop. under 15	34.7%		
Pop. over 65	4.1%		per 1,000 pop.
No. of men per 100 women	101	Crude birth rate	24.9
Human Development Index	82	Crude death rate	4.7

The economy

GDP	Bs5,359bn	GDP per head	$2,835
GDP	$59bn	GDP per head in purchasing	
Av. ann. growth in real		power parity (USA=100)	37
GDP 1985–93	3.5%		

Origins of GDP[a]

	% of total	Components of GDP	% of total
Agriculture	5.5	Private consumption	72.9
Industry, of which:	45.2	Public consumption	8.3
manufacturing	14.8	Investment	18.1
Services	49.3	Exports	27.4
		Imports	-26.6

Structure of manufacturing

	% of total		% of total
Agric. & food processing	21	Other	65
Textiles & clothing	6	Av. ann. increase in industrial	
Machinery & transport	8	output 1980–92	2.1%

Energy

	'000 TCE		
Total output	223,471	% output exported	67.7
Total consumption	64,884	% consumption imported	0.5
Consumption per head,			
kg coal equivalent	3,214		

Inflation and finance

		av. ann. increase 1989–93	
Consumer price			
inflation 1994	60.8%	Narrow money (M1)	23.2%
Av. ann. inflation 1989–94	47.2%	Broad money	37.1%

Exchange rates

	end 1994		end June 1994
Bs per $	170	Effective rates	1990 = 100
Bs per SDR	248	– nominal	40.6
Bs per Ecu	210	– real	91.9

Principal exports[b]

	$bn fob		$bn fob
Petroleum & products	11.2	Chemicals	0.3
Metals	1.2	Total incl. others	14.0

Main export destinations[b]

	% of total		% of total
United States	50.8	Japan	3.0
Netherlands	7.8	Brazil	2.2
Germany	4.4		

Principal imports[b]

	$bn cif		$bn cif
Machinery	3.8	Metals	1.0
Transport equipment	2.6		
Chemicals	1.4	Total incl. others	12.7

Main origins of imports[b]

	% of total		% of total
United States	47.7	Italy	4.7
Germany	6.1	Brazil	4.1
Japan	6.0		

Balance of payments, reserves and debt, $bn

Visible exports fob	14.0	Overall balance	0.0
Visible imports fob	-11.1	Change in reserves	-0.2
Trade balance	2.9	Level of reserves	
Invisibles inflows	3.3	end Dec.	9.8
Invisibles outflows	-8.1	No. months import cover	10.6
Net transfers	-0.3	Foreign debt	37.5
Current account balance	-2.2	– as % of GDP	64.3
– as % of GDP	-3.8	Debt service	3.9
Capital balance	1.8	Debt service ratio	22.8

Family life

No. households	3.5m	Divorces per 1,000 pop.	1.0
Av. no. per household	5.1	Cost of living, Sept. 1994	
Marriages per 1,000 pop.	5.4	New York = 100	47

a 1991.
b 1992.

Principal exports[d]

	$m fob		$m fob
Copper	1,001	Crude petroleum	227
Diamonds	240	Total incl. others	**2,138**

Main export destinations

	% of total		% of total
Belgium/Luxembourg	46.0	Italy	5.0
United States	22.0	Japan	5.0

Principal imports[d]

	$m fob		$m fob
Imports for Gécamines[e]	362	Transport equipment	95
Petroleum products	169		
Agric. products & foodstuffs	147	Total incl. others	**1,539**

Main origins of imports

	% of total		% of total
Belgium/Luxembourg	24	South Africa	7
Hong Kong	8		

Balance of payments[d], reserves and debt, $bn

Visible exports fob	2.1	Overall balance	0.1
Visible imports fob	-1.5	Change in reserves	0.1
Trade balance	0.6	Level of reserves	
Invisibles inflows	0.2	end Dec.	0.05
Invisibles outflows	-1.6	No. months import cover	0.4
Net transfers	0.1	Foreign debt	11.3
Current account balance	-0.6	– as % of GDP	...
– as % of GDP	-7.9	Debt service	0.03
Capital balance	-0.1	Debt service ratio	...

Family life

No. of households	5.7m	Divorces per 1,000 pop.	...
Av. no. per household	5.4	Cost of living, Sept. 1994	
Marriages per 1,000 pop.	...	New York = 100	...

a 1989.
b 1992.
c 1986.
d 1990.
e Gécamines is the giant government-owned mining company, producing all Zairean cobalt, zinc, coal and copper.

ZIMBABWE

Area	390,310 sq km	Currency	Zimbabwe dollar (Z$)
Capital	Harare		

People

Population	10.6m	Life expectancy: men	50 yrs
Pop. per sq km	27	women	52 yrs
Av. ann. growth		Adult literacy	68.6%
in pop. 1985–93	3.1%	Fertility rate (per woman)	4.5
Pop. under 15	44.6%		
Pop. over 65	2.8%		*per 1,000 pop.*
No. of men per 100 women	99	Crude birth rate	36.0
Human Development Index	47	Crude death rate	13.2

The economy

GDP	Z$37.5bn	GDP per head	$541
GDP	$5.8bn	GDP per head in purchasing	
Av. ann. growth in real		power parity (USA=100)	10
GDP 1985–93	2.0%		

Origins of GDP		Components of GDP[a]	
	% of total		*% of total*
Agriculture	14.4	Private consumption	52.3
Industry, of which:	28.9	Public consumption	23.7
manufacturing	21.7	Investment	23.3
Services	56.7	Exports	29.4
		Imports	-28.7

Structure of manufacturing

	% of total		*% of total*
Agric. & food processing	29	Other	48
Textiles & clothing	16	Av. ann. increase in industrial	
Machinery & transport	7	output 1980–92	1.9%

Energy

	'000 TCE		
Total output	6,383	% output exported	4.0
Total consumption	7,634	% consumption imported	20.9
Consumption per head,			
kg coal equivalent	721		

Inflation and finance

Consumer price		*av. ann. increase 1989–93*	
inflation 1994	23.0%	Narrow money (M1)	25.9%
Av. ann. inflation 1989–94	24.1%	Broad money	19.4%

Exchange rates

	end 1994		*end June 1994*
Z$ per $	8.39	Effective rates	*1990 = 100*
Z$ per SDR	12.24	– nominal	...
Z$ per Ecu	10.36	– real	...

Principal exports[b]

	$m fob		$m fob
Tobacco	437	Nickel	72
Gold	164	Total incl. others	**1,528**
Ferro-alloys	113		

Main export destinations[bc]

	% of total		% of total
South Africa	14.5	United States	8.1
United Kingdom	12.1	Japan	7.8

Principal imports

	$m fob		$m fob
Machinery & transport equipment	809	Chemicals	259
Manufactured products	316		
Petroleum products & electricity	261	Total incl. others	**1,782**

Main origins of imports[b]

	% of total		% of total
South Africa	24.2	United States	6.4
Argentina	12.0	Japan	5.3
United Kingdom	9.0		

Balance of payments, reserves and debt, $bn

Visible exports fob	1.6	Overall balance	0.2
Visible imports fob	-1.5	Change in reserves	0.2
Trade balance	0.1	Level of reserves	
Invisibles inflows	0.4	end Dec.	0.5
Invisibles outflows	-0.9	No. months import cover	4.0
Net transfers	0.2	Foreign debt	4.2
Current account balance	-0.1	– as % of GDP	78.5
– as % of GDP	-2.0	Debt service	0.6
Capital balance	0.1	Debt service ratio	32.3

Family life

No. of households	0.1m	Divorces per 1,000 pop.	...
Av. no. per household	...	Cost of living, Sept. 1994	
Marriages per 1,000 pop.	...	New York = 100	47

a 1990.
b 1992.
c Excluding gold.

Glossary

Balance of payments The record of a country's transactions with the rest of the world. The **current account** of the balance of payments consists of: visible trade (goods); "invisible" trade (services and income); private transfer payments (eg, remittances from those working abroad); official transfers (eg, payments to international organisations, famine relief). Visible imports and exports are normally compiled on rather different definitions to those used in the trade statistics (shown in principal imports and exports) and therefore the statistics do not match. The **capital account** consists of long- and short-term transactions relating to a country's assets and liabilities (eg, loans and borrowings). Adding the current to the capital account gives the **overall balance**. This is compensated by net monetary movements and changes in reserves. In practice methods of statistical recording are neither complete nor accurate and an errors and omissions item, sometimes quite large, will appear. In the country pages of this book this item is included in the overall balance. **Changes in reserves** exclude revaluation effects and are shown without the practice often followed in balance of payments presentations of reversing the sign.

CFA Communauté Financière Africaine. Its members, most of the francophone African nations, share a common currency, the CFA franc, which is maintained at a fixed rate of 1FFr = 100 CFAfr by the French treasury.

Cif/fob Measures of the value of merchandise trade. Imports include the cost of "carriage, insurance and freight" (cif) from the exporting country to the importing. The value of exports des not include these elements and is recorded 'free on board' (fob). Balance of payments statistics are generally adjusted so that both exports and imports are shown fob; the cif elements are included in invisibles.

Commonwealth of Independent States All former Soviet Union Republics, excluding Estonia, Latvia and Lithuania. It was established January 1 1992; Azerbaijan joined in September 1993 and Georgia in December 1993.

Crude birth rate The number of live births in a year per 1,000 population. The crude rate will automatically be relatively high if a large proportion of the population is of childbearing age.

Crude death rate The number of deaths in a year per 1,000 population. Also affected by the population's age structure.

Debt, foreign Financial obligations owed by a country to the rest of the world and repayable in foreign currency. **Debt service** consists of interest payments on outstanding debt plus any principal repayments due. **The debt service ratio** is debt service expressed as a percentage of the country's earnings from exports of goods and services.

EU European Union. Members are: Belgium, Denmark, France, Germany, Greece, Ireland, Italy, Luxembourg, Netherlands, Portugal, Spain and the United Kingdom and, since January 1 1995, Austria, Finland and Sweden. EU data in this book refers only to the first 12 listed member countries.

Ecu European currency unit. An accounting measure used within the EU and composed of a weighted basket of the currencies of 12 EU members.

Effective exchange rate This measures a currency's depreciation (figures below 100) or appreciation (figures over 100) from a base date against a trade weighted basket of the currencies of the country's main trading partners.

Efta European Free Trade Association. An organisation of West European states that are not members of the European Union. Members are: Austria, Finland, Iceland, Liechtenstein, Norway, Sweden and Switzerland.

Fertility rate The average number of children born to a woman who completes her childbearing years.

GDP Gross domestic product. The sum of all output produced by economic activity within a country. GNP (gross national product) includes net income from abroad eg, rent, profits.

Import cover The number of months of imports covered by reserves, ie reserves ÷ $\frac{1}{12}$ annual imports.

Inflation The annual rate at which prices are increasing. The most common measure and the one shown here is the increase in the consumer price index.

Life expectancy The average length of time a baby born today can expect to live.

Literacy is defined by UNESCO as the ability to read and write a simple sentence, but definitions can vary from country to country.

Money supply A measure of the "money" available to buy goods and services. Various definitions exist. The measures shown here are based on definitions used by the IMF and may differ from measures used nationally. Narrow money (M1) consists of cash in circulation and demand deposits (bank deposits that can be withdrawn on demand). "Quasi-money" (time, savings and foreign currency deposits) is added to this to create broad money.

NMP Net material product. The equivalent measure to GDP used in Eastern Europe and certain other economies. It differs from GDP in excluding certain services and in deducting capital consumption. In general, NMP is between 80-90% of GDP.

OECD Organisation for Economic Co-operation and Development. The "rich countries" club was established in 1961 to promote economic growth and the expansion of world trade. It is based in Paris and now has 25 members.

Opec Organisation of Petroleum Exporting Countries. Set up in 1960 and based in Vienna, Opec is mainly concerned with oil pricing and production issues. Members are; Algeria, Ecuador, Gabon, Indonesia, Iran, Iraq, Kuwait, Libya, Nigeria, Qatar, Saudi Arabia, UAE and Venezuela.

PPP Purchasing power parity. PPP statistics adjust for cost of living differences by replacing normal exchange rates with rates designed to equalise the prices of a standard "basket"of goods and services. These are used to obtain PPP estimates of GDP per head. PPP estimates are normally shown on a scale of 1 to 100, taking the United States, where the average standard of living is highest, as 100.

Real terms Figures adjusted to exclude the effect of inflation.

Reserves The stock of gold and foreign currency held by a country to finance any calls that may be made for the settlement of foreign debt.

SDR Special drawing right. The reserve currency, introduced by the IMF in 1970, was intended to replace gold and national currencies in settling international transactions. The IMF uses SDRs for book-keeping purposes and issues them to member countries. Their value is based on a basket of the five most widely traded currencies: the US dollar, Deutschemark, pound sterling, Japanese yen and French franc.

Sources

Asian Studies Centre, The Heritage Foundation, *US and Asia Statistical Handbook*

BP, *Statistical Review of World Energy*

British Mountaineering Council

Corporate Resources Group, *Quality of Living Report*

The Economist Intelligence Unit, *Cost of Living Survey*

The Economist Intelligence Unit, *Country Reports*

The Economist Intelligence Unit, *Country Risk Service*

Euromonitor, *International Marketing Data and Statistics*

Euromonitor, *European Marketing Data and Statistics*

Europa Publications, *The Europa World Yearbook*

FAO, *Production Yearbook*

Financial Times Business Information, *The Banker*

GATT, *International Trade Statistics*

Gold Fields Mineral Services Ltd.

ILO, *Year Book of Labour Statistics*

IMF, *Balance of Payments Statistics Yearbook*

IMF, *International Financial Statistics*

IMF, *World Economic Outlook*

International Cocoa Organisation, *Quarterly Bulletin of Cocoa Statistics*

International Civil Aviation Organisation, *Digest of Statistics*

International Coffee Organisation

International Cotton Advisory Committee, *Bulletin*

International Criminal Police Organisation (Interpol), *International Crime Statistics*

International Finance Corporation, *Emerging Stock Markets Factbook*

International Road Federation, *World Road Statistics*

International Rubber Study Group, *Rubber Statistical Bulletin*

International Sugar Organisation, *Sugar Yearbook*

International Tea Committee, *Annual Bulletin of Statistics*

International Wheat Council, *The Grain Market Report*

International Wool Textile Organisation

Lloyd's Register, *Statistical Tables*

Journal de la Marine Marchande et du Transport Multimodal

OECD, *Economic Outlook*

OECD, *Environmental Data*

OECD, *Health Systems*

ISTA Mielke, *Oil World*

Taiwan Statistical Data Book

The Times, *Atlas of the World*

Time Inc Magazines, *Fortune International*

The World Almanac

UN, *Demographic Yearbook*

UN, *Energy Statistics Yearbook*

UN, *Statistical Chart on World Families*

UN, *World Population Prospects*

UN Development Programme, *Human Development Report*

UNCTAD, *Handbook of International Trade and Development Statistics*

UNESCO, *Statistical Yearbook*

Union International des Chemins de Fer, *Statistiques Internationales des Chemins de Fer*

US Department of Agriculture, *Rice Report*

WHO, *World Health Statistics*

World Bank, *Atlas*

World Bank, *World Debt Tables*

World Bank, *World Development Report*

World Bank, *World Population Projections*

World Bureau of Metal Statistics, *World Metal Statistics*

World Resources Institute, *World Resources*

World Tourist Organisation, *Yearbook of Tourism Statistics*